Myron Adams

Creation of the Bible

Myron Adams

Creation of the Bible

ISBN/EAN: 9783337171605

Printed in Europe, USA, Canada, Australia, Japan

Cover: Foto ©Lupo / pixelio.de

More available books at **www.hansebooks.com**

CREATION OF THE BIBLE

BY

MYRON ADAMS

AUTHOR OF "THE CONTINUOUS CREATION"

BOSTON AND NEW YORK
HOUGHTON, MIFFLIN AND COMPANY
The Riverside Press, Cambridge
1892

The Riverside Press, Cambridge, Mass., U. S. A.
Electrotyped and Printed by H. O. Houghton & Company.

PREFACE.

THAT creation which speaks for itself in the lowest forms of organic life in due time manifests the wisdom of the Creator in the high department of morals and spiritual development. Religion falls into line as the last of a series of creations. If the time has already arrived when thinkers abandon the long-accepted dogma of creation by fiat, adopting in place of it the philosophy of creation by development, it will not be long before it will be seen that religion is also developed, and that revelation grows. The latter begins in the narrow, the confused, and the primitive; it advances in proportion to the moral, intellectual, and spiritual advancement of men.

"Like every other product of man's spiritual activity," says Professor Abraham Kuenen, "the Israelitish religion has its defects, its one-sidedness, the faults of its virtues." Nothing is so important to us as Israel's religion, and that other and better religion which has grown, and is still growing out of it. That the revelation contained in Israel's religion, and in the Christian outgrowth, may be studied in the light of its historical development, a number of books have recently been written; the present volume is a contribution to the same purpose.

To read Kuenen and Wellhausen with attention, and appreciation of their devout and excellent scholarship, is to acknowledge the truth of some of their conclusions; and no careful investigator can now undertake the study of the construction of the Old Testament without consulting these eminent authors.

More than that: if the philosophy of evolution be accepted by any one, as the only reasonable explanation of the Cosmos, no theory concerning the Bible which is invalidated by that philosophy can be maintained by him.

To those who are satisfied with the old views, an attempt to find better ones must seem audacious and perilous; but there are many who are unable to content themselves with the notion of the infallibility of the writers of the Bible; to such this book is addressed by one who has pursued the study for the satisfaction of his own mind.

He does not profess to be a critic, but one who has resorted to the critics and historical criticism for help.

He has been aided, so far as the present volume is concerned, by such authors as Professors Wellhausen, Kuenen, Sanday, and Toy, Canon Driver, President Cone, Dr. Gladden, and others, both progressive and conservative.

CONTENTS.

		PAGE
I.	THE NEW METHOD OF STUDY	1
II.	DIVERS PORTIONS AND MANNERS	10
III.	EZRA THE SCRIBE	21
IV.	HISTORY-MAKING	32
V.	TRADITIONAL SOURCES	44
VI.	LEGENDARY ELEMENTS	56
VII.	PROPHECY	68
VIII.	FROM GODS TO GOD	81
IX.	THE LIMITATION	93
X.	THE FICTION	106
XI.	THE POETRY	119
XII.	GREEK INFLUENCE	132
XIII.	OTHER INFLUENCES	145
XIV.	THE NEW AGE	157
XV.	THE FIRST CHRISTIAN WRITINGS	170
XVI.	THE SPIRITUAL BASIS	183
XVII.	THE MIRACLES	196
XVIII.	INFALLIBILITY	209
XIX.	PAUL AND THE SECOND ADVENT	222
XX.	THE APOCALYPSE OF JOHN	235
XXI.	THE CERTAINTIES	248
XXII.	THE FOURTH THE GOSPEL OF THE PRESENT TENSE	261
XXIII.	AUTHORSHIP OF THE FOURTH GOSPEL	274
XXIV.	CONFLICT AND HARMONY	287
XXV.	THE SOCIOLOGICAL RELIGION OF JAMES	300

CREATION OF THE BIBLE.

I.

THE NEW METHOD OF STUDY.

BIBLE study has come to be of two sorts. Until recently it has been understood that its one object is to discover what the Bible contains. Numerous questions ask themselves continually in the world of human experience. What answer does the Bible offer? In order to attain satisfactory information concerning the answer of the Bible to our questions, and to know very exactly the precise meaning of the answer, a most thorough investigation of the language of the Bible and of its grammar has been undertaken. Accordingly, the literature of comment, exposition, and textual criticism is exceedingly abundant. The painstaking care expended upon criticism of the text is of a sort to cause astonishment. Every field of collateral usage has been ransacked to find material bearing on the subject. The microscope has not been employed more abundantly by experts of science in physical research than the microscopic vision has been in Scriptural investigation. It lieth not within the wit of man to tell the greatness and the minuteness of the work done. But in respect to that department of Bible study it would not be rash to declare that it has already been carried very nearly if not quite to its limit. It does not appear probable that much more light will be shed upon the text of the Bible.

Having gone thus far in that direction, Bible study has recently taken another. Let us be careful just here to make a necessary discrimination. I speak of a new department or direction. Attacks have been made upon the Scriptures from the time of their appearance among men. Christianity at the beginning of its course was the subject of a great literary attack, remnants of which remain. Of course the books of the Christian literature formed to some extent the basis of that attack. That, and all of a like nature which has followed it, I do not speak of as study of the Bible. That study is carried on by those who find a value in the Bible; who wish to secure that value, whatever it may be. It is not the object of any Bible student, properly so called, to destroy the Bible or to undermine its proper and reasonable influence. His object is to discover just what the Bible is, and how it came to be what it is.

The easy way has been almost universally to assume that the Bible is the infallible word of God. It is such an assumption as has been made by millions in the case of the Koran and in the case of other revelations. Joseph Smith was informed by an angel that at a certain spot he would find a book. He proceeded to that spot and found a book composed of gold pages; and these pages were covered with some sort of unintelligible writing. By the aid of a pair of supernatural spectacles he was enabled to translate this tongue into the vernacular. Thus came to human knowledge the Mormon Bible.[1] How many thousands of people have assumed that Joseph Smith did not tell a lie about the matter, I am unable to say. We assume, I suppose, that he did lie, or that some one did. We have, on the whole, a better ground for our assumption than they have for theirs. Upon them lies a burden of proof which seems never to have been appreciated by them.

Upon modern Christian scholarship has been found to rest an obligation not imposed upon our fathers, an obligation to offer some proof as to the alleged nature of the Bible. Such proof was not definitely called for while people were yet superstitiously inclined to accept things unquestioningly. It certainly is called for now, and it is responded to by an increasing number of Christian scholars and believers in the authenticity and value of the Bible. Thus has arisen that phenomenon which has taken, perhaps somewhat fortuitously, the name of the "higher criticism."

Many reasons exist why the Bible should now be studied in the new way, but there is one which possibly includes them all. An English writer offers a suggestion bearing upon the point. He says that all progress is coördinate.[2] "The consequence of this is," he goes on to say, "that a barbarous age must have a barbarous jurisprudence, and consequently a barbarous theology. We must see and admit that culture in one direction presupposes culture in every other." He then cites the fact that transubstantiation, or the corporeal presence of Christ in the bread and wine of the mass, did not strike the religious

---

[1] Dr. Gladden's *Who Wrote the Bible?* p. 3.
[2] J. B. Heard, *Old and New Theology.*

people of the tenth century as absurd, because they believed in the transmutation of one metal into another. Their science affirmed this transmutation of metals; and their theology affirmed the transmutation of bread into flesh. Bad science helped thus to make bad theology, or at least the two were coördinate. Now the idea has prevailed largely in the best portion of the world that the creation of the earth was a sudden work of supernatural power, effecting the immediate result of a very complex world, composed of divers elements, and all produced out of nothing. The notion of almightiness was such that it was supposed to be quite easy for God to make something out of nothing. If something could be made out of nothing, were that something no more than a grain of sand, it followed that the making of a vast globe would present no insurmountable difficulties to the divine power; and so the world came into existence.

That was the science of the past; and the religion of the past corresponded therewith. Here is the Bible, which is recognized by the Christian population of the world as the revelation. While there was no definite knowledge of how it came to be, it might have been claimed that it too was made out of nothing. God put commands and ideas into the mind of Moses and others. He put them thus in the mind, without reference to anything precedent. Thus the law of Moses descended out of the residence of God in the sky, as by a burst or sudden irruption of it upon the people gathered at the foot of an Asiatic mountain. The revelation was therefore created, not out of materials already existing in the world, but out of that which up to that time had not existed below the sky.

It seems to have been reserved for the present century entirely to reverse the old conception of a more ignorant science in regard to the creation of the earth. The earth grew. The theory now is that it was created, by coming to be in its present forms, through perpetual modifications of previous forms.

The corresponding theory in regard to the Bible, considered as revelation, is that it also grew in human thought, that it grew out of previous and more imperfect thinkings; and that by changes, adaptations, and by what we may call the editorial work bestowed upon it, it became in due time the book we now possess.

A peculiar sentiment in respect to the Bible has been influential throughout Christendom. The sentiment, like most of our sentiments, has not been definite and accurately describable. It expresses itself in words which separate the Bible from all other books. Other books are men's books; the Bible is God's book. Other books are of a sort to be known as secular or even profane. The history in the Bible has been called sacred; and the history outside of it has been known as profane history. And thus the Bible has had a place accorded no other book in Christendom. If God has given us a book, we must treat that book with more reverence than any other. We must hold in check our criticisms of it. "Who art thou that repliest against God?" If the Bible makes a declaration, it must be humbly accepted as a final declaration, from which there is no appeal. We may do what we please with other books; but we must treat God's book with the respect due the revelation of the Almighty.

Such has been the sentiment. If any persons have not shared the feeling, they have been classified oftentimes as profane and infidel persons and scoffers. It is possible that some of them deserved such classification. It is probable that such a classification does many of them rank injustice. Anything presenting itself to us for our inspection is likely to encounter in us the feeling of approbation, or the contrary. We use our judgment upon a phenomenon and make up our minds as to its character. If we so hold it aloof from our judgment as to neglect to consider its character, then it is of little moment to us.

Now the Bible is a book found in almost all households. It is bound in a cover, it is printed in a language; it publishes certain propositions of various sorts. It is precisely as much subject to our judgment as are the rocks which lie underneath the soil, or the plants which grow in the soil. If it is said "God made the book," and we are to reverently recognize his hand in it, it ought also to be said that God made the rocks and roses, and we ought reverently to recognize his hand in them. When God makes anything he invites our judgment upon it. As a matter of fact, we have always been very free in our notions of nature; and men have gone so far as to regard nature in a serious sense accursed. They have blamed wind and weather, and grumbled unceasingly and without the suspicion of irreverence at many things. Yet these things were in verity God's things. To take exception to the book has not been tolerated. That shows a confused state of mind. We need clearance of that confusion. If God had authentically written every word of the Bible, if he had caused all the printing, and the arrangement of it, and the very binding itself to be done in heaven, it would be still open to men for their inspection and criticism. Our irreverence consists in being slaves to God, or thinking ourselves such, and not daring to use the gifts he has bestowed on us, and so increasing them.

The Bible was not written in heaven. God did not write one word of it, except secondarily. The only theory which has had any real ground in intelligent modern thought is that God did inspire the people who wrote the Bible. Moreover, it is part of the theory of modern times that inspired men, like other men, are subject to error. It is conceivable that one might have particular power and discernment in one direction, or as to some special subject, but be quite uninspired in regard to other matters.

He who excels in mathematics does so because the power is bestowed upon him. He did not create the power. He is not an independent being, standing alone and original. His excellence in one department may go with defect in other departments. Now the highest excellence is a divine product in human character and thought. It is inspiration, but it does not guard the subject of it from that human defect which we are compelled to recognize everywhere.

Our experience is that human beings are imperfect. That is one thing of which we are sure. There is another thing of which we have come to be equally sure, namely, that the human race has once been far behind its present knowledge of all things. Our human notions have been changing, slowly at first, more rapidly now.

It is by this change we approach more perfect knowledge. Thus it is that the more primitive men spoke from least information. They spoke as moved by the Holy Spirit, we are told, but the Holy Spirit moves in a realm of the incomplete.

It is proposed in this book to give in a simple manner some view of the results of recent Bible study. In doing so, certain principles of interpretation and criticism will be employed: —

First. The Bible is a part of creation.

Second. The order of creation is one of progress and improvement.

Third. All progress is coördinate.

Fourth. The Bible is to be studied as any book would be studied. It is properly subject to human criticism.

Fifth. Its contents furnish to a large extent the means for its investigation.

We study the earth by that which we find it contains. We have made out its history in the vast periods of the past by the things which remain. We know that some geologic periods were earlier in time than others. In the same manner we study the Bible. It is literature. It is a group of separate documents gathered from human experience covering a period of a millennium. There is little contemporaneous literature in the light of which we may investigate the earlier portions of the Bible. A period about eight centuries before our era marks the place at which modern scholarship begins the study of the Biblical documents.

We now come to the object of this sort of study. It is thought that the religious nature of man has nothing to do with criticism. Our Bible is given for the support and instruction of a religious life, and if we are led off into investigations of a critical sort, we shall lose religious fervor. The objection, while it may have a certain force, is oblivious of the fact that much of the religion of the present rests on false bases. Everything has been taken for granted. In the divine Providence it has now come about that much of the devout scholarship of the world is engaged in restatements. Conservatives have been afraid of the results of the newer scholarship; have been timid in letting people know what is going on.

It seems to me high time that the people should have information concerning the movements which have not been exposed to them. That they should have a clear understanding of the main features of the work of the great scholars. Cardinal Newman had the fear that truth itself might make a damage in the world, if it were too freely spoken. He acquired the habit of asking of a truth whether it was safe or not. It was that habit which led him to relapse into the bosom of the mediæval church. We need have no such fears. Religious truth, truth concerning the Bible and its origin, the method of its creation so far as we can discover it, must be of advantage to all who acquire it. Therefore I invite attention to the studies of the scholars who are making a new Christian scholarship, the real end of which is to enable us to live more intelligently and more religiously, and less superstitiously.

II.

DIVERS PORTIONS AND MANNERS.

Two questions in respect to the Bible, scholarship has asked, and is now endeavoring to answer. The importance of the questions is that upon their answers depend the idea we shall have of the nature of the Bible. These two questions are, first, "When was the Bible written?" and, second, "How was it written?" Let us give heed at present to the first question, and the answer furnished by modern religious scholarship.

In the first verse of the Epistle to the Hebrews these words occur: "God, having of old time spoken unto the fathers in the prophets by divers portions and in divers manners." God did not speak all at once, and once for all, but distributed his communications in the manner indicated. For a very long time, therefore, there was no Bible. There came to be a Bible-making age. When that age arrived, then the things which were said in divers portions and divers manners by prophets and others were collected into one collection, known first as the "sacred writings," or for the most part, simply as the "writings," or Scriptures. There came a time when some person of adequate genius and comprehensive skill undertook to make a Bible out of materials scattered and incoherent. This person massed together that of human experience which appeared to him most important, and thus came into existence a collection of before disconnected writings and traditions, in a form which became the nucleus of a nation's hope and aspiration and religious feeling. That is the natural way of explaining the method in which the Bible came into existence.

If a man constructs houses, he goes to one quarry and gets stones fit for foundations; to another quarry for a finer quality of stone, fit for the upper portion of his building. He goes into one forest and gets trees of one sort, for one purpose, into another forest and gets a different quality of wood for other purposes. He mines down in the earth for iron, and makes both tools and materials. Thus from that which had been in divers portions and manners, he constructs an edifice which had not been in existence before. (It can hardly be doubtful, I suppose, to the student, however doubtful it may be to others, that the Bible was constructed as really as any court-house or music-hall is constructed. It came into being as a human production as really as anything else which has ever become extant among us.

When were these various portions written? I mean, of course, with relation to each other. Were the first five books written first? Were the next two written next? and so on. It has become possible to answer these questions. A vast amount of knowledge comes to us, directly and indirectly, from comparing things with each other. We go all over the earth, and compare the products of different regions with each other. We compare climates, for one thing. We compare the animals and the plants and the various tribes and races of mankind with each other. No one can doubt that it is a most useful process.

Then we proceed to compare the habits and doings of people. We look at the dwellings of people long dead, and arrive at some knowledge of how those people who occupied the dwellings must have lived. For instance, we go into New Mexico and gaze upon the old habitations of the cliff-dwellers. We distinguish them from all other people, and identify them as cliff-dwellers. They contrived to climb up the precipitous cliff, and burrow in the rocks there, making for themselves a kind of nest, like the bank-swallow, at some height above the common level. Now in their domestic economies, people have never been in the habit of doing very many unnecessary things, and persisting in so doing. Therefore we search for the necessity of the great exertion required by these people in hollowing out these dwellings, perched thus on high. They proposed to make them inaccessible. They had that way of defense against roving and warlike tribes. They themselves, we therefore infer, were not so warlike and fierce as their neighbors; they were more defensive than aggressive. We go on by comparison and reach a certain definite knowledge of these people, who may have long since become extinct on the earth. Then other peoples have built their dwellings on the level, of branches and twigs of trees, covered them with weather-proof clay, and erected a kind of stockade around their village. In certain localities that sort of erection marks a period of the development of the people of that region.

Along the valleys and passes of the mountain regions in Europe, crowning every spot of vantage, stands the ruin of a castle. That ruin marks a period known as the feudal. It locates itself at a certain definite time in the annals of the world. Equally, the remnants of dwellings built upon posts driven in the water on the shallow margin of Swiss lakes mark a far earlier mode of defense. The men of each period, — perhaps very widely separated in time, — being dead, yet speak to us by that which remains; but lake-dwelling, cliff-dwelling, and castle become obsolete, and pass into the stage of record and ruin.

If the dwellings and defenses of ancient people tell us a story which we can read, much more does the literature of a people tell us its story. If literature begins in some kind of sign language and hieroglyphic art, in tomb and temple inscriptions, it goes on to embody itself in larger and more enlightening form as time goes on. It is in the literature of the past that we discover the most clear and comprehensive record of the feelings and philosophy and religion and morals of an age. Moreover, it is by the literature of a people that we are able to identify the time of the golden or most progressive and prosperous age of that people.

But we must not expect exactness. We go to a considerable extent upon the ground of probability and inference. This has its disadvantages, especially to a certain class of minds, but it really makes no serious defect in the method itself. If our knowledge is simply approximate, so is the knowledge of the astronomer.

A journey of a hundred thousand miles undertaken by one of us would be a very great affair indeed. We might have to encircle the world with our tracks several times; but for a ray of light it is no great matter. In the ethereal distances we do not lay much stress upon the inaccuracy of a hundred thousand miles. We have not yet determined the distance of our planet from the sun in anything less than millions as the unit. The students of history, if they go back far enough in the annals of time, find themselves unable to give us the dates we would perhaps like to have. Events came to pass, we know. Before them were events of which we know simply that they were antecedent; and that, for very distant events, is practically all we require to know.

Literature known as sacred, or other, has its eras. A certain method of literature belongs to certain periods, as the Elizabethan era, and the like. We know, it is true, the date of the issue of some of Shakespeare's plays; we know the date of other important writings. Contemporaneous with the English period mentioned there was an era somewhat similar in the Low Countries. We have ascertained by the critical work of our scholars that Milton wrote "Paradise Lost" and other poems after the Dutch poet Vondel had written poems upon the same themes. Further than that, it is quite evident that Milton must have been a reader of Vondel before he wrote "Paradise Lost," or while he was writing it. Milton nowhere tells us that he read Vondel, and, so far as we know, none of his contemporaries have recorded such an opinion, but the student of the subject to-day is quite as certain that Milton had read Vondel as if Milton had declared the fact in plain language. So, then, it might be established beyond a question that a certain two poets were contemporaries, and that one wrote a little before the other.

Among our facts gathered by inference, but quite as surely known as almost any other facts, is this, that the Homeric poems antedate the Greek dramatists. As it is with other writings, so is it also with the sacred Scriptures. We are able to discover, from internal and other evidence, relatively when the books which compose the volume were written.

As illustrating the mode of ascertainment still further: certain words have recently come into vogue which were not coined a century ago. If, therefore, a poem were published in some volume of old poems, or purporting to be old poems, issued now as a new edition, and if this poem bore the date of 1780, for example; and if in the poem were found the words "telephone," or "phonograph," or "steam-locomotive;" or if allusions were made to Abraham Lincoln, Queen Victoria, the battle of Waterloo, Black Friday, or Prince Bismarck, we would know at a glance that the date was wrong. It might be a mistake of the printer, or the date of one poem had been applied to another; or through ignorance, or willful purpose, or jest, this misplacement of a date had taken place; but the evidence that there was an error would be absolutely unmistakable.[1]

There are many ways of determining whether a document was written after or before the beginning of the Christian era, just as there are means of determining, incidentally, that Paul was an earlier writer than Peter, for Paul's epistles were already extant among the people when the author of Peter's letter wrote. It must have been so from the evidence afforded by the incidental remark of Peter that in Paul's writings were things hard to be understood. He had therefore read those things and found them difficult.

I have thus sketched those common methods which are employed by students in determining when different portions of the Bible were written, but I have given only a few specimens of the ways of literary critics. All we require to know is that there are

[1] Dr. Gladden gives a more striking illustration, *Who Wrote the Bible?* p. 174.

modes, dictated by common-sense, and of universal application, which are used in the study of the Bible.

By study it has become ascertainable that the first parts of the Bible were not written first. When we take up a book, if we read the preface first, because that first stares us in the face, we involuntarily think of that as having been first written. Probably, in nine cases out of ten, it was written last. Usually, a man does not know how to write the introduction to his book until he has found out for himself what his book has come to be. Now we open our Bibles, and first of all begin with the beginning. We naturally suppose, from the arrangement, that the first word was first written; but the student brings a great many tests to bear upon that matter, and by his tests, which are required by common-sense and literary criticism, he becomes very sure that the first book in the Bible was by no means the first produced. Beginnings do indeed come first in the order of nature, but not in the order of thinking. That is to say, description of beginnings comes late because such description is difficult, and much has to be learned before one knows origins and beginnings.

The common notion, gained we hardly know how, has been that a great man of the remote past, Moses by name, wrote the book of Genesis for our Bible. This notion has become so embodied in religious thought, and so belongs to reverence for the Bible, that a distinguished theologian of Princeton not long ago asserted that the Bible would be gone from us, and religion with it, or somewhat to that effect, if Moses did not write the books commonly attributed to his authorship. That statement is instructive, but it also escapes being amusing by only a little. For it might be paralleled with a saying that if Shakespeare did not write the plays credited to him we should have no book of that title left, and the dramatic art itself would suffer destruction. I think we might deal with any assertion of a similar kind in the same way. If the old notions of the substance of the earth came to be put aside, as they were, we still have the earth left, and can manage to live upon it after some fashion.

It seems to become plainer every day to critical and Christian scholarship that Moses did not write the five books which have been ascribed to him. To the rationalists among the critics it is quite as evident that Moses did not write the book of Genesis and the other books of the Pentateuch, as that nails of the sort known as "cut nails" were not made in the earlier times. The material which goes to the construction of the cut nail is very ancient, but the making is modern. As the age of nail-making by machinery is comparatively recent, so the age of Bible-making came long after the time of Moses. Probably that would be admitted by the most strenuous advocate of the conservative view. At the same time such an advocate would affirm that Moses wrote that portion of the Bible — or at least edited it — which is known as the Pentateuch. This is becoming more and more doubtful every day. The reason why that doubt grows to a certainty is that the time of Moses did not admit of such writing or such editorial work as has been attributed to him. If we find that the earlier part of the Bible was spoken of in the New Testament as the work of Moses, if we find that Jesus speaks of "Moses and the prophets," it will be well for us to remember that the fruits of an age are not infrequently grouped under the name of some great personage of that age. The age of Pericles, or of Charles the Great, is identified by the great names of the great personages. It is a matter of convenience, and not a matter of critical accuracy.

It is natural to look for the best literary work of any people, not in their less mature period, and not while they are most busily engaged in wars of conquest or defense, but when they have acquired their best experience, and have developed their best moral and intellectual strength. The evidences are abundant that Israel did not reach its best until long after the time of Moses.

An incident in the history of that people had a most important bearing upon the future of the world. This incident was looked upon as a cálamity, and was in fact such; but calamities, personal and national, may prove of the utmost importance in the work of a person or a people. There came a time when the Jews were overpowered by the superior forces of the Eastern empire, and were reduced to vassalage. There is something almost unique in this experience. The tradition runs, that when the progenitors of the twelve tribes went into Egypt, during a famine, and were hospitably received there, they were afterward reduced to slavery, and that of the most bitter sort. The ancient way of disposing of conquered peoples was at one time to kill them. Afterward the modification of that cruelty was to make slaves of the conquered.

It is noticeable that when the Assyrian army compelled the surrender of the Jewish capital, they destroyed the city and the sacred temple, deporting the more valuable of its contents, but they did not make slaves of the inhabitants. Indeed, an imperial policy, which policy was then new in the world, favors the welfare of a conquered people, so far as that is consistent with the welfare of the empire. The Jews, therefore, were treated with consideration, although from motives of policy they were removed from the soil, and taken to the Babylonian provinces far to the eastward. This, which was to the Jews a fearful calamity, and all the more sorrowful to them because their affections and their religious feelings were so intimately associated with the temple, was nevertheless a very great blessing. It broke them out of their narrow exclusiveness, and brought them in contact with other peoples, who were perhaps foremost at that time in philosophy, art, and learning.

Our world is small, so long as we remain affixed to the soil where we were born. It is the old story of the eagles, securely nested and content, finding their nest broken up, and themselves pitched out of it and compelled to fly. It is a hard ordeal, but it is what makes eagles of the young birds. Judah, conquered by the imperial army, its old habitation broken into and broken down, and its people deported to the plains of Shinar, received an impetus which served it in its mission as nothing else at that time could. It had preserved an exclusive spirit and a spirit of hatred toward other nations.

There were surprises in store for it. There was a new mine of learning opened for its seers and wise men. Moreover, the humanity and even religious earnestness of the Persian conquerors of the Assyrian empire, by their friendliness, threw new light on old laws. The old narrowness was invaded by breadth.

Cyrus was reckoned to be within the mercy and purpose of Jehovah; he was a man girded divinely for his work.[1] After the days of the captivity were over, those patriot Jews who returned to their old home had more light than their captive fathers had possessed. They, or their leaders, wished to commit the old religion to a form more permanent than the old and somewhat chaotic traditions. They wished to put the new light into the old thoughts. It is evident enough, if one will be at pains to examine, that at the close of the captivity, Judah had arrived at the beginning of a golden period of Bible-making. (It was then, for the first time, that the "scribe," or literary man, made his appearance, and began his work.)

Far more than the old temple and the old city walls and the old houses were rebuilt. The old law, and the old Mosaic traditions, and the old chaotic and scattered chronicles were also rebuilt, and the glory of the later house in that regard was vastly superior to that of the earlier house. The library of sacred literature was made. The hymns and the proverbs, and the laws and the legends, and the greater poems were made, not out of new material, but of the material afforded by the national traditions and feelings.

So we may say with a degree of certainty that the Bible as we now have it began to be made, not in the days of Moses, and not in the days of Samuel and David and Solomon, but long afterward, in the days of Ezra the scribe, or the first literary men of Israel.

[1] Isaiah xlv. 1-5.

III.

EZRA THE SCRIBE.

It may be said that two Bibles were in use at the time of the opening of the Christian era. It is true that the one which was used in Jewish synagogues was still in an unfinished state at that time. There was some dispute among the learned as to the admission of some of the books we find in our Bible into the list of the sacred books. So that the question was still open as to what the Bible actually was. There was another Bible somewhat different from the Hebrew, and which was published in Greek. The Hebrew was mainly the language of religion, — as is the Latin in the Roman Church. It was not the language commonly spoken by the Palestinian people. They used a tongue known as the Aramaic. For more common use, as in the households of the rich, or in schools, it is probable that the Greek Bible was most in vogue. It was this Bible from which the larger portion of the quotations made by the apostles and Christ came; but this Bible, written in the Greek tongue, differed in important respects from the Hebrew scrolls. It differed chiefly in containing much more than the Hebrew Bible.

We discover in our Bibles at present one book of Ezra. It is a short book of ten chapters. In the Greek Bible, from which Jesus and some of the apostles quoted, there are in addition two books of Ezra.

These additional books are quite lengthy in comparison. In the Bibles which contain them they are called the books of Esdras. Esdras is simply the Greek way of spelling the Hebrew word Ezra. Moreover, the genealogy given of the supposed writer, Esdras, is the same as that of Ezra, in the short book in our common Bibles.

Now the fact that Jesus and his apostles made somewhat copious quotations from this Greek Bible gives rise to the probability that it was in more common use than the Hebrew Bible, of which it was supposed to be a translation. Ezra certainly appears to have occupied a very important place in the annals of the nation. He was not only a great reformer, but in an important sense a prophet; but his peculiar value to the Jewish nation seems to have been connected with his literary work. If we are to give any credit to the books in the Greek Bible which bear his name (even though written later than his time), it will become evident that his work was second in importance to no other in all the history of Israel.

It is an orthodox opinion (or has been until recently, and now it is a little difficult to tell precisely what an orthodox opinion is) that because Jesus referred to the Old Testament, and drew many things from the Old Testament, therefore the Old Testament as we now have it must be an infallibly true document. Since Jesus appears to have been acquainted with the Greek version of the Old Testament, and inasmuch as this version contains much that we now commonly reject, it is quite evident that there is no proof of infallible truth in the fact that Jesus quoted from the Bible then in existence.

Many things in the writing of Ezra, contained in

the two long books bearing his name, appear incredible, and there need be no quarrel with those who determined what the Old Testament should be, because they rejected these books. Yet these books contain statements which throw light upon our Bible, and also show the eminent service of Ezra the scribe.

It appears that Ezra was born and was educated in Babylonia; that he had his training with a number of other remarkable men. The probabilities are that he above all other men of his nation had the instinct, if we may so say, of literature. He responded to the influences around him. His fervent religious spirit found a task for him; it was to give to his nation the teachings of Jehovah, and of the wise men of the past, in the more durable form of a sacred collection.

Now the wise men of that age, as well as other ancient ages, were accustomed to speak much in an oracular form. In all the ancient literature, the priest, or prophet, or the sage consulted by the people as a guide, had a peculiar method of speech. (He did not tell his story in plain language, but in figures of speech.) So much was the figure of speech the mode of such talk that we, in our time, think the ancients were always speaking fables. The prophet or other guide of the people, who was subject to vivid impressions, put forth those impressions in statements we find hard to believe; indeed, it is quite impossible to believe them. As I read the books of Esdras, it seems almost probable that it was never intended that the statements should be believed in their literal form. The words of wise men were given for wise men, that is, for those who could seek the meaning couched in parables, stories, and fables.

Ezra tells us that he was sitting one day under an oak, and that there came a voice out of a bush near by. This voice called him by name. Ezra arose and answered, " Here I am, Lord." Then the Lord answered him out of the bush, reminding him that it was from a bush God had talked with Moses long before: it was from the bush Moses went to lead the people of Israel out of bondage into Canaan.[1]

It was time for the same thing to happen again. Israel was in captivity, though not of the bitter sort, and the period of the captivity had elapsed. There must now be a new Moses to lead the people out of captivity back to the land of promise. The voice speaks to Ezra, and Ezra answers. It is through this conversation that one may learn the state of things in Israel at that day. Ezra is to go upon his mission, and to make a new start for the nation. He tells the Lord that the law is burnt, and therefore " no man knoweth the things which God does." The idea conveyed is that the precious scrolls or tablets had been destroyed. If Moses had committed anything to writing, or if his successors had done so, the remnant of that had suffered destruction in the calamities which had come upon the house of Jacob. All that work must be done over again.

Therefore, as the story goes, Ezra is directed to gather the people, and bid them let him alone for the space of forty days. It was for the same space that Moses had been away from the people in communication with God. Having thus warned the people, Ezra is directed to prepare suitable materials for writing, and take with him five ready writers. He did as commanded, and the next day heard a voice bidding him

[1] 2 Esdras xiv.

drink what should be offered him. What he drank was of the appearance of fire. After drinking that potion the spirit of understanding was strong in him, and he spoke many things. The Highest gave understanding to the five men, and they wrote the wonderful visions of Ezra. Ezra tells us that his memory was strengthened, and that as a result of his visions a large number of books were written during the forty days of his seclusion. We are unable to determine whether the number of books thus prepared was two hundred and four, or nine hundred and four; but it was a large number. It is in such a manner that we are told of the making of a collection of sacred books. We infer that for a long period, lasting at least seventy years, the sacred scrolls and other materials of the Jews had been out of existence. It is very natural to think that when a city has been destroyed by conquerors, its temple and other buildings razed to the ground, its sacred scrolls would be burned, or otherwise disposed of. So that if Moses had written the five books of the Pentateuch, as many think he did, and if later writers had written other books, such as the books of Gad the seer and Nathan the prophet, and the like (which books are mentioned in our Bible as having once existed), it would appear probable that these books had all suffered destruction. The tradition which is embodied in the books of Ezra alludes to the strengthening of the memory of the scribe. The use of memory is not to originate something, but to recall the events and sayings of the past.

Before we dismiss the feat of memory displayed by Ezra, it will be well to remember that the Buddhists believe that the works of Gautama, the Buddha, were not committed to writing by him, but that they were learned by his disciples, and passed along down by the effort of memory alone. This is not impossible. It is known that the Vedas were handed down in this manner for many hundreds of years, and no one would now dispute the enormous powers of memory to which Indian priests and monks attained, when written books were not invented, or only used as helps to memory.[1]

If we leave the extra books of Ezra which are not found in our version of the Bible, and turn to that book of Ezra which our common Bibles contain, we shall come upon facts suggestive of the proposition that to Ezra we are indebted for the making of the Bible, in its first form.

In the first year of the reign of Cyrus the Persian, a decree was issued for the rebuilding of Jerusalem; and the work was undertaken. If we follow the common chronology, this was in the year 536, or thereabouts, B. C. Afterward, during the reign of Artaxerxes, a coalition was formed against the pious Jews, who were engaged in rebuilding their city. The conspirators complained to the king that Jerusalem had always been a city of rebellion, and that if it were built again it would seek to become an independent power, and therefore the king's revenue would suffer, and the like. The king caused the records to be searched, found the charge substantiated, and ordered the work to cease. Afterward, however, Artaxerxes was induced to modify this decree, probably through the influence of Ezra, and the scribe was himself commissioned to press the work of restoration forward. The copy of the letter given by the mon-

[1] Rhys Davids, *Buddhism.*

arch to Ezra is contained in the book of Ezra. "This is the copy of the letter that the king Artaxerxes gave unto Ezra the priest, the scribe, a scribe of the words of the commandments of Jehovah, and of his statutes to Israel. Artaxerxes, king of kings, unto Ezra the priest, a scribe of the law of the God of heaven," etc.

It is the opinion of some of the foremost and most expert scholars that about this time the Bible took tangible form, and the Jews began to be the "people of the book." It is quite impossible to fix with entire certainty upon the man, or master spirit, who did the most in reducing to proportion the Holy Scriptures, but certainly the indications point to Ezra more than to any other. The eminence of this man is somewhat obscured to Bible readers by the inferior place and space accorded him in the Bible; but it accords well with the spirit of the prophets, earlier and later, to keep themselves and their particular work in the background. If we look for qualification for the enterprise of Bible-making, we find no one superior to Ezra, a man recognized by decree of the king as a writer of the laws of Jehovah.

He may have been one of a number engaged in that important and pious enterprise, which was primarily to recover the people to obedience and righteousness. In order to that, it was needful that the law should take a more tangible shape, and moreover that it should be placed in its appropriate historical setting. It was necessary at last that Israel's story should be told, as only a scholar and a trained man of letters could tell it. The indications are that Ezra had five colaborers in this work, and that their work was of a magnitude greater than any previously undertaken. The materials were abundant. There was first of all the prophetic work of the period beginning, say, two and a half centuries before. There was then the historic work which had been going on during the period of exile. There was the vast body of tradition, and no people have been better furnished with tradition than the Jews. Let us suppose that the Assyrians had also their body of traditions. They had their story of the creation of the world. Perhaps it was during the exile that the Jews became acquainted with the story of creation. Or if they possessed their independent traditions, they were modified by the Assyrian ideas. Whatever the Assyrians had in the way of creation-story could, readily be appropriated by the Jews, inasmuch as their progenitor was an emigrant from that very region.

According to the researches of recent students, it becomes more and more probable that the story of the creation was first written in the form we now possess at the time of the exile. Inasmuch as the account bears evidence of being composite, that is, of being drawn from different sources, one may almost see the places where the primitive Assyrian and the primitive Israelitish versions are joined together.

It will be noticed that all along this way of study we are following the line of the greatest probability. There is absolutely no other way of studying such matters. The old method of maintaining that the Scriptures came into being miraculously is a following of a way of improbabilities. Study proceeds along such a course with immense difficulty at present.

At any rate, it is in evidence in these later days that Israel's story became connected with the Assyrian story. The Assyrian influence demonstrates itself very fully. It is well to bear in mind the difference between history and myth. The two are connected in the earlier ages of the world; but it is our work, with the light we have, to distinguish between the two. The reverent study of the Bible does not consist in shutting our eyes to the facts, but in being very closely observant of them. When we undertake the study of the life of Israel, as a whole, tracing it from its early beginnings, we are very sure to encounter statements which are historical, and others which are unhistorical. That the children of Jacob were in bondage in Egypt is history. That they came out of Egypt by the hand of a strong leader is also historical, and that this strong man enacted suitable laws for their conduct is historical. They came into the land of Canaan, and dispossessed the inhabitants. In the telling of the story there is a great amount of what we have learned to call "folk-lore" connected with it.

Jehovah was recognized by Israel as their national God. Other nations had their gods also. In time there grew up the purer conception of the universal domain of the God of Israel, Jehovah. Traces of the growth of that conception are found in the wonderful little book of Jonah, and in the prophets of the eighth century B. C.

Since Jehovah was the God of Israel, it came about that their God was concerned intimately in their deliverance from the house of bondage, and in their entry upon the land of Canaan. So we have the truth of God's dealing, his government set forth in terms of the folk-lore. Moses, the great deliverer, went up to the top of a lofty mountain in the wilderness, and there he met God. There God gave him the set of laws which were to be the code of the people. These laws God had engraved on two tables of stone. God engraved them with his finger. A man would have to use tools, but God does not need them. Moses meets God in the top of this lofty mountain, and is there with God for forty days, and then comes down and delivers the law. That seems to have been one version of the folk-lore. There was another, if not several others. Another account declares that God came down to the top of the mountain, and there in a mighty voice spoke out these laws to the trembling people below. When at last the work of making the history of Israel began, it was not found necessary, as it now would be, to reconcile these various accounts. They are woven together, as though they were not contradictory, as we may see them to be. History was in its infancy then, and there was no such skill in it as would be demanded of the historian now.

Stories had grown in the mind of the people for hundreds of years, and had been rehearsed by parents to children. Part of the stories were historical, and part the dressing of the idea of the interest of Jehovah in the people. That such stories had been passed along the centuries, from parent to child, from one generation to another, without subtraction, or addition, or other modification, is simply incredible to the historical student of this time.

During the captivity, the past glories of Israel, its mighty triumphs in the power of Jehovah, and its sufferings and deliverances had been dwelt upon. The example of the past furnished the hope of a deliverance still in store. We may think of the experiences of Israel as becoming panoramic in the mind of a man of letters, like Ezra. The laws were forever associated in all minds with the name of Moses, but the writing of the laws and of the history in which they were environed is of the time of the exile, long after the days of Moses. So much emerges to very high probability in the study of the present time.

It will be asked, " Did Ezra, or some other man of letters, manufacture the history?" Certainly not in the sense of inventing it. Prescott's " Mexico " and " Peru " are not invented history. The accomplished historian relied for his data upon such facts as were accessible to him. He gathered them from all attainable sources. We have later discovered that some of his sources of information were untrustworthy. Yet his work was simple as compared with that of Ezra, the scribe. The Israelitish folk-lore was so abundant, and had so taken hold of the thought and life of the nation, that no historian could have gone free from its commanding influence. I take it that Ezra did faithfully choose out of that mass the very things which were to him the most true and important.

IV.

HISTORY-MAKING.

THE making of a history does not come early in the literary accomplishments of a people. If primitive people knew how to tell a connected story of their experiences, and make books, they would not deserve to be called primitive. Such work they know not how to do. They commit to such writing as they possess the art of, their simple philosophy, their poetry, their sayings, which have a recognized value, like proverbs. They do not make their history. It seems to be a pity, because we have a curiosity concerning early beginnings. We would be glad to know all the facts of the forgotten centuries, if that were possible. We certainly find that it is impossible. A text of Scripture is quoted, as showing that what things are impossible with us are possible with God. It might be applied to the matter in hand. 'It is impossible for us to know the early beginnings of history, except in the most general and vague way." It is possible, so we have been told, for God to make these early beginnings known to us by inspiration. If God inspires a man to tell things about which he has no other information except inspiration, why should any one find fault with that? Certainly no one ought to find fault with it, if it is true that God has proceeded in that way.

Let us suppose that inspiration is the quickening of

one's powers of memory, or of reason, or of all the faculties. That is a reasonable supposition. Inspiration, then, would be different from hearing something from another person, or reading something from an inscription or a tablet. If God, or the Jehovah of Israel, were like a man, if Jehovah were possessed of a body like a man's body, in every way except that his body is invisible to our senses, and if God were to speak to a man, say Ezra or Moses or another, out of a bush, in an audible voice, so that the sound of the voice came into the man's ears, like any other voice; and if God should in that way tell the man how the earth was created, and how man was made, and why man is so often bad in his character and conduct, — that would not be inspiration. If the man could understand the meaning of the words used, and if he could catch the ideas of the sentences thus delivered, he would not have need of inspiration, in the sense in which that word is usually understood. The Christian theory has been that Moses and Ezra, and many others, were inspired men. That they did not have things told them by some voice speaking outside of themselves. It seems to have been the notion of the Apostle Paul that the men who wrote the Holy Scriptures were inspired men. If he was right about it, then these men were quickened in their faculties, and did not have new or extraordinary faculties given them.

Now among other of our faculties is that of imagination. We are justified in concluding, are we not? that if God wished to communicate anything to any person, the communication would be made in that faculty we call the imagination. It may be said that God communicates with us by means of conscience, and by means of the judgment, but without imagination we should make nothing of it.

Very well. The question pertinent to our present purpose is this: How did the historian of the Jewish people — the man who extracted history from the tangled mass of tradition, folk-lore, legend, myth, and all the like, and made a veritable historical construction of it — accomplish his work? Did he employ his imagination or not? All will probably confess that he must have used his imagination, because in literary work of all kinds, and especially in the historical kind, imagination is indispensable.

On the other hand, were facts communicated to him in some other way than that by which we arrive generally at knowledge of facts? Are we to suppose that Jehovah came to him, and told him, in so many words, or at least in substance, that the first human being was made of the dust of the ground, that he was moulded in the shape of the human frame, and that afterward a rib was taken from his side, and made over into a woman? It would be difficult to believe that Jehovah told him that story in an audible voice, or wrote it on tablets, or otherwise.

The features of the creation-story were in the ideas of men, and had been so lodged in the human mind for a long time. It is probable that many persons of different generations exercised their imagination upon the subject of the creation. How did things come to be as we see them? How was the sky stretched out, and how were the stars set in it? How did the waters come to be gathered into one place, and the land in other places? Are there windows in the sky through which the rain is dropped? It seems so. By thinking on these subjects, generation after generation, there must arise an imagination of the manner of the creation. Man did not make himself, and he did not always exist, therefore he must have been made. How was he made? Why, there is no better way, before we know to the contrary, than to judge according to the appearance, and make up our minds that the Maker of man took the dust, and made a man and a woman out of it, and that thus began the human race.

God never told any one so in any direct way. We have found out more about creation during the past half century than all the ancients and moderns put together ever knew. We have an immense array of testimony to the effect that our present theory is the true one; but among the people of old Israel there was never any proof that the old theory was correct, except the ideas of men who supposed that appearances were safe to go by.

The historian, say of the time of Ezra the scribe, undertaking to construct out of the material at hand a history of the past, did faithfully apply himself to his task, and culled out of the mass of ideas, facts, and other material, his story of the beginning of things and the continuance of them in the nation of Israel. There was a demand for a history, and he was prepared to meet that demand. His memory, his imagination, and all his faculties were placed at the service of that demand, and there resulted those books of the Old Testament which we distinguish as historical.

The work of the historian is not easy, it is difficult. One difficulty may be specified. An observer, standing high above the level of the ground, as on the top of a mountain, enjoys a larger view of things than that of the observer lower down. He has a wide prospect, and all that he sees gives a true idea to his mind. The farther away his eye roves from the objects in the immediate foreground, the less he can discern of details and particulars. Near him lie stones of a definite shape, containing so many cubic feet and inches; here and there are masses of snow, accurately measurable. If the observer is of the critical sort, he can treasure up in his mind the definite and smaller facts. As regards the distance, his observation is limited to outlines, and a general idea of color and form. If he beholds a patch of snow miles away, it is vastly larger than the small patch at his feet, although it seems to be the same in size. If the point of view were shifted, the scene would be very different. The shapes of objects would change.

The historian is the man who goes up to a high point of observation, and takes his view. The things which are nearest him he perceives with entire clearness. The things which are far from him in time, he sees faintly. He can perceive outlines, and he feels the necessity of filling out these outlines to make them correspond in detail with the time he knows best. The first historians attribute to men of a distant era the feelings and purposes and the intelligence which belongs to their own era. The first historians are therefore unskillful. If there is a truth in the statement that human nature is the same the world over, and in all times, it is a truth of limited range. The fact is that human nature changes in important ways as time goes on, and that our environment has a great deal to do with our nature. The first historian of the Jewish people did not know that; even Milton did not know it.

The work before the historian of the Jews, at the time of the exile, was to connect the present nation with its past, and to connect both with the beginning of things. The national divinity, Jehovah, had become more to some of the prophets and seers of that period than one of the gods. They were thinking of Jehovah as the Creator of all nations, and the rightful Sovereign over all. They were at last emerging from the narrowness of their ancestors.

So the historian, who had acquainted himself with the learning of the ancients, knew his field, even to the beginning; for the wisdom of the ancients included everything, even the first things. Thus he begins with the first man, who was as real to him, perhaps, as any other in the series. The first man being, so to speak, a ready-made man, a man made all at once, was complete from the day his eyes first saw the light. His name was furnished, too. It was, in English, The Ruddy.[1] It was quite natural that a man thus made should have such a name. It was further natural that a man thus completed at one stroke should be able to reason consecutively, and to give names to the various animals by which he was surrounded. He could attend to the horticultural work demanded by the garden in which he found himself. He could cultivate the soil in such a way as to increase the value of the trees. All this presented no insurmountable difficulties to the historian, and it presents no difficulties to a great multitude of honest people now.

There was a difficulty, however, in the mind of the historian, such as might arise in the mind of any thoughtful person of ancient times, that is, the necessity of attributing to Jehovah a bad creation. Mat-

[1] Or perhaps Red Earth.

thew Arnold has said a very helpful word to us in telling us that to Israel, more than to any other people, belonged the intuition of righteousness. Jehovah was righteous, and was able, after he had finished the work of creation, to pronounce everything he had made good. A righteous Creator would not make an unrighteous world. Yet the hard fact stares us in the face, that unrighteousness prevails widely, if not universally, throughout the world.

The wisdom of the ancients had furnished a way out of that serious difficulty. The man was forbidden to eat of the fruit of a single tree in the garden. That tree was the knowledge of good and evil; by abstinence from that tree the man could be perfect, or right: the moment he ate of that tree he would become wrong. That is to say, before eating of that tree he should know nothing of good and evil, any more than a bird flying in the air and alighting on the branches. We should not now regard him a moral being, in that case. Yet it has long been the theory of religion that Adam, before he knew the difference between right and wrong, was a good being.

Now Ezra, if he was the historian, as we may assume for convenience he was, was not very expert in making distinctions which would occur to almost any one now who gave heed to a matter. He was solicitous that God should be right, and his creation should emerge from his hands perfect; but he had to account for evil in some way; and the legend of the serpent, which may have belonged to various peoples, came to his aid. Jehovah had made the serpent. He says: "The serpent was the most crafty of all the brutes on the earth, which Jehovah made."[1] This ser-

---

[1] The LXX., Bagster's edition.

pent had either partaken of the fruit of the tree of the knowledge of good and evil, or in some other way had acquired the knowledge, and came and talked with the woman whom Jehovah had made for the man's companionship. If all the rest of creation was fair and good, here was one part of it which was not good. Moreover, the evil which was in this serpent was more powerful than all the good which Jehovah had made, but that did not occur to Ezra. He had to account for evil, and here was the way of it, ready furnished by the legends of the ancients.

The serpent talked to the woman in a tempting manner. That a serpent should talk, and that in a language which the woman could understand, did not trouble the mind of the historian. It was contained in the learning of the ancient world, and since it fitted his purpose it was available.

We may have been accustomed to read into this simple narrative something which we have found necessary. We may have incarnated a malignant and very powerful spirit of evil in this brute. It is sometimes necessary to read meanings into the language of the ancient sayings in order to save them. Whatever we may do, however, it is improbable that our historian saw these meanings. He was making the history of his people, and from the beginning of time; and he was choosing from the material afforded by the wisdom of the world that which was fit for his purpose. While he was doing that work he was in the hands of that Providence which is ever providing. Out of roots of past thought spring flowers of later and better thought. After we have the later and the better, we can read into the earlier the best we know. The wise man can read the tulip in the bulb and the oak in the acorn. That has nothing to do with the historical work of the historian. He connects the reputed founder of the Israelitish tribes with the first man. He has the names of families. Genealogies have been preserved, as such things are preserved, when people learn their value. The names belonging to the earliest periods may well be unhistorical. The mixture of the historical with the purely mythical was inevitable to the historian of that time.

If we bring to bear on this subject the faculties of judgment we are in the habit of applying everywhere (except, perhaps, to the Bible), we shall be compelled, for various reasons, to hold the beginning of the history in the Bible to be mythical.

If we were to meet anywhere, outside of our Bible, a story of a serpent talking to a woman, uttering articulate words with sense in them, we should hold that to be an ancient myth. We should never for a moment mistake it for history. If in any language we read the story of a god making a woman out of a single bone taken from a sleeping man, we would not for a moment hesitate to call it a myth. Why should we hesitate to do the same thing when we discover such a story in our Bible? If we are to hold our reason and judgment in abeyance when reading that book, how will we be able to get good out of it? How shall we maintain anything like mental integrity?

The first portion of the Bible presents to our view the work of a historian who is not able to distinguish actual history from legend. Stories were extant which were venerable, and commanded the assent of the wise. These stories helped him to the data he was seeking, and which were necessary to the completeness of his work. By their means he saw, as he supposed, how man was made from the dust of the ground, and how woman was made from the rib of the man. He found how evil came into the world, as well as how Jehovah kept a seed of righteousness alive. For some purpose he saw the necessity of attributing a life of great length to these early dwellers in the land, and discovered legends to that effect. All of which, when we come to examine it in the light of historical criticism, is simply and unmistakably mythical.

The first chapter of Genesis may be interpreted in many different ways. However it may be interpreted, it is a work of the imagination. It really has no historical basis whatever, — it is in the nature of guesswork. Ezra regarded it as historical material. Doubtless he supposed other things equally untenable. He imagined that the sun revolves around the earth. He thought that God commanded the people to offer sacrifices, although sundry persons of a period earlier than his own, by a century or more, disputed it.

Now guesswork has its value. If guesswork is serious and skillful, we now call it "hypothesis." Newton guessed at the solution of one of the great problems of the universe. Darwin guessed at the solution of another. It is in the work of hypothesis that inspiration becomes, so to say, most apparent. Let us admit that in the cosmogony of Genesis we have not history, but inspired hypothesis. The value of it is demonstrated by the scientific opinion of experts that no such good account of creation has appeared in the annals of time, up to a recent date, as that contained in the Bible.[1]

[1] The Dean of Peterborough quotes Haeckel as affirming that "from Moses, who died about 1480 B. C., down to Linnæus, who was born 1707 A. D., there has been no history of creation to be

The historical character of the books of the Bible is invalidated, however, by the discovery that the very material which has been supposed to be history is not, and, in the nature of the case, cannot be history. When we reach the period of the Flood we may be said to approach that which has some elements of actual history in it. Such a flood as is described may be set down as an impossibility. Mr. Gladstone thinks it was possible, but then Mr. Gladstone has proved himself far from expert in many things; whereas the scientific experts show us why the flood, as described, could not have occurred. If it could have occurred, then natural laws were set at defiance, in which case we have nothing to go by. That there may have been a flood, of a local sort, such a flood as has since devastated many a fair portion of the earth, seems not unlikely. That this local flood was an important event in the history of mankind may also be admitted. All that we can say is that the account contained in the historical work of Ezra shows us how he made his history, and history made in that way is not reliable.)

There is this line of righteous life which the historian finds must have been maintained. The line reaches at length to Abraham, who becomes the founder of a great nation. The same thing which characterizes the history before Abraham is also continued afterward. The mythical element is introduced at every point in the narrative. It was so in the history of all peoples.

The food of mankind, so far as it grows out of the soil, comes to us by growth. We have wheat; the wheat does not appear in the world in the naked seed:

compared to the Biblical." Professor Sanday's *Oracles of God*, p. 10, note.

it grows in a protecting envelopment. When the time arrives for that envelopment to be stripped off, then the wheat is ready to fulfill its mission of feeding the world, but not before. For Christendom the Bible has grown up as food for the spiritual nature. It has been growing, and it has been preserved in its integrity. Now it seems its integrity is being broken. Criticism is disengaging the real food — food for the spirit of man — from its sheath of untrustworthy history. We see that it is unverifiable history. That is the first step. Until it is seen that the history is subject, and properly, to our reason, to our judgment, we do not get into the real intent of the Bible as a revelation. "He will burn the chaff in the unquenchable fire," said John of the coming Son of Man. What if the fire be already kindled in shape of that searching, merciless, and scrupulous criticism which has newly come into play?

V.

TRADITIONAL SOURCES.

To many, doubtless, the critical examination of the Bible appears to be simply a process of tearing the Bible to pieces. It offends the religious sense, and the feeling of reverence which has been inherited, or has otherwise gained possession of the mind. Such offenses must needs come, but woe to them by whom they come. We are in the habit of admitting the validity of a principle, but when we behold the application of it we are troubled, and thrown into an offended state. We may be quite willing to admit that the Bible is subject to critical study, and ought to be critically studied; yet when by such critical study the Bible is found to be no flawless and infallible revelation, but a human book, — a book produced by fallible men; good men, and inspired men, but not necessarily accurately informed men, — a sense of bereavement and loss comes upon us. If it is shown that there are mistakes in the Bible, the inference to which some minds swiftly move is that it therefore becomes an unsafe guide in religion. Moreover, if the Bible is God's book, how is it possible that it should contain errors?

A distinguished bishop[1] has recently and explicitly told the clergy of his diocese that the doctrine of the church is that the Bible contains two elements, the

[1] Bishop Potter.

human and the divine. He says it is one error to suppose that it is all God's book, and another error to suppose that it is all man's book. The doctrine of the church is that it is both human and divine. Now it is proverbial that to err is human. If there is a human element in the Bible, there are errors in it. It may be that they are not important, but the discovery of an error is a real discovery, important or not. As a matter of fact, such mistakes are plainly discoverable.

It may be a thankless task to ascertain the true nature of the Bible, or to attempt it, but it is a task demanded imperatively by the age in which we live, and by the peculiar crisis which has come in our religion. There comes a time in the experience of men when idolatry meets its overthrow. It is a hard ordeal to see our idolatry broken down, but if we do not flee from idolatry, we may find ourselves dispossessed of our idols. The Bible is a created thing, and we have worshiped and served the created thing rather than the Creator when we have worshiped the Bible, or maintained in the face of the evidence that it is infallible.

The idea of an infallible guidance, and from a book, belongs to a social state different from ours. It belongs to a less individualistic social state. Moreover, the Bible is of too composite, not to say self-contradictory, a nature to furnish an infallible guidance for any one. Recognizing which fact, the leaders of religion have made the creeds for our guidance. The existence of a creed has been demanded by an actual deficiency of the Bible; for the Bible presents a mass of material which the common mind has not been able to deal with. The uncommon minds have drawn principles and theories out of this mixed material for the guidance and government of men.

Some religious men have stubbornly closed their eyes to the discrepancies in Bible narratives. They have declared that there were no discrepancies; but it requires no very great learning to find them. Persons who have been attentively reading the sacred writings of Israel in the original tongue have clearly made out the presence of two elements in large portions of the Bible. To an inattentive reader of the Bible in the English these two might not appear. If one were to read any of the books, or the encyclopædia articles bearing upon the subject, the matter would become quite plain. The two elements are manifest from the two words applied to Deity.

The Hebrew word for God was El, and the plural of that is Elohim. The gods of the Phœnicians would be spoken of as Elohim. There was another word which was applied only to the God of Israel, and that was Jehovah, or, more simply, Jahveh. Now these two words are not used interchangeably, but their use indicates that two original accounts are put together. If we were to adopt the distinction now made by our scholars, we should say that there were Elohistic Scriptures, or Scriptures in which the word Elohim was applied to God, and Jehovistic Scriptures in which the word Jehovah is applied. It would appear that there were people among the religious leaders of the Hebrews who did not know of Jehovah, and others who did. Inasmuch as the idea of Jehovah was not the first, we may conclude that some time elapsed before the people were believers in Jehovah. When people had learned to think about Jehovah, they would write that name, instead of the older name, Elohim. There is something peculiar in the use of the plural word, (which would properly be translated " gods,") which, however, we need not enter into now. Suffice it to say that these two words indicate different original writers of traditions, and that the historian endeavored to put together in some sort of harmony things which were irreconcilable.

The river Rhone issues from Lake Geneva, a clear stream. Before the Rhone falls into the peaceful bosom of the lake it is full of the material made by the grinding of the rocks in the glaciers; but all that impurity is left in the lake, and when the river flows from the lake it is pure. A short distance below it is joined by the river Arve, which takes its rise chiefly in the glaciers of the Mt. Blanc region. The Arve is a muddy stream, and where it joins the current of the Rhone, the waters do not mingle, but there is a line of demarkation between them. The two streams flow between the same banks, and make one river, but the waters are different, and their difference is plainly to be seen, — which things, as Paul would say, are an allegory, or parable. Let us say that the Elohistic idea, that is, the idea of gods or superior powers, is that far from pure theistic conception which primitive men acquire. That is the idea which Israel, in common with other peoples, inherited; but falling into the experience of that peculiar people, there gradually emerges the pure idea of Jehovah, one God, who is creator and sovereign of all. This seems to have been the pure conception of the prophets of Israel, or of some of them.

Now, in constructing the history of the nation, the historian does not begin with Jehovah, but with Elohim. The two streams, the Jehovah stream and the Elohim stream, are brought together in one current of history, but they do not mix. The Elohistic account of the creation is given in the first chapter of Genesis. At the fourth verse of the second chapter another account appears. There the word Jehovah is introduced for the first time. The second account does not harmonize with the first. In the first account the Elohim causes plant life to precede animal life. In the second account Jehovah first creates man of the dust of the ground, and afterward causes the plants to grow. The first is the Elohistic account, and the second is the Jehovistic account, and the second contradicts the first. So that although the two run together in the same historic record, they are as distinct as are the waters of the Arve from those of the Rhone. In the first account, as any one can see by simply reading, God commands the plants to grow. In the second, Jehovah causes a mist to rise from the ground. In the first account the lower animals are created before man. In the second account man is made first, then the lower animals, and afterward woman. One does not require learning in the Hebrew or any other ancient tongue to be able to see these facts. All that any one needs is an honest endeavor to see the facts as they are, and to understand the significance of common English words. For our translators have performed a service for us, in many editions of the Bible, in translating the word Jehovah by the word LORD, and have caused it to be printed in small capitals. When, therefore, we see the word LORD in small capitals, we can know that the Jehovistic account is introduced there.

Thus it is seen that in the religious treasure of Israel at least two, if not more, sorts and series of traditions were contained. Proof of this emerges from the stories which are told, now of one person and now of another. The Elohistic tradition will attach itself to one name, and the Jehovistic tradition to another.

An instance of this is found in a tale told of Abraham, in the twentieth chapter of Genesis. The same tale is told of Isaac, in the twenty-sixth chapter. Abraham commands his wife Sarah to call herself his sister, fearing that Abimelech, king of Gerar, will kill him for the sake of his wife. The same story is told of Isaac and his wife, and in each case Abimelech is the king of Gerar. That a like experience of a domestic sort should happen to father and son is not improbable; but because the second tale makes no allusion to the first we reach the probability that the first is the same story as the second, only applied to different persons. Yet when we see that the first story uses the word Elohim, and the second Jehovah, it becomes quite evident that we have in the incident only one account, given, however, in two traditions. It is related that Abraham digged a well at a certain place, and called the name of the place Beer-Sheba. It is related that Isaac digged a well in the same country, and called the name of it Sheba, and the historian adds: "Therefore the name of the city is Beer-Sheba unto this day." We perceive the great probability that the different traditions attached the names of different persons to the same incident in this case also.

The two traditions are closely joined in some places, as in the account of the Flood. The Jehovah narrative and the Elohim narrative are dovetailed into each other, but they do not match as to the facts. The Elohim narrative says that the animals are to be taken into the ark two by two. "Two of every sort shall come to thee to keep them alive." The Jehovah narrative says: "Of every clean beast shalt thou take to thee seven and seven, the male and the female, and of the unclean beasts two, the male and the female." A discrepancy manifests itself to the most unobservant observer. There is a difference between twos and sevens, which is represented by the number five. This discrepancy arises from the bringing together into one history of two traditions which contradict each other.

The Apostle Paul seems to have been in the habit of introducing parentheses of exhortation into the current of his argument. He wished to anticipate objections. He desired that those who read his letters should be in a right frame of mind. Following his example, it may be well to anticipate the objection, which is not unlikely to arise, that the method here pursued tends to tear the Bible to pieces. Surely that is an objection well worth consideration. All nature is studied. We look as closely as we may into the developments of nature. It is well that we should do so. While we study nature we at the same time, and to an extent, reverently be it spoken, study God. Now the student of nature, one who has informed himself concerning the rocks and the layers of them which underlie our soils, has attention called to some lofty and magnificent bridge. There is a great arch spanning a chasm. In this arch he discerns two rocks firmly cemented together. They differ, perhaps, in color and in texture.

He looks upon them, and declares that one belongs to a period of the past, say the Eozoic, and the other to a later, say the Mesozoic. One was made thousands of years before the other, yet here they are joined together very firmly in one structure. The man does not have to get powder, or other explosive, and blow up our noble bridge, with its wide arch, in order to identify these different stones, and declare that they have been fitted together by human art and ingenuity. He does not have to say that the builders of the bridge were dishonest because they joined the stones of different periods in their arch. If the Laurentian stone and the Jurassic stone are in the arch, and if it stands secure in spite of their conjunction, and fulfills its purpose, the man does not destroy the bridge by his geological statements. It might indeed appear to him that the arch would possibly have been better built with stones of the same period, but the bridge is what it is, and he recognizes and states the fact.

The Bible stands before us as a literary construction. Every intelligent person as well knows that it is a construction as that men builded the bridge. The Bible was built out of materials in the form of traditions. Some of these traditions are older than others, belonging to different periods, and yet they are wrought together in the same structure, and those things which did not originally belong together are made by the historian to stand together. Now if we seek to identify these various parts and analyze the Bible, the fear seizes the mind of the timid that the Bible is being torn to pieces; but the Bible will not be torn to pieces. It long since took the form which it will doubtless maintain as long as the earth lasts.

There is, however, something which will doubtless happen, and that is a change of opinion about the Bible. There has happened a very great change of opinion about the earth, and the stars, and the relation of the earth to other bodies in space. The old heavens have passed away, and the old earth, if we speak in the language of poetry. Certainly the earth has not changed so much as our ideas of it have, and our ideas have changed in a way most profitable to us. We can employ the powers and forces of the universe far better than our fathers could. I think it must be the same with reference to the Bible.

Matthew Arnold says this: "At the present moment two things about the Christian religion must surely be clear to anybody with eyes in his head. One is, that men cannot do without it; the other, that they cannot do with it as it is." There are many reasons why they cannot do without it, and certain reasons which are now rising into prominence why they cannot do with it as it is. Among these latter is the fact that the Christian religion, as it has been professed, joins in an artificial unity those things which have no real or vital harmony. We have one of the parables of Christ to the effect that a man who hears his sayings and does them not is like one who builds his house upon the sand: the house falls down when the storm comes. The parable has a wide application. It is precisely what our Christian religion has done, and is still engaged in doing. It has claimed to have an infallible revelation from God covering the facts of creation and the history of the people of Israel. It has demanded of its adherents that they accept for truth those things which common experience either denies or is doubtful about. It has attached an importance which they do not deserve to the confused traditions of a people whose inspired thinking was provisional, and almost all of whose ideas are revised by later experience. The result is a dubiousness in the mind of intelligent people concerning the validity of the religion of Christ. If that religion compels us to believe that contradictory things are not contradictory, that seven is the same as two, and that the impossible has happened, then it is doomed to go down in proportion to the rise of rational intelligence; but the foundation of the real religion of Christ is not of such incoherent material. It does not rest on the confused and primitive traditions of a people of whom Jesus said that they made void the word of God through their traditions.

Let us return to our main line of illustration of the fallibility of the work of the sacred historian. One may select at random, from numerous instances, illustration of the unskillful method of the editor of the Old Testament Scriptures. A code of laws seems to have been given the Israelites in the desert, upon their flight out of Egypt. Some account of that we have in the second book of the Bible, the book of Exodus. But a fuller exposition of the laws appears in the book of Deuteronomy, the fifth book of the Bible. It has been supposed always, or since the Bible has been read by the people, that this fuller expression of the laws of Israel was written by Moses, and only a little later than the account given in Exodus. Evidence has arisen that some of the laws contained in the book of Deuteronomy were devised long after the time of Moses. It may be that these laws were many or most of them devised hundreds of years after the flight of Israel out of Egypt, and it may also be that some of them have no historical basis whatever.

We will note that there grew up in Israel, in later times, a great hatred of other nations, and of some other nations in particular. This feeling expressed itself in some of the laws and usages of a later period. It was assumed by the historian that Moses gave these laws, yet it is curious that the law-abiding people near the time of Moses acted as though they had never heard of these laws. For instance, there is a law against any fellowship with the Ammonites and the Moabites: "An Ammonite or a Moabite shall not enter into the assembly of the Lord; even to the tenth generation shall none belonging to them enter into the assembly of the Lord forever."

But in the days of the judges, which was not long after Moses, a Moabitess was married by one of the chief personages of a certain locality, and no word of disapproval seems to have been uttered by any one. Indeed, this Moabitish woman was the ancestress of the great king David. This is a mere incident, to be sure, but it is one of many which shows how the book of Deuteronomy was composed, of how diverse elements, and how widely some of its parts are separated in time. If some future historian of the United States were to tell the incident of the murder of a certain Boston man by a professor in a medical school, and were to add that this professor was punished by electrocution, it would be open to the critic to show that electrocution became a law in the State of New York long after the Parkman murder, and that the historian mistook a law of New York for a law of Massachusetts.

The work of the historian was not accurate historical work. We have a history containing most serious flaws. These frankly exhibit themselves to anybody who will look at them, and by their existence two things would appear to be demonstrated: first, that accurate history is not necessary to the real religion of Christ; second, that the traditions which include accounts of miracles, such as the changing of rods into serpents, the standing of water "upon an heap" in the bed of the Jordan to admit the passage of Israel dry-shod, the standing still of the sun, and the like, do not furnish us with the substance out of which a real history can be made. All that we can know by them is what the people of old believed in regard to such things, and how easy it was for the most improbable stories to command assent.

Meanwhile the Bible, which contains the religion of Christ, and that other religion upon which the religion of Christ was founded, while it becomes less and less to us a book of history or of science, will be likely to become more and more a book of religion and of the development thereof in the thoughts of men.

VI.

LEGENDARY ELEMENTS.

TRADITION has favored the idea that Ezra the scribe is to be credited with the formation of the Old Testament canon. We have seen that the work of Ezra, or some contemporary, was of a more general character than that. It may be said that the Old Testament made its appearance in the world for the first time under his hand.

No historian creates history. His imagination is not employed in devising facts; he takes the facts as he finds them, and brings them together, not into a mere mass, but into an organic whole. History is not like a catalogue. It is not a list of things which have happened; it is not a heap of stories; it is a kind of body, instinct with life. In that body the past speaks. The history is wholly made of material already in existence, not evolved from the inner consciousness of the historian. The historian chooses and prepares his material. He condenses this, and enlarges that. According to his best judgment, he finds the relations of the facts, which experience has supplied. He may not always get the right relation. The less skill he possesses the more liable will he be to go astray. The result of his work will be a connected tissue; a real fabric, woven together. (No man has ever yet written a perfect history; it will be long before such a history can be written. If it were written, it would not be a mathematically exact reproduction of facts as they occurred; for that would be no history, perfect or imperfect.

Perspective comes in the work of the historian as really as in the art of the landscape painter. The Chinese painters give a very faithful picture of details. The Chinese artist's fisherman is undoubtedly accurate, and the boat which he paddles. The mountains are good and the representation of water and all the like; but the Chinese painter is most faulty in perspective. That is to say, his fisherman will be about as large as his mountain, and the fisherman's boat would never be able to get through the mouth of one of his rivers. The artist undoubtedly proposes to do ample justice to the man and his boat; we must be able to see the features of the man, and the cracks and knots in the boat; but that necessitates making the man and the boat so large that the rest of the landscape is thrown into fault thereby. It might be better, for the purpose of art, to make the boat by one little indefinite stroke of the brush, and the man by another. So it is in history-making. That is a work of high art. What we require in history is that it shall be a picture; that it shall not be an endless chain of stories of particular individuals with no attention to perspective. Ezra wished to put Israel's truth, that truth for which it stood, in a setting of past events. The setting was now felt to be necessary. The law of right conduct must be traced, and through the mazes of genealogies, legends, creation-hymns, and tales of heroes he traced it. When we require of him that his history shall be authentic even to the beginning, as history, we require too much.

Our scientific teachers tell us that the young of a

species epitomizes the history of its race. The young frog is first a young fish, and afterward a young something else. The young child is like the young human race. It has its life and its experience, but of this experience it can give very little account in after years. Its earliest months are real enough, but when the child, grown up, undertakes to tell the story, there is a point where definiteness begins. Behind that point, all is indefinite. Of the months succeeding its birth it has no memory whatever. Then there arises some one incident which makes sharp impression upon the child's mind, perchance some little matter of domestic discipline, or some beginning of a moral perception, and that is retained in memory. It is at that point the historical material begins. After a while something else occurs, which makes an addition to the small historical stock. Later a more closely connected view of incidents, and acquirements, and the like arises; but the early things will forever be shrouded in the mystery of infancy.

So it is with the human race. For a long time after the race is born, as a human race, it has no history which can be told. Then incidents come which are made much of. These are out of proportion to the place accorded them. They are explained in the way children explain things. Thus arise the legend and the myth. What is true of one portion of the human race is true practically of all. There is a battle fought between one tribe and another. The daylight seems to be protracted beyond its usual length. This is felt to be to enable the victors to pursue their victory more thoroughly. Thus grows up the legend of the standing still of the sun. A legend of a flood which is so great that it covers the whole earth with its waters, and rises above the tops of lofty mountains, a flood which destroys all living things, except the marine, has for its basis some disaster in the shape of a flood. Which actual flood, however, does not rise above the tops of the mountains, and does not cover the earth, and destroy all land life.

Such incidents, built up into such legends, adorn the pages of all the first attempts of men to tell about the first things, or the things of man's infancy. As the race grows older, it becomes more discriminating. Its historians grope patiently in the mass of the early things, and confess that we are ignorant of the actual occurrences in the childhood of the world. In the legend they recognize a basis of incident which made impression upon a time, so that it was pushed forward into prominence and embalmed in the myth. This brings to our view something of importance, namely, it is the duty and privilege of a child to learn by experience, and to outgrow its earlier and more crude interpretation of things. The same duty belongs to the human race.

There are many intelligent persons who somehow or other hold it to be a sort of duty to believe, or to profess belief of things which their sober and trained judgment refuses to accept. They do not proceed in that way with reference to the practical affairs of life, but only with reference to religion. Thus their religion becomes a sort of invertebrate religion, — a religion which has not real stamina, and sturdy, independent uprightness. It is never safe to tamper with the truth and accept fables. Wherever you find the fables, it is safe to recognize them as such, and to make use of them as fables. It is not safe to call them the facts of history, because in so doing one becomes careless about the truth of a thing. He renders himself incapable of adhering to the truth through evil report and difficulty. It is held to be an act of piety by some to believe every statement made in the Bible, even if it should transpire that the statement could not be true, taken in its literalness. Pious men deny the discrepancies in the Bible genealogies and other accounts. They start with the proposition that the Bible contains no error of any sort, and then they hold to the proposition in the face of the plainest evidence. Now they do themselves a moral damage, and are acting impiously. There is a lack of candor and truthfulness in them, which makes the very root of religion unsound.

Let us consider for a moment the martyrs. A multitude of heroes have died rather than live a false profession. Such stout honor redeems our race. They have faced the beasts of the arena, and the fires of persecution, and the loss of friends and of all things, in order to be true to their convictions. Such men were not well informed, but so far as their information went, they did strictly abide in their truth. A certain light had broken in upon them in the progress of God's creation, and that light they welcomed, and embraced, and stood by. Their fellow-men crucified them, or burned them, or tortured them, or flung them to the lions. Whenever a man obstinately stands against the light, and will none of it, he takes his stand against God, for it is God who pours the light down. It is God who builds new ages upon the ruins of old ages. It is God who makes increasing revelation of himself and his truth, as time goes on.

Professor Sanday quotes from the Table Talks of Luther: " Melancthon, discoursing with Luther touching the prophets, who continually boast thus, 'Thus saith the Lord,' asked whether God, in person, spoke with them or no. Luther replied: 'They were very holy, spiritual people, who seriously contemplated upon holy and divine things; therefore God spake with them in their consciences, which the prophets held as sure and certain revelations.'"[1] It is a reasonable view, and of great consequence. For all men who studiously contemplate any of the things of God in any department of his creation will be not separate from, but closely in line with God's revelation. It is thus the revelation has been made from time to time. Thus and not otherwise Johann Kepler thought God's thoughts over after him. Others have seen the light of his truth in like manner.

[It has been complained that the religious world obstinately opposes the advance of truth in the world. Modern astronomy had to fight for its life, and geology had its struggle for existence. Modern biology has been compelled to fight its battle. Why? Is it because men, as men, are always opposed to progress? Is it not rather because religious men and men of the Bible have been opposed to the new theories? The new astronomy was contrary to the Bible, the new geology was opposed to Holy Writ, and biology does not harmonize with Moses. Religious people were afraid of the light of new discoveries. The Bible proceeds upon the general theory that the earth is flat; and the religious world said to the discoverers that they must not prove the earth's rotundity. It was not a question of truth, but of what the Bible was supposed to say; and what the Bible said was to end all dispute. We have learned

[1] *The Oracles of God.* Preface to the second edition.

surely that the earth is not flat. So much light God, through the astronomers, who contemplated his truth, has set shining among us. The truths of geology and of biology are each a light God sends to us. By reason of a false notion of the nature of the Bible many have set God's light at defiance.

It is a strange thing that men should have used the Bible thus obstructively, and fenced out God's light with it; that is, however, precisely what they have done, and are more or less continuing to do. Jesus boldly revised the law and the prophets of Israel. He learned from them their truth, but he brought forth new truth, and was thus a light in the world. The upholders of the sacred traditions were roused to great wrath by his conduct. They spoke of him as a blasphemer, while he on his part told them that they refused to come to the light because they preferred darkness. The severity of the reproof justifies itself. Any person who prefers the statements of the Scriptures to the knowledge which now enlightens the intelligent world shows the same preference for darkness which characterized the defenders of the old faith.

We talk of the Scriptures as sacred. There is a reason why we should so speak of them, but we ought to lay it well to heart, and it would be a bright day if all mankind could once grasp the thought, so late in making its way, that what makes the value of the Scriptures or of anything extant among us is the truth, not the error, they contain. The really and eternally sacred thing is truth. Now truth is no mere rock-like and stable substance, but it is a growing plant. It is apprehended, not by those who love statements for themselves, but by those who love truth. To those who love truth for its own sake, nothing will stand in the way. The truth they will have if it is procurable. They will not let words of the wise, long spoken, stand in their way. They will not permit the traditions of the past to hinder the truth which walks to-day.

We make a far-reaching mistake when we attribute to anything more than properly and naturally belongs to it. The Israelites took trees and lopped off the branches, and then drove the trunks into the ground about their altars. They are called "groves" in our common version of the Bible. Really these were emblems of the goddess Ashera, and the goddess Ashera represents the "female side of the beneficent and fertilizing sun-god." These wooden posts were only wooden posts. They had grown as trees, under the kindly influences of nature, but when men had wrought their devices upon them, to make them signify something more than trees, they fell into that curious something we have learned to call idolatry. Under the influence of the sun, the trees do actually grow, put forth their leaves and the buds and fruit. It is right to recognize the fact, but when the trees are set up around the altars to receive the worship of mankind, they make for idolatry, which is confusion.

There is a more subtle and refined idolatry to which our Christendom is no stranger. A book is set up to be our infallible guide and God's speech to us. What the book declares in any portion of it is to be taken to be God's truth for us. To inquire further or to doubt is held to be an evil, involving a distrust of the Most High. That is attributing to the Bible more than belongs to it. More than could possibly belong to it, for is not the book a device of men? It grew in men's thoughts, through the illuminating influences of the

Spirit of God, no doubt. These thoughts, more or less appropriate to their time, have been extended or diminished so as to fit that structure of revelation in which we find them.

Pillars of stone were set up in various places in the borders of Israel. It is perfectly right to have pillars of stone erected for certain purposes: the common purpose is of a memorial nature. There were some of the Jews, at least, who thought of these stones as simply memorial and nothing more. There were others who regarded them as the abodes of this or that deity. These last attributed to the pillars that which did not and could not belong to them, and were idolaters. There are beautiful images of stone and bronze erected in the streets and parks of cities. They serve for the most part a memorial purpose. They are so far superior to the images worshiped by heathens, that a heathen visiting London, for instance, might be powerfully moved to fall down and adore the mere statuary of the place. His mistake would lie in attributing to the work of art somewhat more than he ought. It might be to him, if he were far down in the ranks of heathenism, the abode of a deity. There is nothing to be complained of in the images, nothing whatever. It is well to have monuments as memorials of great deeds and great events, but they ought to be regarded as memorials.

The Bible is a memorial, a monument, the very best literary product of ancient times. There are blemishes in it. It tells us of the thoughts of men of an early time. These men were strongly influenced by the higher motives through which God blesses our humankind. These higher were in struggle with all sorts of lower motives, but the motive of righteousness came to prevail more and more. That is the crowning glory of the Bible. The book itself indicates to us that the higher motive emerged by slow process, painfully fighting its way against the opposition of mankind. The higher was always beset by the lower. The grander apprehension of the best men, who felt that God is a Spirit, and must be worshiped, not in particular places and by particular performances and by a specific set of men, was continually obstructed and silenced by the people who wished to be idolaters. They must have their spectacular shows. They cared more for the dress of the priest than they did for the character of the suppliant. They cared more for the external order of the sacrifice than for the feeling of the heart. Therefore it was that the man of the greater apprehension was compelled to complain that they drew nigh God with their lips, while their hearts were far from him.

The Bible presents to us not only a memorial of the grander apprehension; it also gives, and in tedious detail, the lower and spurious apprehension of the idolaters. We have their version of God, as well as the better version. What it all comes to is this, that we have the responsibility of making proper choice for ourselves, and with such light or lack of it as we have of the things the Bible tells us. When we conclude, as many seem to have done, that in this memorial of the religion of the past God dwells; when we are told, as we have been, that God is in the book, in the sense that God's Spirit in some way pervades its pages, so as to make it different from any other book, we are attributing to the book that which does not belong to it, and we are making an idol of it. Now the idolatrous worship of the book is the real religious sin of the time; and this idolatrous worship of the book goes with much careless reading of it, and therefore a superficial knowledge of its contents. But it is of that with which men have a shallow acquaintance, that they can make the most sweeping assertions. They can say, if they know nothing about the facts of the case, that there are no mistakes in the Bible. They can say with great confidence that all its prophecies have been fulfilled, or, if not, that they will be fulfilled. I think we discover that those who know the most about anything are apt to talk about it in somewhat guarded terms. The wide-sweeping statements which we are accustomed to hear and read about the Bible are the most untrustworthy of all statements, because they show a lack of knowledge.

There are in the historical portion of the Old Testament two sets of national traditions regarding the government of Israel. In one of these we read that under stress of peculiar circumstances King David purchased a field and a threshing-floor of a Jebusite. The king wished to make a sacrifice, and he proposed to have it no mere cheap sacrifice, made by another man, but by himself. Wherefore, although the man offered the oxen of his threshing-floor and all the place to the king to use as it might please him, the king declined the gift. So far, in the main, the stories agree, but as to the price paid they totally disagree. In one account we are told that David paid the man six hundred shekels of gold, and in another that he paid fifty shekels of silver. It is true that the men named in this transaction seem at first glance to be different men, but the circumstances make it most probable that there are two stories of one event. If a man declares, in the method characteristic of the careless and the extravagant, that there are no blunders, and if a blunder is shown him, he may explain it in some manner, but the object of the explanation is to fortify a notion of the Bible which is becoming more and more untenable. The object is to maintain that the Bible is infallible, or without even the slightest error. That attributes to the created thing the quality which belongs only to the uncreated. God is infallible: men are not, and men wrote the Bible. The Bible is the work of men's hands. It is the work of their thoughts, and their imagination, and their consciences; and God works unceasingly in the most enlightened consciences, and in the most consecrated imaginations, and in the most true thought of men so as to give an increasing revelation of himself and his glory.

Another thing. The inaccuracies of the Bible, those very things which lie plain upon the pages of the book, are in respect to things of no practical moment. It concerns us no whit what David paid for a field. It does concern us that David repented of evil designs, and made his effort for righteousness. Whether Moses was a descendant of Abraham, or an Egyptian, really does not concern our character; but that a law of God came to Moses through his serious "contemplation upon holy and divine things" is of very great interest to us. The revelation came that the revelation might continue to come. When we worship the means of the revelation, by calling it inerrant, as the phrase is, we foreclose the farther revelation we might be receiving. For the problems of our time, for our own right conduct and influence in our time, we need not a settled formula of the past, but speech with God in the living present.

VII.

PROPHECY.

THE word prophecy has come to mean more than its original significance. The prophet was God's speaker at first, but afterwards came to be one who could foretell the future. Ability to speak for Jehovah seems to imply an ability to look into the mystery of the future and disclose it. If one is in the counsels of Jehovah, knowing God's mind, it is not difficult for him to perceive what shall come to pass; but it does not necessarily follow that one who knows the mind of God in respect to some things is also informed in respect to all things. It not only does not follow, but it is absurd. There is not a living person, whose intelligence is at all developed, who does not know something of the mind of God. There is no one to whom the world does not express something, and something which is true. All persons know of the alternation of day and night, of seedtime and harvest, and of ten thousand other cosmic facts and arrangements. These things disclose an order and an intelligence. We may not be able to give a very good or sufficient account of that intelligence, or of the order which it testifies to; it is a fact that no one can give a sufficient account of creation. Yet, in so far as we discern order and intelligence in the cosmos, we are let into the mind of God; but that privilege is strictly limited. Those who best see the meaning of present things are likely to know most of the future. The knowledge of the future is not a supernatural gift, or at least it is no more a supernatural gift than the knowledge of the past or the present.

In the Bible we encounter a prominent class of writers, perhaps the most prominent of all, known as the prophets. Soothsayers, necromancers, witches, medicine men, and all the like belong to the history of all tribes of men. Astrologers consult the stars and necromancers the dead, and medicine men go through various frenzied performances to gain some knowledge of the future. These persons attain influence in their tribes and become chiefs and priests and prophets or sages. Israel, while it had its soothsayers and necromancers and astrologers at various times, and possibly in some abundance, presents us with the vision of a higher class. The reason why this class is higher is chiefly that it is more sober, more reasonable, and more solicitous for righteousness.

It is with the prophets who spoke to Israel, and who wrote out their addresses afterward in that permanent form which has survived to this day, that we begin the study of Israel's history. Before them we have confused and contradictory traditions with a large admixture of myth. With them we seem to arrive at the solid ground of reality. These prophets of the beginning of Israel's reliable history do not spring into existence all at once. There are intimations of the presence of prophets in the time of Samuel, that is before Israel became a kingdom. There appear to have been communities or groups of them. These groups we may call "schools of the prophets." And possibly they were like certain communities of monks flourishing in later times, and some of which were devoted to specific objects. These men were known as "men of the spirit," or inspired, and were probably subject to ecstatic visions. They contemplated holy things, and not without result. Thus in due time arose an official class, connected with the government or with the priesthood. There were some who were authorized to speak, and who gave their predictions concerning the outcome of wars and other enterprises. Others commanded a hearing, whether belonging to the recognized prophetic class or not. They were the real, as distinguished from the official prophets. These uttered their warnings and admonitions simply because they had something to say, and were determined to say it.

Perhaps one of the first of the prophets who wrote his predictions was Amos, who flourished a little later than the time of Solomon. He prophesied against Damascus and its sins, against Gaza, Tyre, Idumæa, Ammon, and others, and finally against Israel. He seems to have predicted the downfall of all these. His prophecies have been justified by events: for none of the cities and families against whom he spoke remain, except Israel. Amos uttered his prophecies at Bethel, which was at that time the centre of worship of Israel. The chief priest at Bethel sent word to the king of Israel to inform him that Amos was forming conspiracies against the kingdom, and that the land would be utterly unable to bear his words. Finally, the priest bade Amos go out of the land and live in Judah. "Thou shalt no longer prophesy at Bethel, for it is the king's sanctuary." Amos answered, professing to be no prophet, "I was not a prophet, nor the son of a prophet, but I was a herdsman and a gatherer of figs. And Jehovah took me from the sheep, and said to me, Go prophesy to my people Israel." This is the man who, while disclaiming the prophetic office, claimed the prophetic gift. His theory of the work of the prophet may be gathered from these words, "Jehovah will do nothing without revealing instruction to his servants, the prophets." Nothing more clearly sums up the idea which the genuine prophets had of their own service. Jehovah would as surely reward iniquity, as pain would follow a bruise. Of that there was no doubt in any true prophet's mind. Israel would fall, as Amos declared, nay, in effect was already fallen. At one time he declared that Israel should never rise, but the warning of the catastrophe would surely precede the event.

By such words as these we acquire a knowledge of the field or province of prophecy. Jehovah will do nothing without revealing instruction to his servants, the prophets. If we judge these words fairly, and in their connection, we shall escape that false notion of prophecy which has had so wide a following at various times. The herdsman was attending to the duties of his vocation, and meanwhile meditating upon the state of things in his nation, and in other nations. He was alive to the degeneracy of the times. He saw, as plainly as he could see his flocks, that calamity would follow such degeneracy. Because he saw it, he felt that Jehovah was calling him away from his flocks to go and tell Israel of the woes which should surely overtake the nation, unless it changed. He who sees things of importance to his time, and is deeply convicted of them, leaves his flocks or whatever of personal interest might withhold him, and goes as his conscience, that is to say, as God, calls him.

The scope of the prophet thus called is strictly limited. He is not a fortune-teller. He does not so much foretell future events as describe the certain result of present tendencies. It was characteristic of the Israelitish prophets to declare in a thousand ways that Israel would be rooted up out of its home and carried away. It was the way of conquest in those times to transfer a conquered people from their soil. It is notable that a great military power afterward arose which left the conquered peoples where it found them; but that mode had not yet come. It was easy, therefore, for the prophet to see that Israel would be deported, when it should be conquered. Amos, living before the rise of the great Assyrian sovereignty, saw that Israel would be conquered by some of the surrounding powers.

We have already seen that Israel's writers were clearest in their history in the times nearest themselves; that as they went back into the past they became involved more and more in that inaccuracy which belongs to lack of knowledge. It may be said that their best view of the future was of things imminent, not of things afar off. If they had their dreams of far-off times in the future, they were of such stuff as our dreams of the distant future is commonly composed. We ourselves are not without our prophets, who foretell us the future. Perhaps one of the most widely read of modern books is the dream of Mr. Bellamy. It is a forecast of the time when socialism shall be realized and shall bless the world. Only we are very sure that it can never come to pass, and for obvious reasons. The chief value of the prophecy of Mr. Bellamy does not at all lie in the picture of the end of the twentieth century. That is merely a piece of literature, and of an attractive form. The great value of the book is that it calls attention to the present tendencies. It may not even be a correct view of them, — undoubtedly is an imperfect view, but it is like a voice of warning which startles us, and sets us considering how we may possibly amend matters.

I do not see why it should not be precisely as true now as it was in the days of Amos, that God will do nothing without revealing instruction to his servants the prophets. Yet the limit of the prophetic gift is to be soberly admitted. It is simply impossible for any finite intelligence to pry far into the future; while it is not only possible, but of common experience, that the best instructed men of any age are precisely those who know something of their present, and by light of it are able to discern the near-by future. We may conclude, reasonably, that if a prophet had arisen in Israel who could have foretold the discovery of a new continent, to be called America, and by the energy and skill of a man of one of the western nations, and at a time corresponding with our year of the Christian era, 1492, then we should have to hold that prophecy is of a miraculous nature — a kind of fortune-telling, and that by its aid we may look far into the future; but we find no such definite instance of the scope of the prophecy. What we do find is the prediction of the downfall of Israel, its conquest by its enemies, and that prophecy was fulfilled. There were wise men in our own land half a century ago who predicted the trouble that was rising already concerning the slave. It was given to one statesman to declare, upon a memorable occasion, that between the system of slavery and freedom there is an irre pressible conflict. Yet neither the time nor the manner of the issue of the conflict could be predicted until the time was at hand. God gives us intelligence of things which are shortly coming to pass. Not to the foolish, and not to the indifferent, but to those who love the ways of truth and hate evil, God gives intimation of his work before the work is accomplished. That is what Amos tells us, and that is also what wide experience corroborates.

Our intelligence is of such sort that it does not concern itself altogether with the immediate present. It takes hold upon the past, and lays its grasp upon the future. The wise can always foresee things, and do foresee them. We plan ahead, and we heed the warnings of experience, but if any one projects his imagination too far into the future, and attempts to declare the things which shall come to pass remotely, he is sure to fail in his predictions. Or, if he attempts to use the language of precision, and to describe in detail some far-off events, he will surely blunder.

There is a considerable diversity in the prophets of Israel. It is in the study of this diversity that our scholars have arrived at the degree of probability, which amounts practically to certainty, that our book of Isaiah, in the Bible, is not the work of one prophet. Both of the prophets who were in the main the authors of the book of Isaiah are to be distinguished very clearly from the sort of prophet who wrote the book of Ezekiel. He is more given to ecstasy, and to the Assyrian method, than others of the prophets. He entertains hopes, which lead him to predict things which have not come to pass. We may be quite sure that the things he foresaw, some of them in very detail, will never come to pass. He tells us that the word of Jehovah came to him, to take one stick and write upon it, "For Judah, and those of Israel who were associated with him." He was likewise to take another stick and write upon that, "For Joseph, the stick of Ephraim, and those of Israel associated with him." Now it is plain that by these two sticks, thus named, is signified the two kingdoms into which the original one kingdom of David and Solomon had been separated. Such an allegorical object-lesson teaching was not uncommon in Israel. The people would ask the prophet what the sticks meant, and he would tell them that they meant the divided houses of Israel. The sticks would become one; and so after all the years of division, the two houses would be united again. Of one thing we are very certain, and that is that this union has never taken place. I think it is admitted, even by the most conservative of students, that Israel or Ephraim remained distinct. After the Babylonian exile, it seems that much of that portion of Israel which is represented by the name Ephraim became merged in other peoples, and lost its identity.

Now, if we were to analyze the feelings of the prophet, considering his tender patriotism, and his pious trust in the words of those who had gone before him, we should see that it seemed a very word of Jehovah to him that the sundered Israel would be restored, and that it would take up its neglected mission to the nations, and perform it faithfully to the end. The old twelve tribes, the tribes of the promises which had recently been rehearsed in the ears of the returning exiles, would rise, as out of the very valley of death in which they had fallen, and would be an exceeding great army, enough to conquer the world.

This was the prophet's hope, and it became his prediction, but it was not fulfilled. To-day there is no reason, except the prediction of the prophet, to hope that it will be fulfilled. It were as well to expect that Assyria itself, and the Tyrian, Carthaginian, or old Roman hosts, would rise out of the dust of long-past centuries. Let us glance at it a moment. If there were ten tribes, partly deported to the distant East, and if these peoples became assimilated with other peoples, taking their language and their customs, intermarrying with them, then our tribes become "lost tribes,"— lost by assimilation with foreign nations. It is easy enough to see why it would not require a long period for them to become indistinguishable from others, because they would not be Israelitish after a few generations. We are accustomed to the idea that omnipotence does not make impossibles possibles. To cause a race of human beings, now, or at some future time inhabiting the earth, to revert to ancient conditions, to take the mixture of races, already accomplished, out of their blood, is certainly one of the impossibles, if any such there are in all the wide domain of nature.

An impetuous and almost frantic zeal has been awakened in the heart of many prophetic enthusiasts with reference to the fulfillment of prophecy. They have searched the Scriptures and found the predictions, and having already in mind the fundamental proposition that the Scriptures are all and altogether from the infallible wisdom of God, they have proceeded to predict the regathering of scattered and lost Israel, the coming of the Son of Man in the clouds of the sky, the rapture of saints, the confusion and condemnation of the disobedient. Thereby the study of the prophecies of Israel has been discredited, and fallen into disuse. The richest product of Israel's wisdom and experience has thus become for the most part of no value to the modern religious world. This arises from the notion that prophecy is a miraculous gift, that it is apart from the laws which govern thought and judgment, and that the prophets could view the far-off future; whereas the prophets are the men who perceive the tendencies of things, and the inevitable consequence of the decline of morals and of responsibility. They can look into the future, but they are governed by the laws of thinking. They are as liable to make such mistakes as Ezekiel made as other men of insight are to go astray in their estimates of things.

In respect to prophecy we force our belief beyond the bounds of reason when we consider that men of any age can predict a remote future, except in the most general features of it. It is open to any prophet to maintain the ultimate conquest of good over evil, but to tell us in what form the good shall display itself, or how the conquest shall be effected in detail, is simply beyond that finite knowledge which prescribes our limitation. If ever an infinite being were to be among us, as one of our kind, — which is an impossibility to thought, since such a being would not be of our kind, — then the most remote future might be spoken forth as though it were the present.

By reason of a strange perversity we have been in the habit of ranking the prophets of Israel, earlier and later, with the astrologers and fortune-tellers. We have credited them with an ability which transcends mortal powers. We have read into them more than they could have meant, and we have not dared to revise their conclusions when they required revision. Out of such perversion have arisen the fanaticisms which came with the Reformation, — the vagaries of the fifth monarchy men, — the fright produced by William Miller in the forties of this century, and the various earnest but unreasonable fancies of those who have been looking for the end of the world. Even now, and from the seat of one of our principal institutions of learning, warnings are sent forth that the world is on the verge of ultimate disaster; that the mercy or grace of God is to come to a pause within a few months, and that we have fallen upon the last times. There is much to justify these extravagances in the words of the prophets, especially some of the prophets, but there is nothing to justify them in the idea which the best of the prophets had of their own province. They were called from other occupations, not to predict the fall of empires not yet risen, but to warn people of the impending consequences of their faults. Because they devoted themselves to such a work, adapted to their times, and therefore, in the deep meaning of it, to other times as well, they have given us the word of Jehovah, unto which we also do well that we take heed, as to a light shining in a dark place.

The prophetic gift is not an abnormity. It is more or less put in use in every age. It was exercised by Lord Bacon when he wrote his "Novum Organum." Plato was a prophet when he wrote the "Republic." Washington was a prophet when he wrote his farewell letter. Every great statesman produced by time has been a prophet, or he could not have been a great statesman. The gift of forecast is as natural to man as is the gift of history-making: the one gift is supplementary to the other in many cases. To no class were the people of Israel so deeply indebted as to the prophets; it was not the priests who strove to keep Israel in the paths of Jehovah and his righteousness. It was not the scribes of a later period, it was not always or often the kings, but the prophets, those speakers for Jehovah, whose words move our hearts after so long a time; these were the men of God, the men of the Spirit, the men of the forward look. According to the opening words of the Epistle to the Hebrews in our New Testament, God is said to have spoken, not through the priests and the elders or chiefs, but through the prophets. They foretold, before they came to pass, the consequences of righteousness and of iniquity.

We have the assurance that Jehovah would do nothing without revealing instruction to his servants, the prophets. That seems to hold true all along the track of all ages. The wisest and best of men have foreseen. They have enjoyed the revelation in their own reasons of the doings of Jehovah. They have been able to forewarn the people, and often to avert the disaster which surely follows unrepented wrong. Their function has never been to tell us of the end of the world and of the coming of the Son of Man in the clouds of heaven, when every eye shall see him. That has come through no prophetic gift, but through the frenzy which good men fall into when they transcend their powers of true thinking. We have to distinguish true prophecy from false; we have to apply the test which the prophets themselves give us when they undertake to tell of the things which must shortly come to pass. Under whatsoever figures of beasts and trumpets and horns and crowns and other phenomena they speak to us, they mean that we shall get out of it some guidance for our conduct, some help to our betterment. If any of them transcend that purpose, and serve to gratify our morbid curiosity touching the hidden things of futurity, we shall be neither the wiser nor the better for their imaginations. It is the true prophet who says to us, "Come, let us reason together. Though your sins be as scarlet, they shall be white like wool. Cease to do evil and learn to do well." It is the false prophet who awakens our morbid terrors by pictures of the crash of elements and the downfall of the world in final ruin.

VIII.

FROM GODS TO GOD.

THE ground of authority is not the same to a child and a man. The child is under tutors and governors, who dogmatize. A statement is of authority to a child because it comes from an official person. The parent, the tutor, or the appointed guardian stands in a relation of authority to the child, and the child accepts what is told by this competent person as truth. It is therefore of the very last importance that teachers and parents should teach children, not carelessly, and not ignorantly, but with great prudence and wisdom. When, however, the child becomes a man, the childish things are put away. Then things are not accepted upon the authority of any one, but simply upon their merit. That is the main moral difference between child and man. The ground of authority has shifted. As it is with the individual, so is it with the race as a whole. In the childhood of the race things are accepted upon the dogmatic assertion of some persons in authority. As the race advances, it more and more shifts its ground from the dogma and the speaker to the merit and the thing spoken. The shifting process is one of disturbance and of anxiety. It must needs come, otherwise the race is kept in its childhood, and does not reach its true estate. To the child portion of the religious world, authority is still vested in official persons, and their dogma is accepted with as good a grace as may be. The adult portion of the religious world is at this very day stoutly making its revolt against the child method; so that, to the casual and superficial observer, all authority seems to be set at defiance. To those who look deeper into the phenomenon, there is evidence that we are witnessing in fact no dissolution of authority, but a shifting of its ground. In other words, the child begins to show signs of manhood. The child asks, in respect to any commandment, or proposition, " Who says it ? " The man asks, " Is it true ? " The child has reference to its parents, tutors, or guardians, the man has reference to the merit of the matter. If we observed this distinction, to which I think the Apostle Paul helps us, great confusion, and possibly much heat and anger, would be avoided. Children's things for children, men's things for men. At the same time it ought to be the aim of all men to help the growth of children, so that they should not remain in a perpetual state of adolescence.

Not a few religious people are greatly disturbed by the discovery which begins to dawn upon us that Moses did not write the books which we have ascribed to his authorship. We have been told that with the going of Moses all our religion goes. The child who has not been able to put away childish things cries for Moses. The man who is beginning to put away childish things is less disturbed at the departure of Moses as a dogmatist. The work which has been credited to Moses, and all other work, by whomsoever done, must rest entirely upon its merits. Not so to a child, but precisely so to a man. The authority of the Bible taken altogether, as a great literature of the religious past, is coming to rest entirely on the merit of it. This perhaps were a rash proceeding four centuries ago, when the Bible was dug up out of its burial and put into the hands of the people. A growth has been going on since, more or less apprehended by the more adult portion of the Christian communities, which makes necessary the shifting of the ground of authority. To a child, that is, the undeveloped religious intelligence, the saying of a prophet is the end of doubt. The prophet is recognized as God's appointed tutor and governor. The law is recognized as the schoolmaster, whose word is final. The man forgets the tutor and the schoolmaster, and institutes inquiry concerning the reasonableness of the thing taught. So far have we come in the creation of the world, that men are beginning to assert themselves, and the childish mind of the world is shocked.

My proposition is that the prophets of Israel have a merit which makes their words superior to those of the prophets and diviners of other nations. These words are put into the mouth of Moses, addressed to Israel before they came into the promised land: "For all these nations whose land thou shalt inherit, they will listen to omens and divinations, but Jehovah has not permitted thee so to do." "Jehovah shall raise up to thee a prophet of thy brethren, like unto me; him shall ye hear." While Israel did have its diviners and readers of omens, and other such, by the time of the golden age of prophets there had grown up such a prophetic work as no other nation experienced. How far different this work was from that of the diviners and soothsayers, or fortune-tellers of other peoples, one has only to read in order to see. The diviner does not care to preserve a record of his work. He wishes the public favor and applause. He wishes to be consulted and made much of. Now it transpires that the prophets of the golden age were those who were not made much of except in an unpleasant way; and, characteristically, they were addicted to forfeiting the public favor. They must have seemed to the simple minded of the people to be always engaged in tearing down something. They were precisely that class of malcontents which will not let well enough alone. I speak now of the golden age of the prophets. That age was reached through various experiences. Sometimes the prophets appear as belonging to the popular party as against the tyranny of the kings. They stand for the welfare of the people, and for their liberties or rights. Afterward they take stand alone, each prophet independent, speaking against whatsoever meets his censure.

The diviner is a patriot. He is ready to prophesy against other peoples, but he does not prophesy against his own people. He wishes the success and glory of his own people. It was not so with the prophets of Israel. They stood against the evils of their own people. They loved righteousness better than the fatherland. They devoted themselves, first of all, and most of all, to producing righteousness. In that they shine in the firmament of history more than the seers of other peoples. In them, therefore, Israel has a real glory. It is because of them Christianity could find a foundation. But what did the prophets wish to do? They wished to improve the religion of the people. They appeal with Isaiah to the reason and conscience of men. They endeavor to show that there is only One who is entitled to our worship and service, one God, Jehovah. The people had never attained that conception. They believed that there were other gods beside Jehovah, and often worshiped them. This is evidenced by the words of the prophets themselves. Jeremiah complains that Judah has as many gods as cities; and over and over again protest is made against the gods worshiped in the borders of Israel. What the prophets wished above all things to do was to abolish the idea of many gods from the minds of the people. They resort time and again to the device of sarcasm, speaking of the artificer who takes a block of wood, and with part of it he kindles a fire wherewith to cook his food, and of the remainder he makes a god. The prophets ask whether the gods can help their devotees at a pinch: whether there is any eye fashioned by the carpenter which can see, or any ear which can hear. They at least could not endure the degrading, the besotting worship; because such worship always goes far to subvert the natural ideas of righteousness of the devotee.

The prophets of the golden period proclaimed themselves boldly the servants of the One God, Jehovah, than whom there was no other. The gods of the heathen were but fashioned things. There was no divinity nor even sense in them. Jehovah was righteous; the Creator; the rightful Sovereign of all. Next, Jehovah is not a visible being, — therefore not a being to be represented in any visible form. This was harder to proclaim and gain the assent of the people to than anything else. (The absolutely invisible, to children or to primitive people, is the same as the non-existent.) Therefore the prophets of the golden period were accused of and persecuted for breaking down and setting at naught the holy things. They were the reformers; and no reformers of any period have had a more difficult work than they. Their work was nothing less than to eradicate the primitive and strongly rooted polytheism of the people, and to make them what they never had been, — the people of Jehovah.

Before the time of historical criticism, as applied to the Bible, men have been in the habit of ascribing to Abraham, the reputed founder of Israel, the pure monotheism which really belongs to a much later age. It has been supposed, naturally enough, that from the time of Abraham on, Israel was essentially, or with some breaks and relapses, a nation of Jehovah, believing in one only God. Later evidence seems to run counter to that supposition. The polytheistic word which serves to indicate a plurality of gods was embedded in the Hebrew language. While it became used afterward to apply to one God only, such was not its first use. Abraham, according to the traditions and legends which came down to the time of Ezra and Nehemiah, while he may have had glimmerings of the truth of one God, permits us to see that like the best men of his time he was powerfully influenced by the polytheistic notions and practices of the day. (He offers his son in human sacrifice. His successors easily adopt the worship of the sacred bull.)

It seems to be intimated by the prophet Amos that Israel in the wilderness was not a worshiper of Jehovah. "Have ye offered to me victims and sacrifices, O house of Israel, forty years in the wilderness? Yea, ye took up the tabernacle of Moloch, and the star of your god Ræphan, the images of them which ye made for yourselves." Is it not possible, is it not even probable, that the Israelites, before they became established in Canaan, were almost altogether idolaters, and that their very tabernacle was an idolatrous contrivance? It accords with the truth that a pure monotheism is of late beginning in the annals of time. The true worshiper of Jehovah, such an one as Isaiah the prophet, looks upon the sacrifice of animals upon altars as no requirement of Jehovah, but as an abomination to him.

Nothing springs full grown into being. Israel's true religion, that which distinguishes it from all other people's and makes Israel in reality the people of Jehovah, came to be through long periods of time. We do not fully see what it was until we reach the later prophets. We cannot even tell what were the convictions of the men of an earlier faith. As Abraham is portrayed to us, he confuses us. Even so late as the time of Elijah and Elisha, prophets who did not write or care to preserve the records of their works and times, we find a degree of the same confusion. It is difficult for our most expert scholars to determine with anything like certainty whether these prophets were opponents of certain forms of idolatry, as we certainly know their successors were.

Whatever may have been antecedent to the work of the prophets of the golden period, it is manifest that they boldly and with a measure of success founded the real and final religion of Israel. It was against every obstacle in the way of popular prejudice and of persecution that they proceeded to establish their religion of Jehovah. So bitter was the opposition to them that the memory of it lasted long in the mind of the nation. There was an almost complete gulf between the prophets and the people. The priesthood and royalty, and the people, often at war with each other, were at one against the handful of the prophets. It was to this memory of the peculiar mission of the prophets that Stephen appealed when he accused the rulers and people of his own time: "Which of the prophets did not your fathers persecute?" The persecution was unexceptive, and demonstrates that with the prophets alone was the religion and service of Jehovah. Accordingly, their work was to establish their convictions in the hearts and characters of the people. Nothing less than that.

For a long time the people had held to Jehovah as their tribal god, but that did not hinder them from believing also in other gods. Jehovah was their national god, and dwelt in their house, which they had built at Shiloh, at Dan, Shechem, and Bethel, and finally at Jerusalem. Moab had another god, and the Philistines other gods. These gods, too, were powerful, and might render help if properly approached. What the prophets undertook was to urge not only the supremacy of Jehovah, but to make plain that there is no God but the One; that righteousness is not a variable thing determined by the character of local deities, but is fixed. (Moreover, that it belongs to conduct.) To the prophets good was the same as life, and evil the same as death. "Seek good and not evil, that ye may live: and so Jehovah shall be with you, as ye have said."

It is evident that the people at various times worshiped images which represented Jehovah to them. After the partition of the kingdom, it is related that because the people went up to Jerusalem to worship, Jeroboam, the king of Israel, conceived the necessity of having them stay at home and worship. Because if they continued to go to Jerusalem his own kingdom would of course be lost. He made two young bulls of gold, and placed one in Bethel and the other in Dan, and said to his people: "It is too much for you to go up to Jerusalem; behold thy gods, O Israel, which brought thee up out of the land of Egypt." It is not doubtful that these two images represented the one tribal or national god, the one who had delivered their ancestors from the bondage. There are intimations in the period of the judges, as well as long afterward, that Jehovah was worshiped in the form of the golden calf or the golden bull. There is a similarity between that worship and the worship of Moloch: in either case human sacrifice was probably practiced.

So late as the time of the prophet Micah human sacrifice was in vogue, for Micah protests against it. Abraham is represented as ready to sacrifice his son and is commended for that readiness while hindered from carrying out the project. In the time of the judges, Jephthah vowed a human sacrifice to Jehovah, we are told, and sacrificed his own daughter, because she was the first to meet him on his return from an expedition. Samuel hewed Agag to pieces before Jehovah, and David proposed to sacrifice the seven sons of Saul. These instances suggest, as do the works of Micah, that human sacrifice was practiced, and to a late day, by Israel, as it was by other nations. Moreover, the rite of circumcision appears to be the remnant of an older practice of human sacrifice. In brief, the survival of abominations of cruelty, and that in the name of the religion of Jehovah, awakened in the prophets the purpose of a radical reformation. To abolish the cruelties was to a large extent their aim. Thus we perceive that their notion of righteousness was not a mere abstraction, or a mere assertion of righteousness in Jehovah, which by itself passes for nothing, but it was a positive announcement that the things of their religion which involved cruelty to man or beast were all wrong, and must be stopped.

One cannot help thinking, in this connection, how the cruel dogma of a remorseless Jehovah, inflicting ever continuing pain upon his creatures, has tenaciously held its ground in modern times; and how bitter has been the experience of many who have attempted to reform that cruelty out of the religion of Christ.

We have reached the point where we may say that it was the aim of the prophets to establish humanity, or humane conduct and feelings, in the religion of the people. Of course feelings of humanity came earlier than the time of the prophets, but these feelings did not dominate the religion of Jehovah until their time. Jehovah, like the sun-god and like other gods, was supposed to demand sacrifices of various sorts. He was supposed to demand the cruelties of other heathen worship. In process of time the prophets came and declared that Jehovah requires simply the humanities. Notice the words of one of the prophets which directly affirm this. Micah puts the words into the mouth of an Israelite. "Wherewith shall I come before Jehovah, and bow myself before the high God? Shall I come before him with burnt offerings, with calves of a year old? Will the Lord be pleased with thousands of rams or with ten thousands of streams of oil? Shall I give my firstborn for my transgression, the fruit of my body for the sin of my soul? He hath shewed thee, O man, what is good; and what doth the Lord require of thee but to do justly, and to love mercy, and to walk humbly with thy God?" In such a saying as this we reach high-water mark of the prophetic utterances. Jehovah requires of man none of the bloody sacrifices, requires none of the offerings of one's substance, which were so scrupulously made. He requires the humanities: mercy and justice. It is in the humanities that man walks humbly with his God. It is in the sacrifices and the inhumanities that he departs from Jehovah, and misrepresents Jehovah in the world.

It has been supposed, and the idea has been most zealously supported, that Jehovah gave to Israel a law of sacrifices. That by observance of this law the man could set himself right with his offended God. The sacrifices of the altars have been held to symbolize the sacrifice of the Son of God as the offering for sin and the refuge and Saviour of sinners. Probably in the most recent times there is survival in much strength of the very notions against which the prophets proceeded. We note this survival in the words of formulas of prayer. In so many words men worship God by pleading the merits of the sacrificed Christ. The question asked by the prophet, "Wherewith shall I come before Jehovah, and bow myself before the high God?" is answered, not as he answered it, but as the Israelite answered it. In a form of language, containing some idea at least, men bow themselves before Jehovah, bringing forward the sacrificed Christ. It is supposed and asserted with great stress that God requires that. If at this late day, wherein the humanities have been greatly developed, we fall short of the real religion of the prophets, we need not marvel at the difficulties which beset the prophets in carrying out their sublime aim. For it was their aim to bring about a pure worship, — a worship not of altars and not of sacrifices, but of just and humane feelings and conduct. That was pleasing to Jehovah; all else was not pleasing to him.

While all the prophets did not attain the same high standard of religion, while some of them countenanced the sacrificial forms of worship which belong to polytheism, yet it may be said of the later prophets that they furnish, and they exclusively, the necessary foundation for the Christian religion which was to complete their work. Not that Christian religion which is confused and shows its hopeless confusion by the large number of sects into which it has become split, the Christian religion of dogma, but the religion of the humanities, the religion of mercy and justice and a humble walk with God. Were we to inquire into the development of religion in the world we might divide it into three great stages: First, the stage of fetichism — with remnants abiding to this day. Second, the stage of polytheism. The first is the lowest stage of human attainment. The second is an advance, but leaves much to be desired. In this stage are many gods; gods of nations and families; gods fighting each other in the warfare of their worshipers: this is the stage of sacrifices, human and other. The third stage, of which we may also say that it is the last, is the stage of the unity of God, one and only one God. This being is not to be represented in thought as the golden bull or in any image whatsoever. This is the being who demands of us the humanities, mercy and justice. This is the being in whose image we are being created. Thus the Christian religion presents to us not an unapproachable divinity and not a nature-god, always to be propitiated, but God manifest in the flesh — God in man. God walks in the humble and just and merciful man: for that conception the prophets of Israel more than any other have prepared us.

IX.

THE LIMITATION.

The Jehovah of the earlier Israelites was not, and in the nature of the case could not have been, the same as the Jehovah of a more advanced period. The Jehovah of David was not the Jehovah of Isaiah. It is because the concepts of people change. In respect to all things which engage their attention there is a growing change of opinion; but because of the conservative influence always in more or less force, the change of opinion does not go on uninterrupted. It is a stream frequently blockaded, and the result is that the changes of opinion assume appearance of violent transition.

In Israel's history we note as successive changes of conception those revolutionary periods, such as the escape from the house of bondage; the formation of a kingdom under David; the disruption of the kingdom afterward; the Babylonian exile, and finally the establishment of the Christian religion. All of these changes strike us as being very great, especially the last. They seem to come suddenly. That is because the process of change, which is as continual as the growth of a flower from the seed, was continually obstructed by the conservative feelings of men. Since the changes could not go in the form of an orderly progression, they came in the form of, or accompanied by, national disasters or deliverances.

Now the prophets were certainly ignorant of things which Mr. Darwin could have told them. They did not know that all men rise, but do not descend, from lower ranks of life. They did not know what the theistic evolutionist of to-day sees to be highly credible in the light of what Mr. Darwin has shown him, that all progress goes on by successive changes; or that as it was in the lower orders, so is it also with the higher orders. There were mollusks and there were fishes. The mollusk is a creature far inferior in organization to the fish, and yet God is equally the creator of both. Moreover, each comes in its own time: first the lower, and afterward the higher from the lower. The prophets did not know this, I say. Nor did they need to know it; but if those who had to do with preparing the canon of the Old Testament, and whose duty it was to give here and there a title to a piece of sacred literature, or to indicate something in regard to its authorship, had known it, they would not have made the mistake of attributing to one period that which belongs to another.

Changes in our concepts of things go on, sometimes imperceptibly, but they do steadily go on. These changes make different periods, as really as successive changes in animal structure make different periods in the history of the physical world. We have means of identifying the periods. The historical critics of the Bible are like the geologists; they have discovered how to place the relative time of customs, laws, prophecies, and the like.

It is quite safe to say that the prophetic books of the Bible do not hold a very high place in the interest of the average religious man of to-day. He regards them as sacred books, to be sure, and therefore to be reverenced, but he does not read them with interest. Their language is foreign to his understanding. Their imagery seems to him far-fetched. He knows a great deal more about the parts of the Bible which tell him stories of heroes. He knows of Samson, the Hercules of the Bible, and of Moses, the Nestor, and of the patriarchs. The story of Ruth is attractive to him as a pastoral. He reads the book of Esther, and because it is in the Bible he thinks it is a sacred book. If he were to find it outside of the Bible, he would feel no great regard for it, but might even look upon it as Luther did, a book unworthy of respect. Luther thought the story of Esther ought to be destroyed. The prophetic literature, which is the really valuable literature of Israel, he cannot force himself to take a lively interest in, as a rule.

On the other hand, the enthusiastic study of prophecy is peculiar to certain sects, and to those who look for a speedy downfall of the world. In the prophets there are many things upon which the imagination seizes, as importing the end of the world and the minor catastrophes connected therewith. The study of prophecy is therefore generally understood to imply an interest in the "last things." We cannot help feeling that there is almost always an element of fanaticism in such interest. Those who have entertained the ideas of the modern expositors of prophecy, and who have been thrown out of mental balance thereby, and have tormented themselves and others with visions of an impending sounding of a last trumpet, with the summons to appear before the judge, and receive sentence, etc., have made prophecy seem to us an enthusiasm, and an imposition as well. All this misunderstanding and misapplication has been due to an uncritical study of the prophets. Our enthusiastic teachers have piled up texts on texts. They have made selection of passages, and taken them out of their connection, and have supposed these things all bore on the same subjects. Moreover, they have gone upon the theory that the prophets were men who knew something about the end of the world. A more careful study would have assured them that the end of the world lies beyond the ken of any one, and that while some of the prophets seem to be talking about the end of the world, they are in reality talking of the near future.

We have read the prophets too, without much consideration of the time in which they respectively lived and spoke. Therein we have been unskillful and have suffered for it. Our scholars have done much to clear away these difficulties. We can identify the periods more accurately. In our common editions of the Bible we find the short books of two prophets together. The first is Joel, and the second is Amos. Upon consulting the small figures in reference Bibles, we see that these books were written about the same time, namely about 800 B. C. Of course no dates are given in the text of the books themselves, any more than dates are written in the silurian rocks. The time of the composition of these books has been supposed to be identical. For some reason Joel was put first, and Amos second. If these books had been read in the light of history, and a careful study of history, it would have been impossible to put Joel first and Amos second. It is by the light of historical criticism we find that Amos is one of the very first of Israel's prophets who recorded his thoughts; perhaps the very first of those whose actual words have come down to us. If an attempt had been made to have the prophecies follow each other in a chronological order, Amos would have headed the list, and probably the next would have been Hosea; and one of the last would have been Joel, — for he spoke and wrote in the Greek period, more than two and a half centuries later.

Joel wrote in a vivid style, and is supposed to have written explicitly about the "last days." In the Acts of the Apostles he seems to be quoted as one who foretold the last days. It is therefore well worth our while to read him carefully, to find if he really does that. The immediate occasion of his prophecy is a plague of locusts which devastated the land in his time. His description is at once that of a prophet and that of a poet. The pest is like a fire, moving on to devour everything before it. When the locusts came, the land was as the Garden of Eden, but after their onslaught the land was a wilderness, and nothing escaped them. They were like a great army, conquering, as by spears and chariots and horsemen. All of this, which would be plainly described as a grasshopper plague, he dwells upon and sees in it the devastations of Jehovah, who is offended with the people on account of their sins. The locusts make up Jehovah's army. "They shall run to and fro in the city; they shall run upon the wall, they shall climb up upon the houses, they shall enter in at the windows like a thief. The earth shall quake before them, the heavens shall tremble; the sun and the moon shall be dark, and the stars shall withdraw their shining: and Jehovah shall utter his voice before his army, for his camp is very great; for strong is he that executeth his word; for the day of Jehovah is great and very terrible, and who can abide it?"

Here is a prophet who does not seem to be telling about future events, but about things then transpiring. A plague of locusts is upon the land: it is Jehovah's time, or day, — the day of reckoning with his people. Jehovah it is who is cutting off all the green things from the earth, who is causing the crops of the husbandmen to disappear, who is taking away from the flocks and herds their food; and instead of plenty there is a famine.

In our own West, when the locust plague has come, and the sun has been darkened by the vast clouds of the enemy; when the farmers have seen their toil go for nothing, everything destroyed as by sudden blight, if any among them were convinced that God is punishing the people for their sins, and that God has times of reckoning with the people, and if he were all the time watching the destructive march of the plague, he could speak perhaps in the vivid language of Joel. He could say that the Day of the Lord had come, and that it was a very terrible day, "who can abide it?"

This prophet Joel is not a prophet of woe. He does not dwell on the dark side of things, to magnify that. He says it is right for Israel to mourn, and to clothe itself in sackcloth. Then he raises the song of hope. He begs the people to mourn and lament over their wrong-doing. He begs the priests, the ministers of Jehovah, to put forth their supplications, and say, "Spare thy people, O Jehovah, and give not thine heritage to reproach, that the heathen should use a byword against them: wherefore should they say among the people, where is their God?" For the Gentiles would say of a people so plagued that their god had forsaken them, or that he was powerless to avert the evils thrust upon them by some greater power. The prophet feels that it has all come in retribution for the vices and sins of the people. It is not a time when Jehovah has gone away, but it is his day; a great and terrible day. However, that is not the end of it. He who wounds will also heal. If repentance is had, Jehovah will be "jealous for his land" and will pity his people. "Yea, Jehovah will answer and say unto his people, behold I will send you corn and wine and oil, and ye shall be satisfied therewith." The prophet foresees that Jehovah will drive the invading army of locusts off into the desert. Then the famished beasts of the field will have their pasturage, the tree will bear her fruit, the vine will flourish. The threshing-floors will once more be full of wheat, and the vats will overflow with the oil and wine. By means of this recovered prosperity the nation will know that Jehovah is in the midst of her; and will trust in Jehovah, and serve him.

Thus far in this prophet we have heard nothing about the last times, but only about the times then present. There is the plague of locusts, which, in the vivid feeling of the prophet, makes the earth to quake and the heavens to tremble, and darkens the sun and moon. The destructive army of Jehovah, cutting off our food and making a famine for us, is turning the light itself into darkness. Who can abide the time? The prophet is hopeful. He hopes that his people will repent of their evil courses and turn in humility to Jehovah, whom they have offended, and that Jehovah will forgive and restore them. The prophets of Israel, even those who lament the most and seem to be most impressed with the failure of Israel to follow and obey Jehovah, are yet hopeful.

They seem to see in Jehovah much more than a king; they see one who punishes people for their good, and who works in his people by his Spirit toward their betterment. So Joel, after all that he has said in the other strain, returns to the joyful and triumphant note, "Fear not, O land; be glad and rejoice, for Jehovah will do great things." In place of the famine consequent upon the locust plague shall surely come plenty, and the people shall be satisfied, and "ye shall praise the name of Jehovah your God that hath dealt wondrously with you."

Then comes the song of Israel's triumph. It is in this song of triumph that the convictions of the later prophets spoke. Israel's God is no longer a tribal god, one among many powerful deities. Whatever he had been to earlier prophets, now at last the clear conviction of the monotheist is visible. After Israel is restored, having duly repented of its sins and returned to Jehovah and his service, it should come to the fulfillment of exceeding great and precious promises, as the Apostle Peter said, "And it will come to pass afterward, I will pour out of my spirit upon all flesh." A few in Israel had enjoyed the peculiar favor of Jehovah. The spirit of prophecy did not belong to the people generally, but only to the devoted ones who were persecuted; but all that should be changed. Jehovah would pour out his Spirit upon young and old. Not only upon the free born, but upon the very slaves themselves. Every one should prophesy, young and old, bond and free.

The great thought of the prophet is that Jehovah will put forward his people Israel to accomplish their work. He has not been able to reach the nations with his judgments and grace because of the faithlessness of his people; but with the return of the nation to its fealty, Jehovah would carry out his purposes. Then Jerusalem would become firmly established; and in Mount Zion would be deliverance. For Jehovah dwells in Mount Zion, and from Mount Zion must go forth the laws for all nations.

It requires no violence of interpretation to follow the prophet's thoughts in a direction he himself has indicated. As Jehovah had been dealing retributively, and for the purposes of correction and recovery, with Israel, so would he deal with all nations. As Israel had seen the sun darkened, and had felt the earth quake, by reason of its plague of the locusts; so doubtless other nations should feel the same great trials, and be brought through the same straits, in order to bring them to seek deliverance in Jehovah, who dwelleth in Zion. Israel had experienced a great and terrible day of Jehovah, and other nations should experience like wonders. "I will show wonders in the heavens and in the earth, blood and fire and vapor of smoke. The sun shall be turned into darkness and the moon into blood before the great and terrible day of Jehovah come." Some of our prophetic expositors have seen in this the portents of the last day. They have supposed that the moon would become blood red in the evening sky, and the sun black (how could the moon be red while the sun is black?), and that other signs of impending disaster and final ruin should present themselves to the eyes of the watchful, if not to all eyes. Coupling with all this, too, the apocalyptic visions contained in the New Testament, they have warned us time and again of the dissolution of earthly affairs and the sounding of the last trump.

Joel speaks of the locust plague which destroys

the food supplies of man and beast in the same terms employed to characterize later proceedings of Jehovah with other nations. That is, the turning of the sun into darkness and the moon into blood, etc. He tells us that Jehovah will gather the Gentiles into the valley of Jehoshaphat to plead with them. He will there reckon with them for their treatment of Israel. He will recompense to Tyre and Sidon and all the coasts of Palestine all that they have done. The reckoning of Jehovah with the nations, in the view of Joel, will take the form of a war of Israel with these other nations. And so he calls upon Israel to arm itself. He raises the cry among the Gentiles also to prepare for war. " Beat your plow-shares into swords and your sickles into spears ! " In those days of frequent wars, and when Israel was recovering its strength after the captivity, menaced on all sides by other powers, it was not wonderful that the prophet could foresee a coming strife. He was so full of the thought of Jehovah's might, and of his promises, that in this coming war he could see a great victory for the people of Jehovah, and Israel should regain its old glory. The city of Israel's king should prove to be the city of Jehovah : Jehovah should cry out of Jerusalem. He was the hope of his people; in his might they should conquer. At last it would surely be proved to all men that Jehovah dwells in Zion; that he is not merely the highest, but the only God. In this there is no hint of those last days of final judgment and destruction of the earth which our modern prophets have seen so vividly. The prophet Joel's mind does not concern itself with that.

Nearly contemporary with Joel is the prophet Malachi. He may, indeed, have been a little earlier. He is one of those who speak of a day that is coming to Israel, a fiery and terrible day. The rise of this feeling concerning a day is not difficult to trace in the prophets. If we go back to those first of the prophets, Elijah and Elisha, those prophets who did not write, because writing was not much practiced in their time, but who did sharply rebuke the people for their evils, we shall find growing a sentiment in regard to Jehovah which became most prominent later. The nation was surrounded by powerful heathen kingdoms. There were Egypt and Damascus and Assyria, and others. These powers threatened the peculiar people of Jehovah. The future of Israel was, therefore, very doubtful. Would it be able to maintain itself? Jehovah was indeed very powerful. He had delivered them from the house of bondage and brought them into the land flowing with milk and honey. Why then were they threatened by those powerful competitors? Why were they in danger of being carried off into captivity? They found an answer to that. At least the prophets did. Jehovah was not only strong, but he was also just and holy. If the nation was to succeed, it must also be just and holy, for God would permit it to be defeated and carried into captivity, on account of its follies and wickedness. God required certain things to be done, and if they were not done, he would reckon with his disobedient servants. There would surely come the day of reckoning. It would be a day of downfall to that people, of great trial when it did come. God would sit as a refiner of silver; he would try his people by sifting.

In this country half a century ago, there were prophets, somewhat of the same sort as Malachi, who protested that a terrible result would arise from a terrible crime. It was a national crime, — that of human slavery. If one of them had chosen, he could have adopted the language of Malachi: "Behold, the day cometh that shall burn as an oven." (The day did surely come, a most fiery day, as all of that generation can testify.

Malachi was very sure that Judah would reap the reward of misdeeds, but also, like Joel, he was sure that the people would return to Jehovah, and that all the nations of the earth would have a great blessing because of Judah. "All nations shall call you blessed! for ye shall be a delightsome land, saith Jehovah of hosts." Malachi, however, differs from earlier and far greater prophets in his views of the sins of the people. He wished them to keep the priestly laws very scrupulously, and because they did not, he denounced them. Now the first Isaiah cared nothing for those requirements of the priestly laws, but Malachi was in great offense because the people did not bring their tithes and promptly pay them. He was angry, as well he might have been, because they offered in sacrifice upon the altars the beasts which were not good for anything. He felt that was a direct insult to Jehovah, as indeed it was. The people brought the blind animals, and the lame and the sick; such things as they would not dream of offering to their governor; but these they thought quite good enough for the altars of Jehovah. This so wrought upon the feelings of the prophet, that he could see nothing but ruin and defeat and sorrow ahead, until they should repent. Can we wonder that a man, with strong feelings, and loving Jehovah and his requirements, should have foreseen that the day would shortly come when Jehovah would try all this neglect and contempt most severely, and punish it?

It is evident to any who carefully study these prophets of the later period, that they were talking to Judah of the retribution they were bringing upon themselves for their sins. Malachi may have supposed that Jehovah would send Elijah to warn the people before proceeding to extremities, but Malachi himself seeks to draw attention to the laws which he believed were given to Moses by Jehovah in Horeb. He wished the people to honor Jehovah by obedience of his laws. "Bring ye all the tithes into the storehouse, that there may be meat in mine house, and prove me now herewith, saith Jehovah of hosts, if I will not open you the windows of heaven and pour you out a blessing."

By these latest of the prophets we may perceive that prophecy relates not to another world, and not to the last days of this world, but to those things of immediate import, which concern the people to know. When we read into the vivid language of Joel the notions of last days, we make him demit his real office as an instructor of the people, to be a fortune-teller for later ages.

X.

THE FICTION.

In the development of literature, fiction has a prominent place. The word "fiction" covers all that portion of literature which is invented, or mostly dependent on the imagination. Tales of all kinds, such as stories of the fairies, and fables, and parables, and all dramatic writings, and many poems, may be generally grouped under the head of fiction. We commonly use the word, however, in a more restricted sense, applying it mainly to the kind of books we call novels; but it would apply to the plays of Shakespeare, the great poems of Milton, and the fables of Æsop.

Fiction is an early as well as an exceedingly valuable part of literature. It appears in the mythologies of all religions, in the Greek dramas, in great poems, like the Iliad of Homer, and in all literature of the more popular sort. It may be within the bounds of reason to say that the most important part of the world's literature, in many respects, is the literature of fiction. A writer reaches a public more swiftly and easily and successfully in that way than in any other. Long and involved didactic statements upon any subject are no sooner uttered than they are forgotten by almost everybody. Arguments which have great final effects in the experience of people are not received as arguments, but are reduced to a form more vivid and dramatic before they conquer their way. Therefore, under that Providence which has to do with the flower of the plant, and the flower of speech as well, we are forced to accord a great place in the world's welfare and its intellectual and moral growth to the literature of fiction.

Reluctance has been felt about admitting the presence of fiction in the Bible. Perhaps upon the ground that the character of fiction is not clearly understood. If some ingenious person were to be asked a question by his neighbor, and were to invent the truth of his reply, in the most blunt fashion possible he would be called a liar. He undertakes to deceive his questioner, and bears false witness to his neighbor. Or if a man tells stories of adventure, as drawn out of his own personal experience; if he asserts that he was in this and that battle, and conducted himself in a most heroic fashion, while the truth is he never saw a battle, his tales are works of fiction, but they are made with intent to deceive, and he is a liar.

When we talk of fiction in literature we never mean anything of that kind, and we are not in the habit of attributing ill motives or dishonesty to the author of fiction. The writer of fiction may be, and is held to be (provided his character and work warrant it), as thoroughly honest as the writer of the most carefully exact and unimaginative history. Victor Hugo and Mrs. Stowe and George Eliot tell us of things which never transpired, as though they did transpire. That is the form in which they cast their thoughts, but no one need be deceived by it, and they do not wish any one to be deceived by it. They do not take the pains to tell us that Uncle Tom and Jean Valjean and Adam Bede never existed. In fact, they make them as real to us as possible. Yet, in spite of the fact that they are imaginary characters, and all the incidents imaginary also, we do not complain of deceit.

I am sure if we knew the literature and spirit of the Bible better, we should have no hesitation in finding a plentiful element of fiction in it: and having recognized it as fiction, we might proceed to get the truth it contains. For unless fiction be a vehicle of truth, it is either valueless or worse. Its only rightful use is that it should convey to us, and to all possible readers, the truth it is good for us to know.

We are told that David, the great king of Israel, committed a frightful crime. It would not be regarded such at the time, and was not so regarded by the king himself; but there was one man, at least, who looked with abhorrence upon it. He proposed to tell the king his opinion of it. He felt that he could express God's opinion about it, and that it was his duty to do so. We feel that he was right to think so, but it was a difficult matter to deal with. It has never been very easy to go and tell great despots their faults: one undertaking such a mission was likely to be deprived of all speech thereafter. So the good man invented a story. He prepared a fiction, as being the best means of doing that particular work. He successfully accomplished the difficult mission by means of the little story he invented. A poor man had one lamb, a pet. He derived much of the comfort of his life from that pet lamb; but a powerful neighbor, to whom had come a traveler, spared his own flocks, and took the poor man's lamb, killed it, and presented it to his guest for food. When David heard that story his anger was kindled, and he swore that the man who had done that wicked thing should die for it. Then the good prophet told him he was the man who had done that thing, only in a far worse way. It was a very skillful contrivance on the part of Nathan to invent that story, and by it he accomplished more in the way of truth and righteousness than he could have done in any other way. In the same manner Jesus told the story of the man who had two sons, and the one was thrifty and the other prodigal. The story will last as long as men talk and think, while the lesson given in the way of argument would have died out in a short time. It was a pure work of fiction; and unquestionably Jesus resorted to fiction more than almost any other great religious teacher. He gave to all moral truths the guise and dress of fiction. If the weighty argument of Paul to the Romans and the fiction of Jesus concerning the return of the prodigal were to be weighed in the balance over against each other, the fiction would be found to outweigh the other.

We have been considering the way in which the historical portions of the Old Testament were made. We have seen that there is much of the history which could not pass for history, apart from its connection with the Bible. We have considered, too, how the prophets did their work, their aim in their work, and the fact that they were the great ethical teachers of the Jews; but there was another kind of teaching, neither historical nor prophetic, which occupies a considerable space in the sacred pages. That is the portion of the Old Testament literature which is in the form of fiction.

While fiction may be interwoven with the history, as in myths and legends, it more frankly confesses itself in other portions of the book, — as in the book of Job. Taken by all scholars, now, to be a dramatic poem, with a prose prologue and epilogue, it was earlier and generally taken to be historical narration.

There is no entirely good reason why we should be more stupid about the Bible than about any other book. In fact, there is good reason why we should bring to the Bible a mind which has at least a little clearness. We ought to have just that sort of discrimination which will help us to distinguish between widely different kinds of writing. If any one had taken the pains to think about it he would not have dreamed that the things related in the book of Job ever happened; not because they are miraculous things, but because that kind of writing has never been applied to description of actual events, described in detail. Yet the time is not far past when the opinion that the book of Job is not history, or fact, would have shocked the feelings of almost all religious people. Now it shocks no one, because it has become very evident that it is a dramatic poem. That has been ascertained by attention, by literary judgment, by commonplace discrimination. Educated persons have tried to make out the place of Satan in the general economy of the universe by what is said of him in the prologue to the book of Job. The sons of God came into the presence of God, and along with them came Satan. Perhaps he is one of the sons of God, turned bad. He roams around the earth, seeking who and what he may devour, but he finds time to come to the gathering of the sons of God. He is asked if he has given attention to that very just man, Job. Yes, he has noticed Job, but has no good opinion of him. Like all other men he is actuated by purely selfish motives. He serves God because he can make something out of it. If the reader has not the discernment to discover the fiction form of that story, he is sadly lacking in knowledge of most kinds. The characters of the drama talk in poetry. Men never do that in real life. As well might merchants set their sight drafts to music. In play, children may sometimes carry on a conversation in rude rhymes; but this book of Job is intensely serious. Simply from the evidence of its contents to its character, it is understood by all intelligent readers that it is a made-up story. Nathan made up a story for David, as we have seen. Jesus made up a great many stories for his hearers. This is made up in order to convey a great spiritual lesson, and spiritual lessons are what we go to the Bible for. It seems to have taken us a long time to find out that a spiritual lesson may be as well conveyed in the literature of the imagination — that is, in fiction — as in any other form. Oftentimes it is the best form. The value of the Bible, taken as a whole, is in its spiritual lessons. If it gave us the most unimpeachable history from beginning to end, if it portrayed all the future to us, and failed to inculcate spiritual lessons, it would be of the same value with any other book, of an unmoral sort. But its power, use, and worth lie altogether in its spiritual lessons. If these be conveyed in one form or another, it were well for us to perceive that the form of the conveyance is not of importance, and certainly not to be regarded as at all essential to the validity of the book as a divine revelation.

Job is a work of fiction, and for certain purposes it is not inferior to any other part of the Old Testament. If we get the lesson, or if we fail to get it, the imaginary Job is of quite as much service to us as if he were a veritable man among men.

A work of fiction, as we have seen, is a literary expedient. If it comes in the form of poetry, that is one method; if in the form of a tragedy, that is another; if in the form of a historical novel, that is simply another literary device. All these forms have long been used, and with great and good effect, and, as a rule, we know how to discriminate between the different kinds of literary method. When we look into the Bible, we ought not to lose our literary judgment: we ought not to take for facts of history and biography the things which belong to literary device.

This may be said to be true in respect to the book of Daniel, which occupies a place between the major and the minor prophets. It has proved, I will venture to assert, a far more readable part of the Bible than those portions which precede and succeed it. It is cast in an attractive form and conveys high lessons. The first portion of it, say the first six chapters, narrate the experiences of a Jew named Daniel in Babylon. He and three of his companions are chosen from the captive Jews to reside in the king's palace. These four are said to have been chosen because they were handsome men and expert in knowledge: they were scientific. They were to be taught all the learning of the Chaldeans. It is further said that Daniel, in particular, was skilled in dreams and visions. As we progress in the story, we see Daniel becoming eminent above all his fellows. The nobles of the court are jealous of him, and enter into a conspiracy to destroy him. He has a habit of opening his window toward Jerusalem, and praying to God three times a day. They make this a ground of complaint. They cause a law to be made by the king forbidding any person to make petition to any god or man except to the king. The conspirators get sufficient proof of the praying of Daniel, and present it to the king, who, for the sake of the law, orders the offender to be thrown to the lions. God closes the mouths of the lions, and Daniel is rescued. His three friends are put into a furnace because of their disobedience of the orders of the king: they receive no harm. Daniel interprets the dream of the king and the handwriting on the wall, while all the soothsayers and magicians of the city fail. It is natural that such a man should rise to great eminence, and certainly that he should have a commanding influence with his own countrymen. It is very natural that his contemporaries, and those who came after him, should mention him and his extraordinary deeds in their writings. Yet the great leaders of the restoration, and those who wrote the records of their nation, make no mention of this very eminent man.

We are entirely sure that if any one should undertake to write the history of the United States from the beginning, he would not leave out of his books the story of Hamilton, nor that of General Grant. He would be less likely to do it, if he were a contemporary of either of these distinguished men. But the Jewish historians have not a word to say of this wonderful man, Daniel, who, according to the book which bears his name, was by far the greatest of the Jews at the time of the captivity. All the others sink into insignificance beside him, yet neither Ezra, to whom we are so greatly indebted for the Bible, nor Nehemiah, nor Zechariah, makes any allusion to him. The prophet Ezekiel mentions his name, however.

Ezekiel has a theory which differs from that of those who wrote the story of the destruction of Sodom.

According to that story, if there had been a few good men in the city, Jehovah would have spared it. But Ezekiel declares that if the very best of men were in a wicked place, that city or place cannot escape destruction. The good men can deliver their own souls only. This is the way the prophet puts the case: "Though these three men, Noah, Daniel, and Job, were in it (the place), they should deliver but their own souls, by their righteousness, saith the Lord God." The three men were therefore representatives of excellence. Of course it makes no difference whether they were real characters or the characters of fiction. Once again Ezekiel mentions Daniel, and in a way to indicate that such a character was somewhat familiar to the people of his time. He speaks of the king of Tyre as pluming himself upon his wisdom. He felt that he was as wise as Daniel and as capable of understanding the secrets of dreams, and the like.

From these allusions, we find some reason to think Daniel is not simply a character of fiction. Perhaps we should come near the truth if we supposed him to be a real personage, who was made the hero, so to speak, of an historical fiction long afterward. We are by no means unfamiliar with that sort of literary device known as the historical novel. And we very clearly recognize the book of Job as belonging to that sort of writing, in a poetical form.

There is great reason to suppose that the book of Daniel is a historical fiction in prose form. It is asserted by some rather conservative writers that the majority of the leading Christian scholars of the present day hold that the book of Daniel was not written in the days of the exile, but about the middle of the second century B. C. There are many and sufficient reasons to adopt this view. It appears that the book of Daniel is one of the supplementary writings, not originally included in the Jewish collection of the prophets. Neither Daniel nor the book is mentioned by the Son of Sirach, who wrote about two hundred years B. C., and gave a catalogue of Jewish prophets and great men. Moreover, there are certain Persian words in the book as well as Greek names of musical instruments which were not in use at the time of the exile.

It is a reasonable supposition that some patriotic Jew during the Maccabean period — say about one hundred and fifty years before the Christian era — resorted to that sort of literary device later known as historical fiction, taking a real character as the basis of it, a man whose name was known to some, though certainly not to all the Jews, and that by this means he conveyed to the minds of his struggling countrymen the teachings of Jehovah, important for them at that time. In order the better to effect his purpose, he introduces visions and interpretations, for the encouragement of his people in their great contest for survival and liberty.

Now among all the books of the Old Testament, that of Daniel is peculiar in that it seems to give minute predictions concerning the future. It seems to lay out the plan for the succession of the great world-empires, as the Assyrian, the Medo-Persian, the Greek, and the Roman. As a matter of fact these four great kingdoms did succeed each other in the order indicated in the book of Daniel.

It has been held to be one of the most convincing proofs of the infallible inspiration of the Bible, that a man was able to tell beforehand how kingdoms should rise and fall. In all the other prophetic books, the predictions, as we have seen, are of a general character, far more ethical than circumstantial, and resting upon the basis of profound principles. In Daniel, however, the predictions seem to have been literally fulfilled. If this book was written after the four great kingdoms had actually risen, then we have no difficulty in understanding how their succession could be described. There was no prediction about it. Edmund Burke wrote beforehand the coming French Revolution; but that was prediction based upon principles of foresight understood by the author. If some one in our own day were to write a historical novel, dating it from the day of Burke, and making it a story of Burke; and if the writer of it were to tell all about the brilliant career of the first Napoleon, and the succession of Presidents of the United States, as having been foreseen by Burke, the device would be similar to that of the writer of the book of Daniel. No one would think of attributing dishonest motives to the writer. It is as much a method of instruction and as legitimate as that employed in the literature of letter writing, or the literature of the drama (as in the book of Job), or the ordinary novel of the better class.

The book of Daniel has been misunderstood, and made to teach an important error, because readers have mistaken the time and design of its composition. The nature of inspiration itself has suffered great misrepresentation, partly because this particular book has not been recognized as a literary device; but our Christian scholars are helping us to rectify our errors in that respect by assigning to the book of Daniel a date long after the exile, and even after the rise of the Roman power.

I know of no better way of showing the peculiar value and the commanding influence of the book of Daniel, its adaptation to the needs of the Maccabean times, than by a quotation from Ewald, cited by Dean Stanley in his " History of the Jewish Church," and by Dr. Gladden in " Who Wrote the Bible ? " describing the critical state of the Jews: " Everything had reached that state of extreme tension when the ancient religion upon its sacred soil must either disappear from view completely for long ages, or must rise in fresh strength and outward power against enemies thus immoderately embittered. It was at this crisis, in the sultry heat of an age thus frightfully oppressive, that this book appeared with its sword-edge utterance, its piercing exhortation to endure in face of the despot, and its promise full of divine joy, of near and full salvation. No dew of heaven could fall with more refreshing coolness on the parched ground, no spark from above alight with a more kindling power on the surface so long heated with a hidden glow. With winged brevity the book gives a complete survey of the kingdom of God upon earth, showing the relations which it had hitherto sustained in Israel to the successive great heathen empires of the Chaldeans, Medo-Persians, and Greeks, — in a word, to the heathenism which ruled the world. . . . Rarely does it happen that a book appears as this did, in the very crisis of the times and in a form most suited to such an age, artificially reserved, close and severe, and yet shedding so clear a light through obscurity, and so marvelously captivating. It was natural that it should soon achieve a success entirely corresponding to its inner truth and glory."

The book of Daniel in a peculiar degree sprang

from the necessities of its time. It took the form that would produce the widest influence in the shortest time. It, more than any other portion of the Old Testament, is the prototype of the political and social fiction-literature of our own day.

XI.

THE POETRY.

A CONSIDERABLE portion of the Old Testament is poetry. This is more notable because the New Testament contains little poetry except that which is quoted from the Old. In the Old Testament poetry abounds, not only in the specially poetical books, but also in the historical and prophetic books. One of the most accomplished and eminent of modern Hebrew scholars declares his conviction that the first chapter of the book of Genesis is poetical in form. Short poems are interspersed in the Pentateuch. The book of Job, the Psalms, the Song of Solomon, are unmistakably poetical. The Proverbs, Ecclesiastes, and the Lamentations are also poetical, though in a slightly modified way. Perhaps one would be entitled to say that the prophecies themselves are prose poems. Now the fact that so large a portion of the Old Testament is poetical ought to have weight in helping us to determine more accurately the nature of the volume as a whole. The oldest of the Greek writings are said to be poetical. We may go farther than that. There is a poetical flavor, if one may use the expression, in the orations and council talks of savage chiefs.

In modern colloquial language we are about as far from poetical as possible. We have a plain, direct, and almost mathematical use of language. We expect definite meanings in the papers we read and the talk we hear. If we do not get it we are dissatisfied. We have time for poetry only in our leisure hours. An attempt to express the difference between that direct and clear-cut method of speech to which we are driven more and more by the advance of science and the old poetical method might issue in something like this, namely: we express small and definite ideas in our prose, but poetry expresses great and indefinite ideas. Poetry is the tongue of the man whose thought is too great for any other sort of statement. Whenever we attribute to the poet the small and definite idea which belongs to another kind of speech we do him injustice, and inevitably fail of his meaning.

Wordsworth, Tennyson, and Browning see potential greatness in small things. They help us to see the greatness, too, and rejoice in it. The unpoetical soul sees great things only in bulk, or expressed force. Our poets do not measure with a tape line the dimensions of small things: they are not so definite. They are impatient of the man who in the primrose sees nothing but the primrose. The ordinary man glances at the primrose and sees nothing but the definite form and color thereof. The man of science does much more than that. He pulls the plant of it out of the ground and carefully examines the root, the stalk, the leaves, the petals, and all the parts of it. That is his province. He may go even farther than that, and follow the particular plant down in the line of its origin. His field is a grand one; compared with the ordinary man he perceives great things in the flower. The poet, when he sits down before the flower, contemplates it; and contemplates infinitely more than it. That is his province. It is planted in a background of the infinities: it blossoms as a suggestion of God. He writes his couplet or verse or lofty poem about it. In prose language no man has ever been able to tell us all about such a thing as a primrose. There is no prose which will contain it: you cannot translate the thought into prose: if you try you lose the thought.

Well, the great thoughts of Israel's great men have come to us in the poetical form. It may be said that all of the great thoughts have come in that guise. Little thoughts, such as the priests often had, — little notions of how to sacrifice to Jehovah, and how to make curtains and other things for a tabernacle, or how to make clothes for priests, — really fail to interest any one. The man of the smallest soul can get no comfort out of those portions of the Scriptures which contain the priests' trifles, unless he first tries to swell the trifles to something of proportion by putting into them a prophecy or symbol of the sublime sacrifice of the Man of later Scriptures. They are definite enough, those ancient trifles, — as definite as a treatise on housekeeping: but they fly away from us like the chaff.

The real power of the Old Testament is in its poetry. It constitutes the kind of food which makes the soul great. It pushes us out of our pettiness; it furnishes a balm for our heavy sorrows; it gives us visions; helps us to contemplate, and takes us out of the range of the little and the fugitive. Poetry, therefore, is peculiarly the language of religion. For religion is no hard and fast and dry philosophy. It is the realm of the feelings. Its office is to develop in us great and true emotions, and it may truly be said that we gain our greatest feelings by the help of Israel's poetry. Therefore when we come to the poetry of the Bible we come nearer to God than in history or story or ethical teachings. As we grow able to look in upon the inner meanings of that poetry, the veil of the temple is rent for us, and we gaze upon the Most Holy place.

The truth of poetry is suggested rather than directly expressed, and therefore the poet does not care for the small and definite truth which he seems to be putting into words, except so far as it may serve his purpose in suggesting the great and the indefinite truth. In the use of the poet the incongruous, the extravagant, and the impossible are not rejected. The flood of his feelings knows no bounds. If any one looked upon a vast mountain raising its white spire into the clouds, he would think of that as an immovable mass. Whatever else might move, that would remain and be everlasting; but if the poet were upon another strain, and were thinking of the presence of God, the everlasting hills would cease to be everlasting.

One of the hymns of Israel expresses the fervid feeling of the poet, who sees the mountains skipping like rams, and the little hills like lambs. The sea also beholds something and flees away. The river stops its flowing. What produces all these wonderful effects? The presence of the God of Jacob, leading his chosen people out of bondage. God comes out of his secret place and visits his people, after long absence, and all things witness this awful presence, — the mountains, the sea, the river: the earth itself trembles. This is the poet's feeling of the sublimity of that presence, and it is graphically portrayed.

After we have learned the poet's method we do not speak of the drapery as if it consisted of actual phenomena in nature. We do not think that the sea fled away, nor that the river stopped its flow, nor that the mountains skipped. A great many people have thought so, and out of poetry have made history. But when out of poetry you make history, you destroy the poetry and lose the element of religion it contains. The poet always was extravagant, seemingly. To him, in his vision, the earth trembles at the presence of God, and the mountains skip; the sea is driven back; the river stops flowing. Everything goes out of its course to honor or testify to God. So stood the sun still on the plains of Gibeon, while the leader of God's people sought help from on high; but it was in the vision, and not in fact, it stood still.

The principal poetry of the Jews seems to have been gathered from many sources, and into a number of hymn-books. That portion of the poetry which could be used in worship, could be sung or chanted, seems to have made a hymn collection. That many of the Psalms were so employed appears very natural. There are many things which go to show that the hymns were prepared for chanting. Musical signs were interspersed here and there. The word "Selah," which I suppose used to seem one of the mysteries of Providence, and insoluble at that, is found to indicate simply a pause. And just as we have marks in our staff, — above it, generally, — such as $f.$ or $ff.$ to signify that the passage is to be rendered strongly or very strongly, or *piano* or *pianissimo* to indicate softness, so this hymn poetry of the Jews had its marks.[1] There were time-marks and marks of expression, and

---

[1] See Dr. Gladden's *Who Wrote the Bible?* chap. vii., for more complete explanation.

indications of the kind of instrument to be employed for accompaniment, and all the like, in the Psalms. One easily forgets the names of these various marks, which I suppose every Hebrew student who becomes proficient in the Psalms commits to memory. But these indicate that when we read the Psalms we are reading from the Jewish hymn-books. They had five or six of these books, which were finally gathered into one. Many of the hymns have been credited to David, some to Moses, some to Solomon, and others to various authors; but our modern scholars find it difficult to believe that David wrote any of the Psalms. The compilers of the hymn-books attributed some of the songs to David, and they all came to be known in a general way as "the Psalms of David." There is sufficient evidence that they belong to a later time; but with the question of authorship we are not now concerned. At present we will consider the widely variant conceptions of God which these hymns testify to.

In modern times it seems desirable to have hymn-books which express the ideas of our own particular church or sect. There are some hymns so good and so comprehensive that almost any sect would put them in their book, but on the whole it is desirable, as it appears, for our Roman brethren to have their Roman book; for our Episcopal brethren theirs; for the Presbyterian and Baptist and Methodist and Universalist and Unitarian brethren their own peculiar hymn-books. One does not really enjoy singing bad doctrines, — that is, if he cares for doctrines at all. He would prefer to sing out of the book which his sect approves and publishes. Some hymn-books, adapted to periods of unusual religious excitement, are employed by all the sects which resort to revivals; but they are used, of course, by most intelligent people with more or less mental reservation.

The Jews, however, were very comprehensive in their hospitality to hymns. Their sentiments seem not to have crystallized into doctrines. Least of all were they able to express doctrines in hymns. A dogma in a hymn is a little like a wild beast in a collection of chinaware, very destructive of the beauty of the poetry. The Jews welcomed to their hymn-books religious sentiment, — particularly that of the patriotic order. Whatever the doctrinal drift of a sentiment might be, if it appealed to the feelings, or some of the feelings, it could have a place. For have we not many sorts of feelings? — those of joy, and of sorrow, of peace and of anger, of exultation and of contrition; and having all these, shall we not give them their best expression in our religion? Israel did not tell us so much about God as about its various feelings concerning God, in these hymns. That is what we want to know. We must have our own feelings about God, and others can help us; but God giveth such knowledge of himself as is fit, to each teachable spirit. One poet looked upon Jehovah in one way, another in another way. Each went according to his gift or light. Our modern hymns are usually poor and feeble compared with the songs of Israel. It has been said that the Psalms strike every chord of human feeling, and these chords are struck strongly. There were two things which did not hamper the poet of Israel: the one was doctrine and the other was rhyme. He concerned himself with neither, but did concern himself to speak strongly his feeling or his inward conviction. His poetry was of the kind Wordsworth called "inevitable."

In modern hymn-books are usually at least some bad hymns, — bad because they are neither poetry nor truth. The hymns are not all upon an equality. We do not begin at the beginning of a hymn-book and sing all the hymns through *seriatim*. There are a few which tower above all others. It is precisely so with all the Jewish hymn-books. There are some which help us more, or inspire us more deeply than we can tell. There are others which help us no whit. There are some which appeal to the feelings we ought to struggle against with all our might. In one of the hymns Jehovah is spoken of as the God of revenges, but in another as the shepherd of men. Then the pathos of contrition and humility is mingled in some hymns with thirst for the confusion and destruction of one's enemies.

There is a blemish in many of the hymns of praise. It is the blemish which rises from the fact that Israel was long a military people. No nation can be military in its enterprise except it be to some extent moved by the feeling of hatred of its enemies. And so bitter was the hatred of Israel in the earlier part of its career that it pursued some of its wars to the extent of exterminating those who opposed. There is no question of the bravery of that peculiar people. They bore the onset of the greatest of the military powers of the world. The hosts of Assyria pressed upon them without conquering their indomitable spirit. There was no extreme sacrifice of which they were not capable. Nothing more truly heroic stands in the annals of history than the intrepidity and unflinching courage of the small bands of Judah, in Maccabean times, withstanding the armies before which the very earth trembled. For such a people to be without martial hymns would be an impossibility. Their God was the God of war, the Lord of hosts. Their Jehovah was the great conqueror of enemies. It is the more surprising, therefore, that many of their hymns breathe the spirit of peace and of humanity. It is surprising that any could be found to believe that the earth is Jehovah's, and the fullness thereof; that the sweeter elements which belong to a later time should have found expression in the days of the struggle toward the sovereignty of the world. The better feeling mingles closely with the worse. Jehovah is spoken of as the God of salvation, but God shall crush the head of his enemies. God says that he will again bring his people out of Bashan, that "thy foot may be dipped in blood, and the tongue of thy dogs stained with the blood of thine enemies." And yet in the same hymn is the prayer that Jehovah will scatter those who desire wars.

We are therefore driven to choose out of the hymns of Israel the best and fittest for our help. Some of the sentiments we must resolutely reject. We are compelled to resort to the sifting process; and so all people practically do. Those who would be horrified at the thought of omitting any portion from the sacred canon do, for their own private behoof, and for the development in themselves of comfort, hope, and trust, select those things which help them the most, and read only with reluctance the other things. Doubtless the hymn-books of the Jews were made very much as ours were made, but with a difference. We have our Watts and Cowper and the Wesleys. We have the modern hymn-book poetry, which is intensely dogmatic, and therefore far from religious. We make our sectarian books. It may almost be said that we try to sing baptism by immersion, and baptism by sprinkling. We try to sing the decisions of the Council of Nicæa and the Council of Trent. We have tried to sing the dogmas of the priests about sacrifices. We have sung, too, about probation and the definite end of it. And in all such ways we have fallen far below the standard of Israel. Their hymns were large hymns of praise to Jehovah. Whether Jehovah were to be regarded as the God of revenges, or the shepherd, there were the ever applicable feelings of praise. "I will praise the name of my God with a song, I will magnify him with praise. And this shall please God more than a young calf having horns and hoofs." Our comparatively few hymns of praise are those which vibrate in our souls after the music ceases without.

There is a still higher merit in Israel's hymns. The poet has been said to be the one who sets us free. Perhaps it would be better to say that he is the one who can set free from its latency in our own breast the truth which uplifts us, and makes us see God. To have that truth born into the world, and declare itself, is the greatest blessing we can have. And there is nothing which so declares our inward and latent truth, the truth which connects us with God, and makes us now and then conscious of his presence, as the greatest of Israel's hymns. I think I speak advisedly in this. Back in the pre-Christian times there was some great soul of the Jews, a sort of Schliermacher, or Spinoza, or Goethe, who knew how to free our deepest consciousness of its truth, and bring it out into song. The highest and grandest philosophy accords with the highest and grandest poetry. Disraeli called the poets the unacknowledged legislators of the world. So far as the poetry of the Bible is concerned, the poets have helped many to walk in ways of pain and struggle victoriously.

If you are consumed by anxiety, and fretting yourself about the result of your endeavors, it is the divine poet who tells you to rest in Jehovah, and wait patiently for him. If you feel that your efforts will be misunderstood, and that evil motives will be attributed to you, the poet soothes your heart, and bids you commit your way to Jehovah, "and he shall bring forth thy righteousness as the light, and thy judgment as the noonday." If you feel that there is a hazard in your steps, and you do not know where they will end, although you take them for righteousness' sake, the poet tells you that the steps of the good man are ordered by Jehovah, and that Jehovah delighteth in his way; that if he falls he shall be uplifted, because Jehovah upholdeth with his hand. If one feels lonely and forsaken, and as if all were against him, the poet tells him: "I have been young and am old, yet have I not seen the righteous forsaken, nor his seed begging bread."

These and many other things the inspired poet tells us, not because he is an authorized person and can speak *ex cathedra*, but because he sees these things to be true, and we can also see them to be true, without any proof whatever. In the Psalms we find that highest authority which consists in revealing our own deepest things unto ourselves. We do not ask who wrote a hymn before we are ready to sing it. But if the music of truth is in it, and we have an ear for such music, then we sing it as from heaven. It is a song of Zion to us.

The Jews were solicitous for the authority of great

names, and yet their best hymns are anonymous. In science a great name has deserved weight. We cannot examine the facts of nature in any large extent; we have neither the skill nor the time to do it. There is, therefore, a good reason why we should go to our great lights of science to find out about nature. It is so in civil law, it is so in medicine, it is so in many of the departments of our activity; but so is it not in religion. A mother does not go and ask the authorities about love to discover whether or no she loves her babe. No man goes to a philosopher to discover about the presence of God. Yet if it has come about in the experience of mothers that some one has been able to give the best voice to the mother-love, then all true mothers delight in that voice. The speaker may be unknown, but the revelation is there. If it has transpired in the experience of any one that God is present with him, besetting him behind and before, that will make a revelation of our before latent truth, and that is the kind of authority the Psalms notably have. They expose to us, as almost nothing else does, the things of God latent within ourselves. The moral philosopher can help us somewhat; the scribe somewhat; but, most of all, God's poet blesses us with the blessing of opening to us the primal truths.

A hymn would be written by some person among the Jews, and would be set to such music as they then had; would be gathered later into some collection, to be used in their temple service. This collection would afterward be followed by another. There would be long hymns and short ones. In some, the history would be set forth; in others, there would be little but praise of Jehovah for his wonderful works to the children of men. In a few there would breathe the spirit of malediction. (If religious men had chosen only the good hymns of Israel, and had blotted out of their remembrance the bad hymns, bloodshed and cruelty would have been less in the world's history than they have been.) (If religious men had taken for divine that which inspired their own souls to the best feelings, the Christian church would not have stained itself with the blood of countless martyrs.) Thus by the history of Christendom God hath taught us that it is our duty, as well as our privilege, to make choice of the good and reject the evil, in everything furnished by human experience.)

XII.

GREEK INFLUENCE.

ACCORDING to the popular notion, derived mostly from the numbers of years marked on the margins of the English Bibles, a blank in the history of Israel occurs between the last of the prophets and the birth of Jesus Christ, — a blank of about four hundred years. This period apparently leaves no record of itself in the Bible, and therefore must seem unimportant. So that, whereas there are very clear and definite ideas about the earliest days of Hebrew history, and even of the time preceding Hebrew history, the last five hundred years of that history have received almost no attention from common readers of the Bible.

Recent critical studies of the Bible have gone far to modify this popular notion. In fact, one cannot give attention to the subject without finding that the popular notion is the reverse of the truth. Of the actual early history of the Hebrews we have very slight knowledge, and there is little prospect of an increase of it; and the importance of it from a historical standpoint is quite secondary. By far the most interesting and important part of Jewish history is in the blank space supposed to be left by the Bible.

During a period of about one hundred and seventy-five years, beginning with the last of the eleventh century of the Christian era, eight crusades took place. These were hysterical movements of Western

Europeans upon the Holy Land. (Good results, however, often flow from misfortunes.) From that peculiar insanity of superstition which took the form of the crusade arose this chief result, namely, a better acquaintance of the people of Western Europe with two civilizations more advanced than their own, — the Greek and the Saracenic. Thus a powerful impulse was given both to the literature and the commerce of Europe.

The exile of the Jews from their land gave them a great and new impulse in several ways. They were brought into contact with civilizations and religions in some respects superior to their own. It is true they lost their political independence, and that was a great trial to them, but they gained far more than they lost. They added largely to their before small stock of religious ideas. It is possible to represent the changes they underwent only in the most general way, and as highly probable rather than entirely certain. Before the exile they had been like children. Their national god was for the most part one among many such gods, and their practices were largely such as prevailed elsewhere. There was one element of superiority which we may declare became the seed of future greatness. They gradually came to some ideas of right. And while they were struggling to reach these ideas clearly, they passed through much confusion. (They attributed good to Jehovah, but also evil.) We hear the later Isaiah saying for Jehovah: "I form the light and create darkness; I make peace and create evil: I, Jehovah, do all these things." This is an echo from one of the earliest of the prophets, Amos, who cries, "Shall there be evil in a city and Jehovah hath not done it?" It was natural that they should attribute evil to their god. Many even to-day are unable to extricate themselves from the dilemma which confronted them.

In this as in other respects there came a change, and this change was wrought by new ideas which came to them from the Persians and Chaldeans. They were separated from their place of worship, Jerusalem. Their temple had been destroyed, and its service had ceased; and under such circumstances it was inevitable that their feelings and reasonings should change. Jehovah grew greater to them. They came to think of him as the only God. This was all providential. After one has come to think of God as some of the Jews did, there is no lack of providence, but gradually God's providence fills everything. The Jews found that there was only one God, and that he was a far greater and higher being than their fathers had imagined. But as these feelings increased they found God, their national God, withdrawing from them. He seemed to be farther away because he was greater.

So grew up the idea of God's transcendence. He was the ruler of all. He was the creator of all. The heavens were the work of his hands, as well as the earth. Accordingly we behold in the time succeeding the exile a distinct doctrine of angels. To be sure, angels had been thought of before, but what they were no one seemed able to imagine. They might be like the winds and the fires. After their contact with the Persians angels, which are like men and have human names, are spoken of. The angels were now more necessary to their religious philosophy than they had been before. Because if God were so high above all things, if God were resident, so to speak, in a lofty transcendency, it would be necessary for him to have beings of inferior rank to do his bidding and carry on his affairs. The Persians contributed angels to the Jews when the new necessities of their religion called for angels. There was a distinct necessity for them, because God was no longer a dweller on earth, but far away. God was therefore not alone in heaven, but was surrounded by an heavenly host of swift and powerful beings, by whom he procured his will to be done.

This enlargement of their theology helped them also in other ways; they were no longer compelled to think of God as the author of evil. While God had been receding from them, the ground of their confidence in him had been growing firmer. He was righteous, and could now always be righteous. If there was evil in the city, it was not necessary to think that Jehovah did it. It was not necessary to think that God was darkness as well as light. For the inferior beings, sometimes called the sons of God, were capable of both good and evil. Some of them were reckoned to be good angels. And instead of having a god for each nation, it might at least be conceived that there was for each nation a guardian angel. In the time of great distress and danger, there was comfort in feeling that a mighty angel was guarding the destinies of the people. If there were hosts on the earth in battle array, it was conceived that there were also hosts on high, also in battle array. The good and the evil were fighting there, as good and evil nations were fighting here. These beings of the other and higher order were therefore good and bad. They were respectively instigating their peoples to good and evil.

At the present time the angels are fading away again. It is because of still greater conceptions of God that arise; but at that time the introduction of angels marks a distinct advance and improvement of the religion of Israel.

It is impossible to do more than touch upon the nature of the Chaldean and Persian influence upon the Jews. But, to those who carefully study in the light of modern methods, there can be no doubt of the importance of this influence, and at the very time when it was received.

In that blank space between the last of the prophets and the birth of Christ, the principal preparation was made for the introduction of the greater religion. We are perhaps unable to strictly identify all or many of the influences, but the principal ones are plain. And one of the principal of these moulding influences arose from the association of Jews with Greeks. The outline of the history is somewhat as follows: A certain portion of the Jews had returned to Palestine during the reign of Cyrus, and under his protection. After the time of Cyrus his successors had made the most strenuous effort to conquer the Greeks, but the servile forces of the Oriental monarch found themselves unable to cope with the free Greeks. They met disastrous defeat at Marathon, about 490 B. C., and at Thermopylæ ten years later. The states or cities of the Greek peninsula were torn by jealousies, and by reason of their dissensions were fast becoming unable to carry on their warfare, until they were united under Philip of Macedon. As the Persian ambition had been to possess the Greek territory, now the ambition of Philip was to conquer Persia on its own soil. This design of his was carried out by Alexander, who, in a brief but brilliant career, became the master of the world. Palestine became incorporated in the new universal empire about 330 B. C.

In the course of a century, there came to be Greek communities in Palestine. A large number of Jews went to the new and great city founded in honor of Alexander, and called after him. It is very evident that the Jews were now brought under an influence which was to have a profound effect upon their feelings and religion, as well as the religions which should afterward grow out of theirs.

Without entering upon any examination of the peculiar history of the period, which was one of great trial to the faithful Jews, suffice it to say that they were being broadened, or, as we say, liberalized, by contact with the people who at that time excelled not only in arms, but in the arts and philosophy and polite learning. It is impossible for a people who have any quickness of apprehension, no matter what strength of conservatism is theirs, to escape the influence of such a contact. The Greeks were not haughty and tyrannical, but met them upon grounds of a fellowship which their liberal religious ideas did not forbid. The effect of such influence is seen in a book written about the close of the third century B. C., and which was attributed by its author, according to a literary device of the Jews, to Solomon. In reality this remarkable book does not reflect the times of Solomon, but the times of the Greek dominion. The book of Ecclesiastes is lacking in the religious fervor of earlier and greater books, and there is apparent in it, as most readers have seen, a skepticism which shows that the Greek contact had brought sadness and that shadow which is always cast by materialism. The writer is wearied with the repetitions of nature. The sun riseth and goeth to his place. The wind goeth toward the south and turneth about unto the north; it whirleth about continually. The rivers run into the sea. All things are full of labor; man cannot utter it. This unutterable sameness of things, and of life, and of labor; this everlasting flight of vanity upon an aimless mission; the very effort to find out the meaning of all these things, — it is all a vexation of spirit.

The writer of this belonged, of course, to the wealthy class. He had the time and opportunity to devote himself to philosophy. He gave his heart to know wisdom, and acquired, as he tells us, a great experience above all other men, but he found only grief.

The position of his nation, as conquered, was an affliction to him; but that does not account for the dismal view he takes of all things. For he does not limit his view to his own nation; he takes a keen glance at everything that is done under the sun. And whether it is here or there, it all amounts to the same thing. It is all vanity, and such a realm of vanity is more painful to contemplate than a realm of sorrow itself. He does not know how to account for it. He does not know how it can be that there is a God who is mighty and good, and at the same time such a world as this. He has lost the faith of his predecessors. Not their faith in the existence of God, but their sense of God's presence. God no longer has anything to do on the earth.

It is a curious fact, and worthy of our notice, that he does not seem any longer to care for the Jehovah of the Jews. He never once mentions his name, which was held in such profound reverence. He does not think of Israel as a peculiar people of Jehovah, therefore. The Persian influence has already had its effect, and God has gone off farther and farther into the abysses. "Be not rash with thy mouth, and let not thine heart be hasty to utter anything before God; for God is in heaven and thou upon earth, therefore let thy words be few." Possibly, if this were to be translated into the plainest of our speech, it would be found to be advice not to address words to God, or petitions or praises. God is in heaven and man is on earth, and there is no communication between the two.

It must not be supposed that the religion of the Jews is forgotten by this man, nor that he has become atheistic. And there is another thing which ought to be noted, — his belief in the goodness or righteousness of God. He taught that only by obedience to the commandments of God can we expect happiness. He has lost the enthusiasm, the spirit of trust, the heart of love for God. The truth he sees is like the light of a most wintry sun: it does not warm his soul. It is entirely possible he was acquainted with the doctrine of immortality. In then recent times it had been embraced, but he did not find himself able to believe it. He, indeed, finds that the same event happens to all, both good and bad. "As is the good, so is the sinner. . . . To him that is joined to all the living, there is hope; for a living dog is better than a dead lion. For the living know that they shall die, but the dead know not anything, neither have they any more a reward, for the memory of them is forgotten. Also their love, and their hatred, and their envy is now perished; neither have they any more a portion forever in anything that is done under the sun." If there is anywhere a more distinct disclaimer of immortality than that, it would be difficult to find it. And yet the man believes in that distant God, that awful Power, resident in the distances. He believes, too, in goodness to a moderate extent. For, in spite of his rash generalization of all things under the head of vanity, he is still almost always moderate. This moderation displays itself in the advice he gives to men. Because there is nothing after death, therefore, he says, "Enjoy your life. Eat thy bread with joy, and drink thy wine with a merry heart. . . . Live joyfully with the wife whom thou lovest all the days of thy vanity, which he hath given thee under the sun, all the days of thy vanity; for that is thy portion in life. Whatsoever thy hand findeth to do, do it with thy might; for there is no work nor device, nor knowledge nor wisdom, in Sheol, whither thou goest." The best thing he can think of is the long extension of life. But he has observed that sometimes the righteous man perishes, and the wicked man prolongs his days. His advice therefore is, "Be not righteous overmuch; neither make thyself overwise; why shouldest thou destroy thyself? Be not overmuch wicked, neither be thou foolish; why shouldest thou die before thy time?" Some have spoken of the writer of all this as a worn-out voluptuary; a man who had tried everything of the delights of the flesh, and had found himself disappointed, as all such do. But does he not rather appear to be a man of extreme moderation? He has lost the enthusiasm and fervor of the Jewish religion, and had contracted the Greek flavor. It was perhaps inevitable, but it was in the last degree mournful. This shows us how the notion of the transcendence of God, his work through angels and secondary causes, is likely to sap the enthusiasm and fervor of religion if it develop far enough.

The Greek influence, however, is not all expressed, it merely finds over-expression, in this book of Ecclesiastes. We may well suppose that, while all the Jews responded to Greek influence, not all, and not a considerable portion of them, went the lengths of the author of this book. Indeed, the Greek influence itself is hard to understand, if we do not find more in it than the moderation of this preacher. There had been a great history across the western sea. The statesmen and scholars and poets had been those whose memory the world has delighted to honor, but these great men had all departed. Five centuries before the beginning of the Christian era the greatest of the Greeks had died, sacrificing himself to the welfare of the state.

The Greeks had their priests, as had the Jews, but they also had enjoyed the advantage of one great prophet, — doubtless of more than one; but the one is known to all men. Socrates had been as conscious of a divine call and mission as any of the Jewish prophets had been. He had devoted himself to that mission with a fidelity sealed at last with his blood. Among those born of women hath not arisen a greater than Socrates, with one exception. The mission of Socrates, as well as of his predecessors, and that great successor Plato, to whom the world is so vastly in debt, could not have been lost as the centuries rolled on. To every great river, as it flows toward the sea, there are tributaries; and that great river of religion, which took the name of Christianity nineteen centuries ago, did not then spring in full flood out of the ground. The same river had been coming down through eras of human experience, but this experience was not limited to the one nation. Or, if we suppose that to Israel belongs the honor of the name of that religion, there were other streams which contributed their supply, at fit places in the progress. Israel, with its distinguishing idea of righteousness, was cast adrift from its old belongings, that it might share the riches of the heathen. It was sent into exile, both for its own good and the good of the world, and for the welfare of unborn generations. It was cast in contact with the Persians, to learn of these followers of the ancient and refined religion of Zoroaster what they could teach. It was thrown afterward with those who had felt the influence of Greek thought, then and long the most subtle, the most liberal, the most enlightened in the world.

It would be possible, had one the knowledge and the delicacy of perception, to trace these four great contributing influences in the mind of the writer of the book of Ecclesiastes. The fervor of the Hebrew is toned down by the moderation of the Stoic. The idea of righteousness inherited from the Hebrews is chilled by the feeling of the distance of God in the heavens; or by the loss of Jehovah, the national and present deity. The skepticism of the later Greeks thus makes its appearance as upon the surface, to be the chief feature of the book. All this, nevertheless, contributes to the revelation of God to man. It all prepares the way for the fuller revelation.

In our own time we hear, as it were, an echo of some of the words of Ecclesiastes. We are exhorted by a persuasive and eloquent orator of our own country not to be overmuch righteous; to enjoy life while we may. But our orator does not go quite so far as the author of Ecclesiastes. Of a life beyond the grave he does not profess to know anything; but he would not darken the star of hope which may cheer any soul. The author of Ecclesiastes is persuaded in his own mind that there is no work, nor device, nor consciousness, in Sheol, whither we are all going. He may have darkened the star of hope in many breasts. Yet there is in all such philosophy somewhat of preparation for the coming better religion. The Jewish authorities did not reject such writings from their canon, because such writings as the book of Ecclesiastes contain somewhat of the increasing revelation. It does not satisfy us: neither do any of the things preparatory to Christianity satisfy us wholly.

There is a value in such a book as that of Ecclesiastes, however, which is not lessened by its defects. Together with the book of Jonah, and others which express wide sympathies, it helps prepare the way for the universal religion. When we reach the beginning of the universal religion, the religion not of the Jew, nor of the Greek, nor of the barbarian, but of mankind, we hear no longer the name, Jehovah. If we find fault with the omission of this revered name from the book of Ecclesiastes, what shall we say of the bringer-in of the new covenant, to whom the word is simply a word of the past? — who dares to replace all the names of the past by the term of tender and close relation, Father? Surely the skepticism of this Jew two hundred years before Christ, the sad pessimism of this book, and the development of an all-doubting spirit were not wasted if they helped to broaden the way for the blessing of mankind by a religion which should root itself in that which had come from all nations. Paul acknowledges that he is debtor to both Jews and Greeks; so are we all, and to more than Jews and Greeks, — to those who held partial truths; to those who held errors; to those who doubted the future, as well as to those who expected the future life.

It may be well to open our eyes to the fact that our

Bible is not the product of Jewish thought alone. As its mission is to bless all nations, so it has been made by all nations. God is not alone the God of the Jew, but also of the Gentile.

In that period which has been regarded as blank, between the last of the prophets and Christ, scholars of religion are showing us the preparations of divine Providence for the breaking down of the walls of partition. In the light of their discoveries we may see the Jew bringing to us his sheaves, and the Persian bringing his sheaves, and the Greek his. And the end is not yet. There rises in the West a people before whom the earth is destined to tremble as it has never trembled before; the people before whom the conquering Greek and the already subject Jew must learn to bow. The last of the world empires is to arise before the coming of the world's true king. The Greek is to be supplanted by the Roman.

XIII.

OTHER INFLUENCES.

THE extent and permanence of the Greek influence over the Jews are best shown by the fact that the Greek language, with some local modification, was adopted by the Hebrew people; and in process of time the Hebrew Scriptures, which were begun at the time of the exile, and brought later to a sort of completion, were translated into Greek. The Greek Scriptures came to be of such general use among the people, not only of Egypt and Alexandria, but of Palestine as well, that a large proportion of the quotations in the New Testament from the Old are from the Greek instead of the Hebrew Bible.

Greek customs and Greek thoughts found their way into Hebrew usage and minds, and the old walls of separation between the Jew and the rest of the world began to be undermined. The Jews, as a separate people, under the auspices of Jehovah, had almost accomplished their mission. As we speculate, we find it possible, perhaps probable, that if the history of the Jews could have been long continued under the influence of the Greeks, there would have ensued such a mingling of the better elements of both kinds of religion and philosophy as would have left the Jewish religion much less distinct than it really is.

Comparative quiet had the Jews during the rule,

first of the Persians, and then of the Greeks. And quiet times are favorable for easy and natural assimilation. The old dream of the Jews, that they were the peculiar people of God, destined always to remain peculiar until they should arrive at the control of all nations, was already subsiding. They were learning the arts and sciences of the Greeks, as well as adopting their language.

A certain king, who seems to have been insane with ambition, and who desired above all things to make a brilliant career, took occasion to violently interfere with the religious rites of the Jews, and even went so far as to issue a command that they should worship the gods of Greece alone. The temple on Mt. Gerizim was dedicated to Jupiter, while, upon the high altar of the temple at Jerusalem, swine's flesh was offered in sacrifice, and broth of swine's flesh was sprinkled in the holy place, and over the sacred utensils.

No such successful mode could have been devised to stop the liberalizing process which was gradually leavening the religion of the Jews. They were, of course, aroused to resist these blasphemous proceedings, and the religious sentiment was revived in great power. They became Jews again, and were prepared to stand stoutly for the ancestral religion, which was almost departing from them. The observance of the Sabbath was forbidden and synagogues were destroyed. Antiochus could have taken no course so sure to defeat his ends as this. Yet by taking this course he performed a great service for the world to come, because he prevented the loss of the root of a true religion, the religion of the prophets and psalmists, — the religion which was founded to bless the world, and out of which should grow the Christian development.)

(One of the measures of repression resorted to by Antiochus the Brilliant was to order the delivery to his officers of all copies of the law to be burned. If any failed to obey, they were to be slain. The satellites of the king went prowling up and down the kingdom, violently destroying the remnants of the old religion. To meet such atrocity, the spirit of the people was at length aroused. A considerable proportion of them submitted and became idolaters, but there was a remnant in whom the spirit of the prophets slumbered, in whose breast it was reawakened. The agents of the king, in carrying out their plan, came to a small town, between Jerusalem and Joppa, where dwelt a distinguished priest named Matthias, who was the father of five sons. This man was commanded to offer sacrifice upon an altar erected by the agents of the king, but he flatly refused to do it. Upon his refusal, there advanced from the crowd one of those pliant men of the Jews who were always ready to make favor with the party in power, and he proceeded to offer the sacrifices. Matthias, the aged priest, would not bear that, and promptly killed the man. The officers of Antiochus were killed, the altar destroyed, and Matthias called to him all who were zealous for the law. These escaped into the wilderness, were pursued and attacked, but after a while became victorious. Their numbers increased, and what they lost otherwise, as in weapons, etc., they gained in increased spirit and courage.

They carried on their warfare, after the death of the aged priest, under the leadership of his son, Judas, whose surname was Maccabeus, or The Hammer.

In a series of conflicts which ensued, the Jews were mainly victorious. Jerusalem was retaken, the temple cleansed, the sacrifices resumed. After that manner the religion of Ezra and Nehemiah, the religion of the prophets, which had seemed to languish, which had been almost lost, as the book of Ecclesiastes witnesses, was again established.

By the student of history, and especially one interested in the history of the Jews, and in tracing the rise of the religion of Christ, it must be deplored that the best accounts of these most urgent and significant times, the books of the Maccabees, were excluded from our Protestant editions of the Bible. For they describe the most heroic period of Israel's history not only, but they give us some information of the rise of those religious parties which played so important a part in the time of Jesus Christ. They also tell us of the first association of the Romans with the Jews. Judas Maccabeus heard of the might and valor of the Romans, and how ready they were to make treaties with other nations. "It was told him also of their wars and noble acts which they had done among the Gauls, and how they conquered them, and brought them under tribute, and what they had done in Spain, and how they had conquered every place though it were very remote from them." In a word, Judas heard of the universal conquest of this mighty people of the West. Moreover, there was something new in the mode of the administration of government by this great people. They had representatives — over three hundred of them — to sit in their senate chambers daily, so that the affairs of the people might be well ordered; and one man was chosen each year for the administration of executive functions.

This information so influenced Judas that, being himself in straits because of his enemies the Greeks, he sent a deputation to Italy to propose an alliance with the Romans. Their response to this proposal is given: "Good success be to the Romans, and to the people of the Jews, by sea and by land, forever; the sword also, and enemy, be far from them. If there come first any war upon the Romans, or any of their confederates throughout all their dominion, the people of the Jews shall help them, as the time shall be appointed, with all their heart; neither shall they give anything unto them that make war upon them, or aid them with victuals, weapons, money, or ships, as it hath seemed good unto the Romans; but they shall keep their covenants without taking anything therefor. In the same manner, also, if war come first upon the nation of the Jews, the Romans shall help them with all their heart," etc. So comes the all-conquering Roman upon the ground of the Jew, thenceforth to be inseparable from Jewish history, so long as the nation remained in the land.

Internal dissensions arose among the rival princes of the Jews, and this gave a pretext to Pompey to gain possession of Jerusalem. The priests were slain at the altar, and Pompey drew aside the veil that concealed the most holy place, expecting to find some image there. It does not appear that this act, so profane to the Jews, was anything more than the curiosity of a stranger who had the power to do as he chose, and who wished to look upon the gods of a conquered people. In this act of profanation, as they deemed it, together with later acts of tyranny, such as taking the Jewish ruler and other princes to Rome to grace the Roman triumph, originated the hatred against the Romans, which never afterward ceased nor diminished. This triumph of the Roman general occurred about 63 B. C., and the hatred then incurred had time to root itself deeply in the heart of all classes of the Jews before the birth of Jesus.

In the year 37 B. C., Herod, known as "the Great," became the king of the Jews, — a man of extraordinary talent, as shown by the fact that he was able to maintain his throne during the great changes in Rome, and in spite of numerous and powerful adversaries in Syria. He raised the Jewish state in the respect of the world, making it the political power it had not been before. The old temple he replaced by a far more magnificent structure. He knew how to adorn cities. He had in perfection the Roman trick of securing popular favor by the improvement of streets, the establishment of baths, theatres, and the like. He builded the city which took the name of the Cæsar. He gave a splendor to the kingdom it had not possessed, according to the traditions of the people, since the days of Solomon; but by reason of his foreign birth, and the vices which stained his private character, and because he was a flatterer of the Romans, the Jews hated him persistently. Driven by the necessities of circumstances, as appears, this man slew many of his own kin, including three of his sons, thus testifying to the evils of times which made such crimes necessary in a ruler. Thus the days of Herod were to the Jews days of horror, making them all the more solicitous to maintain the integrity of their own religion.

One can have but a partial and possibly misleading view of the state of the Jews under the Roman rule, and of the condition of things into which Jesus was born, who fails to note the rise and development of three distinct parties among them. It is, perhaps, impossible to trace any of these parties to its origin. But of the existence of the three, the Gospels of the New Testament bear abundant testimony. These three divisions, partly religious and partly political, are respectively named the Pharisee, the Sadducee, and the Essene. In many respects the first of these is the most important, and has the closest relation with the life and teachings of Christ.

The name signifies separation. The Pharisee was the Separatist. Perhaps he began his career in revolt against that rule of Greek influence which manifests itself in the book of Ecclesiastes, and which came to success under the lead of Judas Maccabeus. For under the Greek influence the old rigors introduced by Ezra, the laws against intermarriage and social intercourse with other peoples, had fallen all but dead. The atrocious attempt of Antiochus to destroy the last remnant of Jehovah worship had, as we have seen, awakened a new and brave zeal for the old laws and the old religion. The cry arose for a new separation of the people of the divine promises from the heathen. In the time of Ezra, the same cry had resulted in the violent divorce of Jewish men from their heathen wives. The ties of nature, which are really more sacred than any artificial ties of society or religion, had been ruthlessly violated. Husbands sent away their wives and children in order to become once more loyal Jews. No doubt Ezra, in his pious zeal for the honor of Jehovah, believed that God does require such barbarous things of the children of men. At any rate, the old idea of separation, which had been slowly growing up, revived after the exile, and again revived in the days of Judas, the heroic son of the heroic old priest Matthias. In many ways the idea was taken up by a class of patriotic Jews. Whether they named themselves the Separatists, or were so named by their opponents, we do not know; but they became very strong with the people. In a certain sense, now difficult to understand fully, they were at the same time the progressive party. They were not a set of hypocrites, as we may have imagined. Doubtless there were hypocrites among them, but so are there in any party. What they wished was to assert the preëminence of the Jew over other men. To this feeling they had been stimulated by the book of Daniel, which foretold the supremacy of the Jews in the world (to be shortly realized), and by other writings of a similar character. But if the nation were separated from other nations less holy, or unclean, so also individuals in the nation who aspired to holiness must keep themselves from association with even Jews of lax religion and morals. Those who loved the law should hate those who cared nothing for the law. They should separate them from their company as unclean and defiling. Such feelings grow naturally out of the desire to abide by regulations for conduct. If they are unmodified by other feelings, such as those which make love for God and man the chief element in religion, they will soon develop into excess, and become the most hateful of all feelings. The Pharisees grew exceedingly proud and exclusive. They knew and affirmed their superiority to other men. They could go into the temple and pray, and thank God that they were better than other men, because they kept the laws and paid the taxes.

The Sadducees were of patrician rank; and while

one of their number might be a Pharisee, although he would thereby sacrifice the esteem and countenance of his fellow-Sadducees, no person not to the manner born could be a Sadducee. The Sadducees fell from political power with the beginning of the reign of Herod. From that time on, the Pharisees gained the ascendancy in Jewish affairs which they were able to maintain nearly to the end.

There was another party, of small numbers and of little political significance, but of which Josephus, the Jewish historian, makes much in his Antiquities. The Essenes were the most devoted of all the Jews in their religion; but their religion was of a type not directly authorized by the law. They separated themselves even from the Separatists. They did not frequent the temple, although for a time they sent gifts to its coffers and altars. They may have been indebted to disciples of Pythagoras among the Greeks as much as to the Jewish Scriptures for the distinctive features of their religion. They seem to have lived in small communities, at long distance from the larger towns, and to a considerable extent in the regions of the Dead Sea. They engaged themselves in agriculture, or bee-keeping, or herding. They disdained all adornment, their dress being such as John the Baptist is described as wearing. They were vegetarians, and abstained from wine. They recognized no social distinctions. There were no rich and no poor. They were brethren, and had all things in common. By them marriage was not tolerated.

The three religions were in force at the birth of Christ. They may be called three religions because the adherents of each were separated from the others by distrust, and even hatred. The Pharisees were the most enlightened, the most progressive, and the most engaged in affairs. They were doing the most to shape the religious and social destiny of the nation. They were the ones with whom the coming Christ would have most in common.

Meanwhile, and for a long time, the religious teachers of the people were not absent or idle. The Scribes, of whom perhaps Ezra at the exile had been the first, formed a body of men who paid attention to the explanation of the law and interpretation of its difficulties. They had attained great authority among the people. They sat in Moses' seat. In general there were two opposing or at least unsympathetic schools. One of these schools, or "houses," as they were called, seems to have been founded by a very wise and virtuous man, Hillel by name. This man extended the authority of the Scribes, while at the same time he himself exercised his authority in the mildest fashion. His precepts are some of them of the sort found in the Sermon on the Mount. The Talmud tells us that once, when a heathen asked Hillel to show him the whole of the Jewish religion in a few words, he answered: "Do not unto others that which thou wouldst not should be done to thee: this is the whole extent of the law; all the rest is merely explanation of it. Go now and learn to understand that." A teacher able and wise enough to teach after that manner is one who, like the great prophets of an earlier time, can understand and express the substance of religion, overlaid and obscured as it is by unspeakable masses of tradition and performance.

A very melancholy spectacle was always in sight of the thoughtful Jew during this period. With the advent of the Greeks there had come, as we have seen, an assimilation of Greek ideas and Greek manners and customs. There had ensued upon the Roman alliance a new admixture. Galilee had for a long time been known as a gathering place or district of heathen. Many Jews dwelt in Galilee, but they were mostly infected with the manners, and to some extent the morals, of the heathen. Away from Jerusalem, and in the smaller cities and villages, there were multitudes who had become indifferent to the laws of the Jews. There were many persons who were ready and glad to gain wealth by favoring the cause of the Romans, and to extract money from their Jewish brethren by the taxes.

And so, at the time of the beginning of the mission of Christ, a number of Jews were in the land, disowned by the Pharisees and by the priests, and left untaught and uncared for. There was no religious teacher who seemed to give any attention to this multitude. All that was done was to withdraw from any association with them. They were Jews by birth, but on account of their lax morals, and their inattention to the demands of the law, they were cast adrift from Judaism to fare as they might. To this result had the mixing of the Jews with other nations, during a period of four centuries, brought religion. The religious were few. The people had to a large extent grown cold toward the rites of the temple, and toward the sacred traditions. The advocates of religion, whether Pharisees, Sadducees, or Essenes, had little hold upon these disowned masses. In a way, these Jews were infidels. They were classified as "sinners," and to the pious Jew a sinner was a horror.

But there was coming, and in fact was already arrived, one who was to look upon these disowned multitudes in a new way. He would look upon them as sheep destitute of a shepherd. If the strictly religious people, the Scribes and Pharisees, may have been expected to be the friends and helpers of this new teacher, the expectation will be disappointed. The coming teacher of Israel will find his friends and the subjects of his teachings in these "lost sheep of the house of Israel." Thus a new career will begin in Judaism. Israel, which has been trained for some centuries in the school of a haughty exclusiveness, will give birth to a new and divine teacher, who will go with tender and winning solicitude to these "lost," and thus establish that new religion in which all the heathen, and all the "lost," shall have their part.

XIV.

THE NEW AGE.

AT some military posts, sunrise is greeted with the firing of a gun, and the day dismissed in like manner at sundown. The sun itself makes no noise in its rising, and may be said to be unobserved by the most of people; but military and other persons sometimes make much noise in the world. At certain times their noise is contemporaneous with the rising or the setting of suns. Eras are sometimes ushered in by tumult; by revolution and downfall of nations; and sometimes the new eras come quietly enough. They are not known to have come when they are actually here. It is left to the future to look back and declare that at such a time the new era came.

The greatest era in human history, compared with which all previous eras were relatively insignificant, was born in troublous times, to be sure, but without attracting the attention of any single soul of man. There are stories well known by all Christendom, and made much of by all Christians, of which this is to be said, that they were the growth of later years. To these stories we will give little credit, provided we are studying the Bible as we study any other literature. Precisely such stories we reject as unhistorical when we find them in the scriptures of other Oriental peoples. Now we are endeavoring to study the Bible as we would study any religious book. We are trying to discriminate in its history the things which are historical and the things which are unhistorical. This we can do only as we apply such a mode of investigation as we find best adapted to the purpose of literary and historical criticism.

So we think of the beginning of the greatest era of human history as coming unobserved by the multitude, and really unobserved by any one. The kingdom of heaven cometh without observation. Now there are two widely distinct fields of thought: the one is the physical, including all that belongs to the recurrence of seasons, days and nights, and the events which occur in them; the other is the spiritual, including the principles of religion. It certainly must strike any one who knows anything of the teachings of Jesus that his work and thought were almost exclusively in the spiritual realm. In the physical sense, and as regards the physical facts, he was the child of a humble parentage among the Jews. But with these and such like facts he was not greatly interested. His mind moved in the realm of spiritual verities, the realm which may be called the kingdom of heaven. His conduct and his words were of that realm. He spoke of himself as the Son of God. His assumption of this rank has been regarded as a most serious statement in the realm of physics, both by his followers and by opponents. Yet there is no recorded saying of his which in any measure justifies the belief that he believed himself to be the Son of God in the physical sense. If we, with the light of greater knowledge of things physical than his contemporaries had, are careful to discriminate between the physical and the spiritual; if we are capable of recognizing a spiritual power in ourselves, and a capacity for religion, or the spiritual life, — we need not be puzzled by those mysteries which for many centuries have caused offense to the learned and the thoughtful.

He who makes the claim of being the Son of God when he is not is a deceiver, and ought to be so ranked. That is one evident principle. Another is that, in such an age as that wherein Jesus Christ was born, there are very few who will be able to understand the claimant of a divine sonship except in the physical sense. While an obscurity rests upon the actual history of Jesus during his life in the world, sufficient of the light of his divine life shines out through the clouds to assure any reverent soul that he was in very truth what he claimed to be, the Son of God. The evidence that he was the Son of God in the physical sense is, to say the least, exceedingly slender; but if that evidence were perfect, it would add no weight or authority to his teachings in the spiritual realm.

If in the study of the Bible we had found that all its statements are infallibly correct, so that in no case was a blunder made in respect to any matter whatsoever, there would then be no appeal from the slight evidence given of the divine parentage of Jesus in a physical sense. So long as the Bible holds that place in the regard of any one, that whatsoever is found therein is final and not to be doubted, there will be no question respecting the birth of Jesus. He will be regarded as the Son of God in the sense of religion and in the sense of physics. But once see that the Bible is not infallible, that there are errors in it which confess themselves to any person of judgment, and forthwith the question in regard to Jesus and his relation to nature will arise.

If our study of the Old Testament has been of real service to us, we have seen that above all other books, because it is the book of religion, the Bible ought to be read with discrimination. That is to say, we are not to take all of its statements as of equal value or equal truth. If we do not read it with discrimination, we fail to get at the value of it. It may be said that readers of the Bible read with two different motives: the one class reads for the purpose of seeing exactly what the Bible says, without a care as to the particular nature of the saying; the other class reads to know not only what is said, but if possible why it was said. The one method is that of superstition, and the other is that of reason, and for the purpose of instruction. Now, that all of the statements of the Bible are not of equal truth any one can see for himself, if he will but give attention.

An illustration offers itself. Let any one read the fifty-first Psalm with attention. There is perhaps nothing in the world which will so touch the heart of a sinful man, who is repentant, as that matchless hymn. By some editor of the hymns of Israel it was attributed to David, and surmised that it was written by the conscience-stricken king after the commission of a great crime. It was such a hymn as the king certainly might have written under those circumstances; or any one else, for that matter. But there are sentiments in it which are believed to belong to a later time. However, the hymn was edited, as we shall surely see. It was "improved" by a later hand.

The sentiment of the hymn is one of deep contrition. The writer of it has discovered himself to be exceedingly evil. He is appalled at the vision of his iniquity; and since he has the idea of a holy God, he feels he has offended, not so much against his fellow human beings as against God's goodness. More than all else in the world he desires to be cleansed from his iniquity. He does not see how he can be cleansed. He does not see how he can do it himself, and he prays the merciful and just God to do it. He hopes that God will not hide his face from him; that God will blot out all his iniquities, will create a new heart in him, and renew a right spirit within him. So far we need have no difficulty in interpreting the hymn, which so vividly expresses our own feeling of contrition when we are convicted of our own sinfulness.

The writer, in considering his own case, and how to rid himself of the burden and defilement of his sin, perceives that sacrifices upon the altar will do no good. True, it was an important part of the priestly regulations that guilt would be done away by sacrifices. It was the law which the priestly party had always sought to make binding upon the consciences of the people; but the writer of the hymn, whoever he may have been, did not believe it. He saw no relation between his sinfulness and the sacrifice of animals upon the altar. This is his testimony: "Restore unto me the joy of thy salvation, and uphold me with thy directing spirit. O Lord, open thou my lips, and my mouth shall show forth thy praise. For thou desirest not sacrifice, else would I give it; thou delightest not in burnt offering: the sacrifices of God are a broken spirit; a broken and a contrite heart, O God, thou wilt not despise." The meaning is perfectly plain. It is summed up in the deep sense of evil, in the appeal to God to cleanse the soul from its sin; in the affirmation that God does not wish sacrifices, else would they have been given, and that the sacrifices of God are contrition on the part of the sinner. So far, good. Now comes the later hand to "improve" this beautiful psalm, so that it may properly find a place in the hymns of the Jews, and be acceptable to the priests as well as to the sinners. "Do good in thy good pleasure unto Zion; build thou the walls of Jerusalem. Then shalt thou be pleased with the sacrifices of righteousness, with burnt offering and whole burnt offering; then shall they offer bullocks upon thine altar." Now the contrite sinner said as distinctly as possible that, if burnt offerings had been acceptable to God, he would have tried to get rid of his sense of sin by offering sacrifices; but he was deeply convinced that such things as sacrifices are of no avail. He felt that his own contrition and horror of his sins were precisely the sacrifices God wished, but the man who "improved" the hymn was of a different mind. He believed in sacrifices. He thought God believed in them, too; and, by so much as he could, he unsaid the truth of the hymn, and reduced it to simple absurdity. If the first part of that psalm is true, the second part, the addition or "improvement," is not true. If we accept both as true, then we reduce both to nothing, because these conflicting statements mutually neutralize each other. Now from our experience, so far as it goes, we know that the first part is the truth; and therefore that the addition is irretrievably false, and ought not to be tolerated. It is only as we reject the addition, and put upon it the brand of falsehood, we really believe the truth of the real hymn.

The same principle obtains elsewhere. The editors of different portions of the Old Testament undertook to unsay the things in the writings which were not acceptable to them. In the book of Ecclesiastes, the whole sentiment of which is unmistakably against the hope of immortality, the editor added a few words expressive of that hope. The book was to go into the sacred canon, but the sentiment of it was rejected, and the addition or "improvement" made which would neutralize the objectionable sentiment.

One such illustration is as good as an hundred. We cannot be left in doubt that for the purposes of religion, as well as of accurate knowledge, we must bring discrimination to the Bible, and apply it faithfully. What is true of the Old Testament is equally true of the New. For the New Testament, while it is the book of the new dispensation, or a new era, makes no violent break with the Old. When the new dispensation begins, it begins as quietly as the dawn. It is a forth-putting of the old, in a new vigor and in a better form. The habits of expression, the habits of thought, of the Jew persist. There is not a great blank of centuries between the prophets of the old and the messengers of the new. In fact, the new is brought before us by one in the spirit of an ancient prophet. Where the old age meets the new, we do not enter a realm of things more supernatural than before. We enter a realm in which nature itself begins to assume more of the divine. We do not find the messenger of the new covenant teaching men how they may ascend the height of the heaven, but how they may open their characters and lives to the incoming of the heavenly and the divine.

The first historians and biographers, unlike Jesus, of whom they undertook to tell us, were not free from the notions of their predecessors. They interpret the sayings and deeds of Jesus on the physical side. Instead of being steadied in thought by the vision of the divine presence, they were thrown out of balance by visions of the divine interference, as in occasional spasms. Therefore are we bound, if we would be learners of the truth of Jesus, to bring careful discrimination to the study of the words of his biographers. Here, as elsewhere and as everywhere, it is our reasonable duty to "prove all things, and to hold fast (only) to that which is good."

So far as we know, Jesus Christ made no record of his own birth, life, and deeds. Knowing, as he did, the fallibility of his followers, knowing that they were liable to error in important matters, and being compelled to rebuke them often for such errors, it seems proper to assume that, if he had considered the facts of his birth in this world of great importance in the promulgation of his gospel, he would have taken the work in hand of presenting a veritable autobiography. The truths of his mission, the gospel he came to make in the world, he committed to his followers, bidding them spread them. He seems to have been confident that, in spite of various errors of interpretation, they would give forth those fundamental truths which would redeem the world from its sin and misery. He refrained from writing anything himself. When his followers should have fully come into the spirit of his work, they would be able to carry it on, and to transmit it to their successors. His failure to write is the more remarkable because the age was favorable for writing, and Palestine was full of scribes; but it may at least show us that he trusted to the spirit of his work, and to the faithfulness of his disciples in carrying it on, rather than to writings.

Therefore, for a time, there were no writings of the

new dispensation, as we may call it. It is all but certain that an enthusiastic expectation of Christ's early return to the earth was very prevalent for a few years. If that glorious new kingdom for which they had been taught to pray were really coming in a short time, it was useless to commit anything to writing; and so for a time that important work was neglected. In the course of a few years after the death of Jesus (it has heretofore been impossible to determine accurately how many years, though it may be affirmed that the number was less than eight), a man of extraordinary ability and tireless energy, and of considerable learning, joined the ranks of the followers of Jesus. When we first discover this man, he is a persecutor, and of the most violent type. He is determined to crush out the new religion before it gains such headway as to threaten the religion of Ezra and Nehemiah. To that end he devotes himself with a singleness of purpose, always characteristic of the man.

He is present when the enraged Jews stone to death their first Christian victim, Stephen. He consents to that act, and the witnesses laid down their clothes at his feet. It is probable that this scene, instead of softening his heart toward the Christians, fixed him the more in his purpose to exterminate them. He is in league with the authorities at Jerusalem, and becomes their efficient agent. He does not wish to confine his efforts to Jerusalem and its vicinity, but pushes out into the other cities. He plans an attack upon the followers of Jesus at the distant city of Damascus, and is on his way thither, when he is blinded by a lightning stroke from the sky, thrown to the ground, and then hears the voice of the persecuted Jesus calling to him, and bidding him renounce his course. He goes on to Damascus with his company, but he goes to learn, and not to destroy, the religion of Jesus. His sight is restored to him, and he devotes himself to the study of the new dispensation. He tells us in one of his epistles that he conferred not with flesh and blood, and that he did not go up to Jerusalem to learn of the disciples there, some of whom had become the apostles of the new religion, but that he retired to Arabia. Now, what he did in Arabia we do not know: our natural conjecture is that in solitude he devoted himself, after the manner in which he had been trained in the school of Gamaliel, to the formulation of the religion of Jesus, and its relation with the religion of the Jews. He did not renounce the Jewish religion; but to him, more than to any other, we are indebted for the connection we find between the old and the new. He becomes the master-mind in the new movement. He does not find himself in harmony of idea with the apostles at Jerusalem. He is able to take a far more comprehensive view of the religion of Jesus, as the flower and final expression of the religion of the law and the prophets, than these simple-minded and unlearned Galileans. He perceives that the Jew enjoys this advantage, namely, that to him have been committed the precious legacy of the divine oracles. He also perceives that he has received such trust that he may become a blessing to the Gentiles. In this mission the Jews had dismally failed through their obtuseness. Now the time has come for the old promises to be fulfilled. He himself will become the apostle to the Gentiles. He will be the truer Jew, because he will carry out the long-neglected mission of the Jews. And all this is made possible because Jesus had been born, and taught, and died, a supreme sacrifice for the sake of men.

Paul does not seem to attach so much importance to the teachings of Jesus as to his person. He is altogether entranced, fascinated, and subjugated by the personality of Jesus. He learns to love him with a love as deep and enthusiastic as it is lasting. His greatest ambition, his dearest purpose, in the attainment of which he is ready to sacrifice every earthly advantage, and even his pride in his nation, is to know Christ, — to experience Jesus in his own life, to live Christ, as he expresses it. For the sayings of Jesus he does not so much care; he quotes very few, almost none of them. The person of Jesus is so dear to him that he thinks only of living Jesus' life over again, though he feels that he can do that only in an imperfect and fragmentary way. Such devotion is above that of the other disciples.

Paul began to write. Others may have written before he did, but we have no knowledge of any such. He began to put the stamp of his purpose and his way of thinking upon the early church. It is entirely possible that he created and greatly stimulated the desire of the people to have a written account of the birth and life, and deeds and sayings of Jesus. The expectation of the speedy return of Jesus was waning. Some doubtless held it strongly, but with some it had become a matter of doubt. Thus began attempts to set forth the biography of Jesus.

The study of these early endeavors is involved in profound difficulty. Yet some progress is made. Our scholars have arrived at the almost if not quite unanimous opinion that, of the four accounts preserved to us in our Bibles, the second account is the oldest. It is surmised, and with much reason, that this is not the first detailed account that was made, but it is the first of the four.

Now when this first of the preserved biographies of Jesus was written, the notion that Jesus was physically, so to speak, the Son of God had not attained a commanding influence. In the multitude of stories afloat in the popular imagination, that story may have had a place; but the writer of this first biographical sketch did not credit it, or he did not regard it as important: therefore he omits all reference to it. The birth of Jesus, where he came from, and what he did as a child, or until he began his mission, secured no notice from him.

Those things were before the gospel. The gospel did not begin until John commenced his preaching of repentance in the wilderness of Judea. After John, Jesus makes his appearance and begins to preach in the same strain. That is to the writer of the very first biography the beginning of the new dispensation. If the gospel is tidings of good, then these tidings of good do not commence to be given with the birth of Jesus, but with the beginning of his preaching.

It may be said that this is merely an omission on the part of the evangelist, and that the omission was made good by the accounts of the later biographers. Perhaps it is open to any one to take his choice as to whether Mark made an omission, or Luke and Matthew afterwards made an addition. The way of the Jews seems always to have been to make additions. That is the way they "improved" the writings. At all events, this first biographer, who responded to the wide influence of Paul, and believed it to be his duty to write the account, omitted the things that the church has held to be vital. One might be justified in concluding that these things are in fact not vital, that they truly have no relation to the divine gospel, and that the church has been mistaken in that, as it has been in most matters.

This fact brings to our view precisely what was going on in those days. Many persons were talking over these things, — the life and teachings of Jesus. Many persons were writing accounts or fragments of accounts. (Into these accounts we may be reasonably sure were woven many a thread of myth, as indeed we find and acknowledge in the so-called Apocryphal books of the New Testament.)

Wherefore, if it becomes us to read the Old Testament history and all its divers portions with discrimination, it much more becomes us to use discrimination in the New Testament, and its biographies or biographical fragments. The sublime religion of Jesus will be found to shine out through all the mists of myth, which so plentifully arose in those days; and it is the religion of Jesus we want, for we believe it is the religion of Jesus which is to save the world. That religion has been buried under a copious myth-substance long and weary ages. But, the myths being discriminated from the truths, we may hope to see the brightness of Jesus rising once more upon the darkened world.

XV.

THE FIRST CHRISTIAN WRITINGS.

AMONG the works of creation, none is more interesting to trace than the making of language. The spoken language undoubtedly antedated the written language. The preservation of the experiences and the wisdom of a generation, for the benefit of coming times, was long intrusted to the spoken tradition. The time comes when this is found inadequate, and picture-words come into vogue. Out of the picture-words in due time grow the letters, each being significant, and arbitrarily standing for a distinct sound. Then come the words, made of combinations of these various signs.

For the preservation of these words, certain provisions are made: the picture-words are cut in durable stone; or a kind of clay is found which will receive the impression of a stylus, or other instrument of marking, and may then be baked hard, so as to be as like stone as possible. The numerous tablets unearthed in ancient Babylonia, Nineveh, and elsewhere, testify to the durability of this method of preservation.

The moulding of tablets, and the cutting of inscriptions upon stone, is a slow labor, and after a time proves inadequate for the demands of a people learning to love and use literature. Now it is found that Providence has always something ready to meet the reasonable demands of human beings. Whenever people are ready for the use of that which they do not possess, God inspires some one to look more deeply into the mysteries of Nature and take out of her inexhaustible storehouse the thing that is needed. Therefore after some development of the art of writing, it was found that a reed growing in abundance along the Nile would furnish a supply of papyrus for the writers. The stem of the reed was sliced in such a manner as to make long and narrow rolls of a thin plate, the surface of which, after proper preparation, would take and hold the writing of the scribe. An ink was made from animal carbon and oils, and a reed, sharpened somewhat to a point, was employed for a pen, and so came that form or mode of literature which is fit for libraries. The use of the papyrus spread northward, and had become somewhat common in Greece about the time of Alexander the Great. A considerable manufacture sprang up, and it is said that the reed was cultivated in southern Italy. Rolls or books of papyrus were discovered in Herculaneum, which were found to consist chiefly of works of the Epicurean philosophers. After the early Christians began to find the need of writing the history of Jesus, they had recourse to the papyrus.

It will occur to any one that the papyrus must in the nature of the case prove a very fragile paper. It is very easily broken; if it is passed about from hand to hand, the edges become frayed, and in a short time the writing becomes but faintly legible. It is probable that the poorest paper now used for writing is much more durable than the papyrus. It becomes evident that the first writers of accounts of Jesus used this fragile material for their work, when we become aware that no original copy is extant, and moreover that no trace of an original document of the sort is found in the oldest Christian literature. The end of the second century of our era was a time of great disputation, when men were talking much of the exact readings of texts; for it was then that the writings of the Christian scribes were beginning to take rank in the minds of the Christian leaders with the Old Testament books. Up to that time the writings, such as the letters of Paul and others and the accounts of the deeds and death of Jesus, had not been valued any more than the spoken tradition. Then a new estimation began to be attached to these writings, — a value which the early writers evidently did not anticipate.

Copies of the works of some of the early writers had been made, but the copying was not so carefully done as it had been done by the Jewish scribes, who regarded their office a sacred one, and of a nature that called for the utmost scrupulousness and exactitude. The accounts of Jesus and the epistles of Paul and Barnabas and others were not ranked as parts of the Bible until long after they were written. Hence there was lacking that sense of responsibility in the copyists which would have been very desirable. The time came when better copies were made, and they, while they were copies of copies, bear witness of great painstaking. They were made upon parchment, which is durable, and the letters were each made symmetrically and carefully, and were almost as regular in symmetry and alignment as print. The words were not separated from each other, but the letters, which were all capitals, followed each other, so many on each line, and it was left to the reader to make up the words from the letters. These fine and durable manuscripts, however, were not made until about the beginning of the fourth century, and the papyrus manuscripts are supposed to have perished.

It may be assumed that God prevented any mistake from creeping into the early papyrus accounts; and that he did not permit the copyists to commit any error, however small; in fact just that has been assumed. An assumption, however, ought to have something in it, the validity of which we all ought to see at once. It ought to appeal either to our experience or our intuition, or both. This assumption does not correspond with our experience, certainly. For our experience is that men, good and wise, and even spiritually-minded men, do make mistakes. God does not prevent them from so doing.

The conviction of modern theists is that God is the Creator of the world, and of all things therein. This was also the conviction of some of the ancient Hebrew hymn writers. Yet all of God's work of creation, so far at least as we can discern it, is in the realm of the incomplete, the imperfect. The work of the geometricians comes nearer perfection than any other writing of which we have knowledge; but that is because in their sphere they have to deal with exact terms. Their terms are not approximate and fluid, but definite. The terms of a biography are very different; life is the hardest of anything to describe, and the difficulty of description increases in proportion as the life is higher and more complex. Therefore, we ought to realize that the early Christian writers undertook to write about a life more difficult of description than any other. They vividly felt that difficulty, or at least some of them did. The superiority of that life shines through all the tales they tell of it. The tales are difficult, and to some impossible, to believe, but the life it is impossible to discredit.

John Stuart Mill [1] says: "The tradition of followers suffices to insert any number of marvels, and may have inserted all the miracles which he is reputed to have wrought; but who among the disciples, or among their proselytes, was capable of inventing the sayings ascribed to Jesus, or of imagining the life and character revealed in the Gospels?" Jesus cast forth his sublime thoughts into the mass of humanity about him. Suppose his words had been of the geometrical order, — exact, and not approximate. Suppose that exactness of repetition had been the thing he insisted upon, as necessary to the survival of his religion. Then indeed we might have looked to see all that he said reported exactly. Indeed, in that case, either he would have made his own book, or have secured the service of some one competent to make exact reports of all that he said, and to have set forth the facts of his life as accurately as possible for human pen. But do we not catch the feeling he had in regard to his work and word, in the saying reported: "The words that I have spoken unto you are spirit and are life"? These words of spirit and life are not the words of an exact science, like that infallible science of geometry. They are words which fail of being caught, except in the sense or spirit of them. The words dissolve, just as the living seeds which the sower casts into the ground dissolve. The thoughts expressed filter through a great many minds, and produce varying impressions. The speaker who is most alive, who thrills the breast of his listener with the fire of greatest and most enlightening thoughts, is of all others the one who most eludes accurate report. By reason of the great power of his teaching, and the greater life of it, he is

---

[1] Essay on Theism, cited by E. Clodd, in *Jesus of Nazareth*.

more than any other likely to be misreported. The spirit and the life (and these the speaker values,— these alone) persist. In all the Gospels in our Bible, and in many of the other writings, they have persisted. There is a warmth about them, a vitality, an immortality, which secures their permanence, after the first form of their expression is dissolved away and lost.

Now one fault of our thoughts about the Gospels has been that we have looked in them for a kind of spiritual mathematics. We have not considered the impossibility of accurate reports of such a life as that. In fact, the church has always imagined Jesus and his life and teachings to be less than they were. True, we have glorified him and his words, and paid to them divine honors, verbally, but we have failed to detach the husk of the report from the kernel of the truth in the report. Therefore, since criticism is coming in like a flood, sweeping all before it (that is, all that is affected by the thinking of the time), many of us find ourselves afloat in the rising tide, and not knowing at all what is coming of all this investigation. Of one thing it is possible to be sure: that those who believe in the spirit and truth of the words of Jesus, and to whom his life is a revelation of God in our human society, will discover the truth and life made clearer and more practical to them, by the sifting process now going on. The very object of sifting is to separate, and bring into clearer distinction, the permanent and the transient elements of religion.

It has been held that the four Gospels were written by the persons whose names appear in the titles; but the titles were added by editors. The writers of the Gospels did not attach their names to their writings; but later men, judging by such information as they possessed, added the titles, as we now find them. So it is held that the Apostle Matthew wrote the first Gospel; a man named John Mark, a companion of Peter, and sometime of Paul, the second; Luke, a physician, the third. These three are known in criticism as the "synoptic" Gospels, because the three seem to "see together." Now there is no surety that Matthew wrote the first Gospel, the Gospel which bears his name in the title. It is more probable that Luke wrote the third Gospel, and we depend mainly upon untrustworthy tradition in ascribing the authorship of the second Gospel to Mark. It does not signify very much (except to the critic) who wrote them.

Proceeding upon the great probability that the Gospel ascribed to Mark's authorship is the earliest of the four, we perceive, by a comparison of it with the others, the evidence of a growth of sentiment and tradition with respect to Jesus. The ground, in its most fertile localities, is not more productive of vegetable growths than is the human mind and imagination of notional growths. Jesus had sown broadcast in Palestine, among the common people, the principles of a great religion. His personality had been the most vital, the most influential, the strongest, of any that had ever appeared. That there would not be a crop of stories of multiform sorts after such a mission could be expected by no one. The first account does not introduce any of these stories concerning the life of Jesus before he began his mission. That account of the beginning of that mission shows us the material out of which the larger stories afterward grew.

John the Baptist appeared in the Judean wilderness, preaching repentance to the people; and the people were greatly stirred by him. They felt that such prophetic utterances portended great results. They went out to him in flocks, and listened to his preaching, and were baptized in the Jordan, confessing their sins. This mission of John meant a great deal to the people, but to none could it have meant so much as to Jesus. The fame of it had spread into the north country, and Jesus was impelled to go to John; and with the others he was baptized. That did not excite the notice of John, so far as we know from Mark. The multitudes were baptized, confessing their sins; but it seems that Jesus received his baptism in another way, as a consecration to his own great work. According to the simple account of Mark, Jesus went down into the water, and as he came up out of it, he saw the heavens rent, and the Spirit descending like a dove upon him. That is what he saw; and in the nature of the case it was seen by no one else. The heavens did not rend, because such things do not happen. The sky is not a tent or canopy over us that there should be a rending of it asunder. Here was at last the Man who was able to look into the heavens, whose life was not an earthly one, but destined to be a heavenly one. The fact cannot be stated in terms of physics without setting aside the spirit of the law and the prophets.

But it was the genius of the age to make of such things physical phenomena. The pure and grand and real vision of Jesus, thus beginning upon his great career, was afterward made to be no vision at all, but a happening in the world of matter. As we read the third Gospel, we see the encroachment of that physical idea. Luke tells us that he made great inquiry, and attained a more satisfactory history of the affairs of Jesus than previous writers. It is Luke who contradicts the sentiment of the law and the prophets, or the spirit of them, by adding to the previous accounts the very thing which ought not to have been added. He declares that the Holy Spirit descended in a bodily shape, like a dove. That is like the tales of the heathen, and does not accord with the testimony of Israel. God is not to be represented in a bodily form, since so to represent him is inevitably to misrepresent him. Instead of a vision of the descent of God's Spirit bringing peace, Luke gives an account of the incarnation of God in a bird! This is distinctly heathen, and neither Jewish nor Christian. To the careless reader it seems a slight modification, but to one who absorbs the spirit of the Gospels, and of the revelation before the Gospels, it is a sad corruption.

It will be well to consider, as we may, the earlier history of Jesus. He had this earlier history, and some incredible accounts of it are given; but we can suppose the credibilities; for man's life is a something we know much about. Trained in the synagogue, and becoming full of the feelings of the prophets, Jesus has passed his childhood and youth in the seclusion of his Galilean home. He has thought out and felt out the secret of God. The prophetic utterances have not been mere words to him, but they have enlightened his soul. If we penetrate the spirit of his later years, we at the same time penetrate the education of his earlier years.

"There is a spirit in man, and the spirit of the Almighty giveth them understanding." Jesus reaches the age of manhood, when the young Jewish man attains his majority, but he has no career; and for such as he a career is the one necessity. He can no longer live in quietude and seclusion. He must be about his Father's business. To receive from God is to give. He has not yet received the full vision; he has not yet found his work. Therefore he has had no opportunity of giving.

Meanwhile John is raising his voice in the south. His fame spreads far and wide. He is like one of the prophets of the olden time. He may be one of the greatest of the prophets, risen from the dead. He is not to be silenced. He does not go to the haunts of men; his voice, crying in the wilderness, "Make straight a way for the Lord," is commanding, and calls men out to him. He believes, he of all Israel, the divine promises.

These promises are now hastening to fulfillment. He feels that he is not mighty enough for his work; but there will be another to take it up, mightier than he. This mightier one will winnow the chaff away from the wheat. Jesus comes to him; he has his mission at last. He receives his consecration to it. He finds that the heavens, before closed even to him, are no longer closed, but opened. God is no longer away, or withdrawn. God is present, and God abides upon him. Those whose thinking is more materialistic than spiritual cannot possibly conceive the experience of Jesus at that supreme time. They can think of a dove flying down and alighting on him. They can think of him as driven into the wilderness to be tempted by Satan. But to think of him as retiring to the loneliness of the desert, there to feel the awful pressure of his mission, the awful temptation of it, — the temptation to make use of his great thoughts and powers for his own glorification and advantage, — that they cannot so much as think of. That is a closed volume to them, as it may well have been to Luke.

What things Jesus told his friends — those closest to

him — of his first divine experiences, of his ecstasy, of his peril from real temptation in the desert, they in turn told to others. And so grew up that phantasm of a bodily shape of God descending from the opened heavens; and the visit of the Persian evil divinity, Satan, to confront and if possible to conquer the Son of God. The facts which were inward and real the popular imagination inclosed in a dress at once fantastic and unreal; but the facts are there. Considering the age in which they occurred, we can readily conceive that they could have come to us in no other dress.

But the teachings of Christ, both in letter and in spirit, show us what to do with the fantastic myth-dress in which the popular imagination — and those recorders of the popular imagination, the writers of the three Synoptic Gospels — clothed them. We are to winnow them, if we would know them in their spirit and reality. By such judgment and superior information as God has given us, we are to wisely discriminate between the writers' stories of the incarnation of God in a dove, and the visit of Satan, and the deep experiences of Jesus which gave rise to those stories.

We value the life and teachings of Jesus for their inherent worth. J. Stuart Mill, who does not seem prepossessed in favor of the Christian doctrines, when he reads the New Testament is convicted of the immense value of the real teachings of Jesus, and the loveliness and excellence of his life. The zeal of followers and of their proselytes may suffice, he tells us, for the strange marvels told in the accounts; but underneath these strange marvels is the life, — is the truth. The things told do not seem true.

Suppose we could take one of the Gospels, say the

third, and change all the names of it. The scene is not laid in Judea, but somewhere in central China. We will give Chinese names to the cities and villages, and replace Jewish by Chinese customs and costumes. We will sufficiently change the wording of the parables to retain their spirit, but not their appearance, and then present our book to the intelligent reader. He may be a devout Christian. The great probability is that he will look upon the book as a fairy tale, containing, however, excellent moral sentiments. No conviction of the reality of the marvels told will force itself upon his mind and conscience. He will perhaps wonder where the book came from, and as to its authorship, but it will be a fairy tale, from beginning to end.

Jesus knew the age in which he lived. He was continually combating the unreal ideas of it. Nevertheless, that age was the soil in which he was to sow his life, his character, and his teachings.

The sower went forth to sow. Some of the seed lodged in the good ground and brought forth plentifully. Yet what the sower sows, identically what he sows, never comes up. In the place of the word sown rises the plant of an apprehension of it, and this may bear little resemblance to the original word. The value of it is that it contains the original truth. So we have the vision of Jesus at his baptism, seeing the open heavens, hearing the divine voice, the descent of the Spirit to abide upon him. That is the original truth. Out of that, as out of a seed cast into the ground, grew in after years the divine incarnation in a dove. That is the plant. The plant grows up, and is tenderly cherished, until like other things of a living sort it grows ripe, and ready finally to thresh out: we winnow the original truth, the living germ, from the plant which has come to be dry and unprofitable. When we make our winnowing process thorough, as we are taught to do, we rediscover the truth of the great vision. At the same time, we cast from us the now dried plant, — stalk, chaff, and all, — that being burned in the fire of our reasonable criticism.

Here therefore, at the very outset of the mission of Jesus, we encounter the necessity of discerning between the flesh and the spirit. The kernel and the husk separate and the value is left, and the thing which has contributed to the permanence of the truth, having fulfilled that purpose, goes the way of all transient things.

I take it to be demonstrable that the age in which Jesus planted — Jesus and Paul — was fit, in the main, for nothing but the outward form of a gospel. It was by that outward form the inward fact was preserved: through the ages of Christianity thus far, the truth of God in Christ has been inclosed in legendary wrappages. Again, I take it that God is the ordainer of times and seasons; so that whenever the fit time comes for the re-sowing of the ancient truth in the soil of the whole world, the truth will be made to emerge from its envelopment, and again cast as good tidings of great joy into the mind of the world.

XVI.

THE SPIRITUAL BASIS.

A SUBJECT of peculiar tenderness in the Christian religion is the birth of Jesus. The freedom of speech necessary to its full discussion does not belong to our present public propriety, but is appropriate only to scientific investigation. It is a difficult and delicate matter, and one that might be avoided, except that the creeds of Christendom have enshrined belief in the miraculous conception of Jesus in the dearest regard of the church. There are not a few who feel that doubt of the miraculous birth of Jesus is doubt of the sum and substance of the religion of Christ.

It is generally supposed that the miraculous birth of Jesus is one of the best proven of the facts of religion. The Apostles' Creed, which seems the simplest and most comprehensive of any of the belief statements of the church, puts belief in the virgin birth of Jesus with belief in God and redemption and immortality. Therefore it has assumed the place of a fundamental faith. If any one doubts or disbelieves that, he has renounced the faith. Gradually a change is taking place with reference to the fundamental beliefs of the church. It is not that many deny these beliefs, for that has always occurred in greater or less measure; but that inside the limits of the church itself the inquiry has risen, and is rising still, as to the proof or the necessity for the notion of the virgin birth of the Son of God.

Now when the proof of this teaching is demanded, it is found to be exceedingly slender. The fact that the church has believed the doctrine offers no proof, of course. In matters of science the church, without being necessarily blamable, has held errors as though they were truths. As to the rising and setting of the sun, so common a thing as that, the church was universally mistaken for many centuries. It may, however, be said that the rising and setting of the sun is not a religious matter. True; it is equally true that no phenomenon of nature with which science has to do is a religious matter. The birth of a human being, or a partly human being, from a virgin is a matter not of faith, but of science. It is something which has to do with natural laws in the realm of physics.

If valid scientific proof is adduced that such births have taken place, or that one such birth has taken place, that becomes an established fact in science; but it still does not touch the hem of the garment of religion. Or if it does touch the hem of the garment in which religion has clothed itself, it belongs only to the garment, not to the religion. It belongs to science to determine, if it ever is able to determine, whether such an event as that related by two evangelists and recited in the Apostles' Creed has actually taken place. When it is determined by a perfectly unanimous consensus of all scientific men (supposing such a consensus to be attainable), the matter will still be foreign to the religion of Jesus, it will still have to be classified with the data of science.

If we begin with the belief of the church, it may be as well for us to begin where that belief is the largest. We may therefore say that at the time of the Reformation of Luther there was practically but one opinion in Christendom upon the subject.

Whatever doubt existed was the doubt of a silent infidelity, or so for the most part. The Roman, the Greek, the Armenian, and the various Protestant churches were at one in belief of the virgin birth of Jesus. When, however, we go back to the time of Constantine, at the beginning of the fourth century, we do not find the church unanimous in its belief about anything. And if we go farther into the past, so as to reach the first believers, we find no evidence that any one believed in the virgin birth of Jesus. The first writer of the New Testament is Paul, and he nowhere indicates that he had any such belief. It seems quite incredible that if he had entertained the notion he should not have taken pains somewhere in his many writings to mention it. The second writer, known as Mark, does not mention it; and what is more, later writers, such as the author of the epistles of Peter, of Jude, of John, of the Apocalypse, and of the fourth Gospel, do not make allusion to it. Now the makers of the Apostles' Creed regard the virgin birth a great and necessary doctrine. They rank it with the being of God and with immortality. They place the statement of it in a point of great prominence, as one of the things to be laid to heart. In so doing they depart from the spirit of the gospel by introducing a subject of physical philosophy as belonging to the substance of Christian faith. In thus imposing upon the belief of the church a scientific dogma they change the church into something very different from the church of Paul and the apostles.

There is no difficulty in seeing how the belief came. It can be accounted for as easily as almost any phenomenon in history. Take Mark's simple account of the baptism. Jesus comes to the baptism as no other one did or could. He can look up into the heaven, and can see the Spirit. He can hear the voice, "This is my well beloved Son." He is the first in human history who has been able to look up and see what he saw, and the first in human history to hear the voice of God testifying that he is the Son of God. The way in which Mark tells this story, the emphasis which in various forms the three Gospels lay upon this scene, testify that it was one of great significance to Jesus. Whatever he may have seen and felt before, he at last sees and feels that he is the Son of God. It does not occur to him that he is not at the same time a son of man. It would be foreign to what we know of him, to that light which shines out of him, to think he disowned an earthly father because he asserted the Heavenly Father. Indeed, we may see in his feelings, at the time of his initiation into his work, what we afterward hear from the lips of Paul. Paul is guarded enough in his language, but he does not hesitate to say that a son of God may be identified, simply by his obedience to the Spirit of God. He does not say, and does not think, that a son of God is one who has no human father; that has nothing to do with it; but "so many as are led by the Spirit of God, they are the sons of God." Here is Jesus, who is ready to be led by the Spirit of God, who sees, in his ecstasy, the Spirit of God descending out of the open heavens to guide him, and who accepts that guidance, and thus knows that he is the Son of God. For the acceptance of the Spirit to abide with him brings the voice, "Thou art my beloved Son."

I think we do not measure the greatness of the faith of Jesus, if we look upon him as a supernatural being.

We do not follow him into the wilderness, to his temptation, and find him making a real conquest there, if at the same time we behold in him the superhuman will displacing the human. We shall have something to go by, and a hold will be established upon our sympathies, if we see him bearing the temptations which befall us human beings, and cannot befall God. That which distinguishes Jesus has been made to be some fact, or assumed fact, in his physical nature. It has been held in the dearest regard that he was physically the Son of God, and that he was anointed with the oil of gladness above his fellows because he had no human father. It was the conviction of some one, whose words have come down to us, that he was anointed with the oil of gladness above his fellows, that he had his distinguishing superiority because he loved righteousness and hated iniquity. That turns our attention upon his inward experiences, rather than upon his physical ancestry. (A man loves and hates; if he loves what he ought to love, and hates what he ought to hate, he has that superiority above his fellows which cannot but be recognized. Such an one has a claim upon us: he is made a real authority to us. Such a man becomes God's voice to us. His inward experience, his inward light, his inward love and hatred,— these are of supreme importance; but his earthly father is not of importance.)

(Now since Jesus felt the presence of the Spirit of God, and heard the voice of the Father, addressing him as Son, he went about his work always with that consciousness. He would not have been true to himself, if he had not always asserted his divine sonship. He would not have had a mission to men, unless he had the divine mission. Less than all could he have taught his disciples to pray to the Father in heaven, except he himself felt in all the feelings of his being that God was his Father. His mission was based on that conviction. He came into contact with the multitudes, and to them he spake as the Spirit moved. He did not tell all to them. He came in contact with the religious, the scribes, the pharisees, the priests. He spake to them also as moved by the Spirit, but he did not tell all to them. By word of mouth, by manner, and by the meaning of all that he said, he was always affirming his sonship to God. He went farther than that, and affirmed that he and his Father were one. Then the Jews picked up stones to throw at him. He was a blasphemer because he said that, they thought. He referred them to their own Scriptures, in which they professed to believe so thoroughly, and showed them that if the word of God came to anybody, it raised such an one up to divinity. If anybody could listen to God, as he had been listening to God, he would be able to say, "I am a son of God." In fact, he could not say otherwise and be true.

In a general way, all Christendom has taken up this word "Father" and applied it to God. But Christendom has never used the term boldly; it has been emptied of most of its meaning, when it has been applied to God. We have repeatedly been told, and with many warnings, that when Jesus applied the word "Father" to God, it meant something very different from what we must mean when we apply it to God. We must not dare to apply it as he did. We must first pull the very heart of its meaning out of it, and be exceedingly humble when we use it, and confess that Jesus was the Son of God in a sense impossible to any one else; he was the Son of God in the sense that he was an equal person in the divine Trinity. He was always equal with God, because, except for a provisional humiliation of him, for the purposes of redemption, he was the eternal God, in proper person. What are we, worms of the dust, and creatures of a day, that we should dare for a moment to use the word of intimate relationship as he used it? We must use the word in another sense, — a sense bereft of the great meaning which Jesus put into it. Jesus had no human father. God was his father. But we have human fathers, therefore God is not our father, in the same sense. Jesus is reported to have said a very curious thing in this connection: "Call no man your father, on the earth; for one is your Father, the heavenly." He did not call any man on earth his father; and on one occasion he refused to call any woman on earth his mother. We do not therefore affirm that he had no mother. If his friends had understood him, and declined to call any man on earth their father, but to call God their Father, we should not therefore infer that they were without human parentage.

It is evident that Jesus affirmed his relationship with God in very positive words: he affirmed with equal strength the potential co-relationship of other men with him. This last teaching, however, seems to have been lost sight of, while the first teaching, falling into the ground of a gross age, — not more gross than other ages, but certainly not a spiritual age, — developed the plant of the story of the birth of Jesus from a virgin. This story had not developed in the time of Mark, or if it had, he did not credit it. It came to flower in the account of Luke. Luke faithfully gathers not only such elements of the matter as had grown in the Christian imagination in a prose form, but also certain poems in which the Christian imagination had manifested itself.

Before examining Luke's account, it were well to note that earlier account which bears the name of Matthew. It is much briefer, and it bases the popular ideas of past occurrences, or the truth of them, upon the sayings of the prophets long before. A thorough Jew seems to have been the writer of Matthew's account, — one who delighted in genealogies, and who weighed the words of the prophets somewhat after the manner of the rabbins. To him the proof of the truth of that imagination, which had grown up since the death of Jesus, lay with the prophets. In particular, one of the great prophets had foretold the birth of a son, to be called Immanuel, to a virgin. But that this was a forced way of reading the prophets is at once visible, if one will take the trouble to read the particular prophecy for himself. At one time a certain Ahaz was king of Judah; and against him arose the king of Israel and the king of Syria. They went up to Jerusalem to lay siege to it. The king of Judah was in much disturbance of mind because of this coalition against him, and a prophet was sent by the word of the Lord to talk with him and comfort him, and assure him that the danger would be averted. So the prophet bids Ahaz not to be faint-hearted because "of the two tails of the smoking fire-brands," as he calls the two armies. Then the Lord said to Ahaz, "Ask thee a sign of the Lord thy God; ask it either in the depth or in the height above." Ahaz declined to ask a sign. Then the prophet said, "The Lord himself shall give you a sign; behold a virgin shall conceive and shall bear a son, and shall call his name Immanuel. Butter and honey shall he eat, that he may know to refuse the evil and choose the good. For before the child shall know to refuse the evil and choose the good, the land that thou abhorrest shall be forsaken of both her kings." Now we should suppose, if Matthew had not quoted this passage in a prophecy, to prove that Jesus was born of a virgin, that the prophet meant that before a new-born child should know the difference between good and evil, the danger which threatened Judah would surely be averted. When we know that the word " virgin " is sometimes applied, not literally, but to young women, whether married or unmarried, the statement of the prophet reduces to this word of promise addressed to King Ahaz. The child was to be born soon, and before the child should be able to discern between good and evil, the deliverance should come. Now to take a statement out of its context and make it fit a case in hand may be rabbinical, but it is not safe. If the author of Matthew's Gospel had given the context, he would have been obliged to date the birth of Jesus in the time of Ahaz, king of Judah. For the sign was offered to Ahaz, and before the child could know the difference between good and evil, Ahaz would be out of his difficulty. Here, as in other places, we may conclude that the Spirit of God taught Matthew a new use of prophecy ; or that because Matthew did distort a statement of Isaiah, the seal of divine approval is put upon such distortion ; but if we proceed to read the Bible without discriminating so plain an error in judgment, on the part of the evangelist, we are not likely to read any portion of the Bible with great profit. Because, as we have already seen, the Bible, being the most important of all literature, demands our most careful discrimination and our best judgment.

Matthew embodies in his account of the childhood of Jesus the story of the slaughter of infants in Bethlehem, and refers to a prophecy, of which this slaughter was the fulfillment. He also tells us that Joseph and Mary take the young child down into Egypt to escape the power of Herod. This journey of the holy family, he tells us, was in fulfillment of a prophecy which says, "Out of Egypt have I called my son." Now the only distinct statement of prophecy to any such effect is found in Hosea. Turning to that, we read these words: "When Israel was a child, then I loved him, and called my son out of Egypt." The manner of the prophetic utterance is such that the unprejudiced reader at once recognizes Israel as the son referred to in the prophecy. Israel, in its childhood as a race, was in Egypt and held in a bitter bondage there, as all the traditions of Israel affirmed. Jehovah had mercy on the enslaved people, called Israel his son, broke the bondage, and brought the people out of Egypt. Now the writer who could apply that language to the flight of the parents of Jesus into Egypt proves himself lacking in the apprehension of the prophets. Possibly he had taken lessons from the rabbins, or a class of them, and regarded the prophets as puzzle-makers, instead of teachers of God and righteousness.

— If we read the Bible with the kind of attention we give other books, — that is, with critical attention, or in the use of free judgment, — then it will be impossible not to see the very peculiar character of some of the stories of the infancy of Jesus, told us in the first Gospel. There are magi in the East, — three wise men, learned in astrology, who see the star of a king in the sky. There is no difficulty in identifying such sight as belonging to astrology. These three magi follow the star, which seems to move before them, until it comes to stand over where the young child is. Since astronomy has replaced astrology, and has become a sober science, it is generally understood that our birth under this or that planet or star, and the influence thereof upon our destiny, is purely visionary; or that it belongs, to ignorant superstition, by pandering to which, pretenders extract money from victims. The story of the star in the east is beautiful and instructive as a poem, but it does not appear to belong to the realm of prose facts. We may see in it the plant which grew up after the death of Jesus. To pay divine honors to the Son of God, the King of Israel and of the world, made the composition of such legends necessary, at the time. We have an affectional interest in these legends, but they do not satisfy our judgment.

Luke is very different from the writer of the first Gospel. He is not so wedded to Judaism. He does not find so much in the prophets of Israel. His occupation and his travel abroad among other people broaden his ideas. Therefore he omits the tales of Matthew, perhaps classing them with those more untrustworthy accounts, of which there were many. He accepts Bethlehem as the birthplace of Jesus. That has become firmly rooted in the Jewish-Christian mind. Bethlehem was the place for a prince of the house of David to be born; therefore Jesus was born there.

But we have in Luke the poetry and prose which grew up concerning the events preceding the birth of Jesus and John. Their mothers meet, and have a conversation together. A portion of this conversation is carried on in a very high strain of poetry. To talk in poetry implies the employment of the dramatic art. Both women, if we make history out of it, have studied their respective parts, and committed them to memory, as do players who go upon the stage. To suppose any such thing as that is beneath the dignity of the subject. When we looked into the book of Job, in the Old Testament, we saw plentiful evidence that we were reading a dramatic poem, with epilogue and prologue,— and not history. Why should we fail to discriminate here also in the story of the two mothers, the poetry of the poet, and not the actual talk of two women of Israel? The very fact that we find the poetry, and that it is set in the connection in which it is, ought to show us that we are not reading history, but poetry.

We have been very anxious to differentiate between Jesus and other men. We have been solicitous to make for him a rank above that of any other being in the universe, except One. In that we depart, I am sure, from his spirit. Not only so; in making for him a physical difference from other men, we have been in danger of losing sight of the real difference. That is a moral and a spiritual difference, and not a physical one.

"Being Son of God
By eminence of manhood,"—

as Sir Edwin Arnold puts it, is not being Son of God by having no real manhood. We have all the time been assured that Jesus was true and proper man, but we have been required to believe also in his virgin birth, which, if it means anything whatever, means that he was not and could not have been true and proper man.

Probably there is a much better statement of the

divinity of Christ to be made than that which grew up in the tale of his birth from a virgin. It is to be made in terms of moral character, and not in terms of physical structure. That story did grow, as any student can see; and it became the plant of the idea. The plant grew and flourished, has now apparently come to its harvest time, and if we love the plant, rather than the seed-truth of it, it is probable we shall not seek and find the truth of the matter, which alone is of value.

Stories of the infancy of Jesus were written and read, but the wise counsel of the early church dictated that these stories be not received into the sacred canon. It may have been well that the first and third Gospels were not pruned of similar stories, and that the doctrine of the divinity of Christ should have been permitted to come to us in a form which is actually repugnant to its nature. Whatever was best in the past, it becomes evident that we do not need the story of the virgin birth for the future, and for three reasons: —

1. It rests on exceedingly slender foundation.

2. It departs from the teaching of the Scriptures, which affirm the divinity of man, as man.

3. It shuts us out of sharing the divinity and character and life of the Son of God, and renders fellowship with him in his mission and sacrifice a dream, and not a practical experience.

XVII.

THE MIRACLES.

The study of the making of the Bible involves a consideration of the subject of miracles, which obtrudes itself persistently in our own time. Whatever may be the standpoint of the observer, it is abundantly evident that a change of mind is going on, with more or less rapidity, throughout the intelligent portion of the Christian world in regard to miracles. This may be a change for the better, or, as the ultra-conservative think, a change for the worse; but whether for better or worse, time will definitely decide. Enough for us to know that the change is going on, and ceases not to go on from day to day.

It was only recently said by a thoughtful teacher in one of our great universities, who has achieved a wide reputation as a philosophical thinker, that religion may be said to have already manifested itself in two ages, — the age of cult, that is of ritual, and the age of dogma; but that another age has supervened, — the age of the meaning of things, the age of a philosophical or rational religion. That age is no longer future, but in sober fact is the present. As to whether the world will lose and religion will be damaged by the transition, many seem to be in a state of suspended opinion. It is the idea of most of the Protestants that the day of miracles is over, and that no miracles now happen. It was the idea of the late Cardinal

Newman that the Protestants were in serious error concerning that matter. Miracles as well attested as any, according to Newman, have occurred in recent periods, and some are perhaps happening at present. The Protestants reject these modern miracles. The issue between them and the Roman Catholics is a serious one. Some Protestants are advancing to another position, which promises to still further widen the breach, — to the position that miracles have not happened. Among the Catholics the excellence of a miracle is believed in so much that they desire as many as possible. Among the Protestants, on the contrary, the effort has been, and now is, to have as few miracles as possible connected with their religion. We must try to explain everything that can be explained thus, on natural grounds.

That of itself shows, more than arguments, that a miracle is felt to be a weakness, a something which may prove of damage to us, in the maintenance of its verity. Thus our scholars accept miracles in the Bible, so far as they feel they must, but they continually decrease their number. In the early part of this century, it was universally held by religious persons of all sects that the history of the world began in a stupendous miracle. Out of the heights of eternal space, God spake creative words, and the earth sprang into being, obediently. Until the work was finished a succession of miracles followed each other. The earth and the heaven began in a miracle, compared with which all other recorded wonders are as pebbles to mountains. It may safely be said that the stupendous miracle has been abandoned by almost all intelligent people, and that largely because a way of creation has been ascertained which does not require miracle, and intelligence has welcomed the discovery almost with enthusiasm.) That God, or that being whom religion calls God, as the philosophers say, created the heavens and the earth, is as strongly affirmed as it ever was. Indeed, the affirmation is now made with immense confidence. But that God created the heavens and the earth miraculously is not affirmed with any confidence at all.

That is the change which has come about in our own century, with respect to miracles. A miracle greater than all others combined, a miracle which is attested by plain words of the Bible, has been given up, so that the defense of it is made, for the most part, by religious persons of limited intelligence. We are told that it is not necessary to believe that miracle. By those who strenuously maintain that we must believe certain other miracles, it is admitted that we can go free from belief in that one. Yet if we discredit the great miracle of Genesis, as we now are permitted to do by common consent, there are other miracles which confront us later in the Bible. There is the standing still of the sun at the command of a captain of Hebrew soldiers. Look at it how we may, we are unable to see that it is any easier of credence than the miracle of the creation. Of course we do not need to set limits to almightiness. When we take the liberty of doubting a story, it is not because we wish to diminish the power of God. (Certain inhabitants of Ireland used to think that on St. Patrick's day the sun, after it had risen, always made two or three bows, in honor of the saint.) This strange habit of the sun, however, has been obscured to the vision of most people because upon St. Patrick's day clouds always cover the horizon. The bow is made, but mortal eyes cannot see it on account of the clouds. If any one doubts the fact, as probably we all do, it is not because we would set limits to the power of God; but because it is somehow obnoxious to our sense of the fitness of things, obnoxious to reason and judgment. For that reason we do not give a moment's attention to the subject. Why is not the obeisance of the sun on the birthday of St. Patrick quite as credible as the standing still of the sun at the command of a Hebrew military officer? If we reject the one, we are in a fair way to reject the other.

In the same way the voyage of a prophet inside a great fish, not of the cetacean order, as we are told, — a voyage continued three days, with the ultimate landing of the prophet at his destination, — cannot command our respect. We do not wish to doubt God, because we doubt the story of such a miracle. Perhaps it is because we are beginning to believe in God, and in the laws of God, as governing in nature, that we doubt the miracle of Jonah. There are many other things of a similar sort which attract our attention as we go on reading the Bible. They were all accepted in the belief of the Christian world not very long ago; now they are being more and more doubted, if not positively disbelieved.

Professor Green, of Princeton, says: "The whole of English-speaking Christendom is upon the eve of an agitation upon the vital and fundamental question of the inspiration and infallibility of the Bible, such as it has never known before. The divinity and authority of the Scriptures have heretofore been defended against the outside world of unbelievers, infidels, and skeptics; but the question is now raised, and the supreme authority of the Scriptures contested within the church itself. In the controversies which have agitated the churches of Great Britain and of this country heretofore, the infallible authority of Scripture has been admitted as the ultimate test of doctrine by all contending parties. All made their appeal to this standard. The settlement of every question depended upon its interpretation, or upon inferences fairly deducible from it. But now the standard itself is brought into question. Utterances which fill the air on every side, and are borne to us from every quarter, — from professors' chairs, from pulpits, from the religious press, — show abundantly that the burning question of the age is not, What does the Bible teach? It is one yet more radical and fundamental: What is the Bible? In what sense is it the word of God?"[1] The great agitation upon a burning question is at bottom a question of the validity of miracles. The world was not made miraculously, as we generally admit. Then was the Bible made miraculously? That is the burning question. It bids fair to obtrude itself until answered rationally.

The infallibility of the Bible being established, it is a miraculous book; but the infallibility of it is questioned on all hands. The rise of the study of geology made a sufficient cause for the rejection of the miracle of creation; the rise of other studies, those critical studies of the composition of the Bible, and the proper stratification of the various portions, will probably lead to the rejection of the dogma of the infallibility of the Bible. That is to say, the earth, which may be said to be the revelation of God in physics, being looked upon as not miraculous, much more the

[1] *Moses and the Prophets*, Professor Green's Review of Professor Robertson Smith.

book which is the chief revelation of God in moral and spiritual laws, will cease to be looked upon as miraculous. The tendency of religious thought, as testified to by our Princeton professor, is toward the elimination of the miraculous. It is religious thought which has come into the field of conflict, not to crush the arguments of skeptics and unbelievers, but to affirm the reign of law throughout the universe.

While the tendency is what it is, it must not be supposed that the matter is one to settle offhand. The modification of thought may involve the use of old words in a new meaning. It is possible that the word "miracle" will take on a significance which it has not possessed. It is possible that we shall presently apply the word to the wonderful and the mysterious in nature, rather than to the irruption of supernatural powers within the scope of nature, to change or break the laws of nature. Perhaps it were well also to examine anew this very word "nature" itself, to see what its history has been. It is not to be supposed that ancient people had a clear idea of nature, or that they had any sharply defined limits in mind when they spoke of it. There was an apprehension of two kinds of activity in operation. The English people of the Middle Ages were sure of two kingdoms which interacted. The procession of seasons and days, and the commonplace events which were regularly repeated at proper intervals, — these belonged to one department; the priest, and above all the magician, had dealings with the other department. No one doubted the prevalence of enchantments. There were ogres and giants, and other semi-supernatural beings. There were witches. That is to say, there was an invasion of the powers of the unseen world. Good spirits and evil spirits contended for the mastery in the world. In the unseen world the laws or methods were different from those of the seen world. The magician drew strange figures, and uttered strange words in his enchantments. In order to effect anything, he must be trained in occult science; that is, he must learn the ways of the invisible world. In time these two worlds came to be distinguished as nature and the supernatural.

The world of nature has been growing larger continually, and more heed has been paid to it and the laws of it. The other world has been losing ground. We have, for the most part, dismissed magic and enchantment, and ogres and nymphs and witches and the like, from our thoughts. The result is that "nature" has become an exceedingly comprehensive term. Things which once seemed to belong outside of nature are now comprehended in its scope. The feeling has been growing apace that nature is coextensive with the universe. We do not need two terms, because one will answer our purpose. Yet nature contains vastly more which is unknown to us, and perhaps unknowable by us, than did both nature and the supernatural to the ancient man. Nature is full of mystery, but we feel that it is, so to speak, a regulated mystery, a mystery of laws rather than a mystery of the infraction of laws.

Now, to some minds, possibly, such a view of nature entirely excludes God. There is really no such exclusion. On the contrary, by that dismissal of witches, enchanters, and all of that order, which has occurred, we have really made room for God, or rather we have come to recognize, some in one way and some in another, the presence of God. The superhuman beings which crowded the world ages ago have vanished, having become supernumerary. They are not required so soon as we have made discovery of the presence of the One Power in which we all live and move and have our being. A child looking reflectively at our streets, seeing the great buildings of solid material on both sides, some of them towering toward the sky, and all of them of substantial material, effectively resisting our stroke, would conclude that matter is always of that solid and resisting quality. He would say that the space between the buildings is empty of matter. Here, he would say, is material, and there is vacancy of matter. He is mistaken. Every apparent space between the buildings is packed full of matter, — so full of it that not the smallest fraction of a cubic inch is devoid of it. We have matter in different states of density, but it is everywhere. That which is invisible to us is not therefore non-existent. More than that, because of that matter, which packs all places which seem to be empty, beings constituted as we are can live. Without it we could not live.

There is, however, somewhat else than matter in nature. We call it force. Some manifestations of it are everywhere present. We assume the existence of force everywhere, because all of the universe of which we can get any knowledge is in motion. The stars flit in their courses, and whole groups of worlds move together in a rhythmical way. Moreover, we are sure that the force which is manifested at the farthest visible star is identical with that which holds us to the ground. There is a force in the ocean currents and tides, in the atmospheric storms, and in the light and heat of the sun. There is a force in the growth of the plant, and in the living bodies of fishes and other animals, and in inorganic matter; everywhere force. Now, while we know something of force, we do not know all; this is what we have been learning through painful and slow ages, namely, that force operates in certain ways, which we call laws. We have come to the practical conclusion that each force moves in accordance with the laws which we have studied out. Gravity, for instance, is uniform. We cannot prove that gravity operates in every portion of the universe, as it does here on the earth and in our planetary system, but we are very sure that it does.

It is to be remembered that the ancients, those who wrote the different parts of the Bible, did not know what we know. They had no idea of the reign of law, therefore their explanation of phenomena was not such as we would give now. They thought it perfectly reasonable that God should make an exception in any law of nature when he pleased. Whenever there was a proper time for an exception, they supposed, of course, that the exception was made. If a man was in prison, locked securely there, and God wanted him to get out, it was perfectly easy for God to send an angel, and the angel did not have to pick the lock or open it with a key, because angels are not subject to laws: the angel could open any door, and take any one out of prison. Inasmuch as an apostle had been put in prison, and had escaped from it, in after years they gave the explanation that God had sent an angel. God could always do this and that, if the exigency called for it. Since the necessity arose often, it was natural to suppose that God did take measures entirely outside of the laws of nature.

If a multitude of people were hungry, and food was inaccessible to them, it was quite in keeping with

God's ways to make a large number of bushels of bread out of a few small loaves. We have found, if we have found anything, that just such things are entirely out of keeping with God's ways. The writers of the Bible did not know enough of God's ways to prevent them from making mistakes. Millions upon millions of people have starved because they did not have bread. It is related that Jesus had compassion on the multitudes who followed him out into the desert. Because he had compassion, he enlarged a few loaves of bread into food for some thousands of people; but Jesus was no more compassionate than God is. His compassion tells us of the compassion of God. God has permitted multitudes, just as worthy of compassion as that Galilean multitude, to go without food.

He has permitted people to be shut up in prison just as the Apostle Peter was. He has not sent angels to open the doors for them. Tens of thousands of people have been in slavery of the most cruel sort. They have pined for deliverance. Their condition has made a strong appeal to God's compassion, but God has not delivered them. He could have delivered, if power is all that is required: he could have sent cohorts of angels: he could have dissolved their chains. The fact for us to consider is that he did not so act; or we may sum it all up in a single proposition, namely, it was within the scope of God's power, as we suppose, to make our race perfect at the outset, and to keep it perfect, and then no wickedness and no starvation and no cruel inhumanity would ever have stained our human annals.)

According to modern philosophy as understood by the theist, our Creator does not create such a being as man from without, by a kind of plastic art, but from within, and by development. Man must grow to his manhood. The race must grow to its consummation and destiny. Man must learn his lesson as a race. He shall become perfect only through suffering. He must bear his hunger; he must learn to supply it. However desirable it must seem to us at times that God should make an interference in our behalf, and break some laws of nature, the very lesson we are set to learn is that of obedience to the laws. It is by obedience, cost what that may, that we reach our estate and accomplish our destiny. The divine interferences were always supposed by the ancients. They prayed and sacrificed to obtain them. To learn the great lesson of obedience was beyond them. Now, obedience is better than all of these supposed interferences. The law of God, the great comprehensive law of creation, which has been opened to us in recent times, converts our soul to the thought of the presence of God at all times and under all circumstances. If we are in prison, God is not absent from us; and if we are delivered in any wise from captivity, that is God's work. It is not the work of secondary beings, — though they may be concerned in it, — but it is the work of God.

What the writers of the Gospels did not know, through our increased knowledge of God's great laws we do know. With that knowledge comes a far greater revelation than was possible in the past. In place of divine interference, the newer revelation substitutes divine presence. In other words, the revelation of to-day is so much greater, so far grander, than that of the past, that we may say of it that God ceases to be an occasional visitor, or a mere governor of angels and other forces, by becoming involved in every part of creation. The few miracles are replaced by the fact, greater than all miracles.

The fuller revelation of to-day, a revelation which is coming in volumes of demonstration, will of course be resisted, as all fuller revelations always have been. So resisted they the old revelation, and so their fathers resisted the still older revelation.

We have the story of Jesus' life and teachings woven in the web of a miraculous narrative. At first glance it seems to be impossible to detach the miracle from the teaching or the conduct of Jesus and have anything left. That is what we have been told over and over again; that if we are going to dispense with the miracles, we must also dispense with the teachings; that if the body of Jesus was not raised from the tomb of Joseph of Arimathea, after the death of Jesus, then the whole matter resolves into mere fable unworthy of any confidence. This we are told, not by enemies of the Christian religion, but by its professed friends. So was it said before the days of geology, in regard to the account of creation, and even since those days.

There was a lesson of Jesus which might have an application here. It cannot be too much insisted upon that such things as the fate of a physical body after its death are not a subject of religion, but of physical science. The enemies of Jesus tried to entangle him in his talk. They asked about paying tribute. "Ought we to pay tribute to Cæsar, or no?" He called for a piece of money, and asked what mark was upon it. "Cæsar's image and superscription," he was told. Then he said, "Render to Cæsar the things which are Cæsar's, and to God the things which are God's."

Science in our later days has been taking many things out of the domain of religion and placing them in its own field. It has put its image and superscription upon them. We may render therefore to science the things which belong to science, and to religion the things which belong to religion.

There is something in which Biblical scholarship has so far made little or no progress, and that is in respect to that core or vital element of truth which accounts of miracles inclose. As before suggested, we have by no means fully explored the domain of nature, nor have we yet measured man's power in that domain. We catch vague hints of the existence of powers which elude our satisfactory examination. The scope of the mind, the agencies it employs, and the strange effects it may produce, have their limits, but we do not know precisely where to place them. In respect to these strange occurrences, of which we occasionally see accounts in the newspapers, it is necessary that they be attested in the strongest possible way, and by persons who know the difference between the natural and the unnatural. Now, one trouble with the miracles recorded in the Bible is that they have no scientific evidence. They are told us, not by eye-witnesses, and not by persons who know anything, beyond the common, of a natural order. So far as the form of them is concerned, we may fearlessly render them to the scientific Cæsar to whom they belong. So far as their moral and religious inner meaning is concerned, that is something for us to gain a knowledge of as our light becomes greater.

XVIII.

INFALLIBILITY.

In nothing is assured verity so important as in religion. So far as possible, we require certainty in the most important interests; and, rightly understood, there is no interest more important than religion. If our religion depends upon that which can have no verification in this stirring age of the world, we are likely to be left with a religion in the air, unfounded, or a superstition.

The reactions from superstition are deplorable. It happens often that one discovers his religion to be incapable of verification, and on the whole quite barren to him, and he not only leaves it, but abandons the very idea of religion; all religion is classified as superstition. That is a deplorable reaction, from which it behooves us to be on our guard, because, while there is no more ground for abandoning religion because some religion is superstitious than for abandoning medical practice because some medical practice is quackery, yet multitudes do proceed upon such insufficient ground to the abandonment of religion as worthless, and without stopping to consider that a true religion is of first necessity to moral beings. (A counterfeit bill ought to render us the more careful, not to reject all bills, but to qualify ourselves to discern between genuine bills and counterfeits.)

In order to give us that assured verity so necessary

in religion, we have been advised that God has given us an infallible standard of truth, and that this infallible standard is the Bible. So far good. It is the thing we require, and the thing we require is presented to us; but is the infallible standard, of which we may be sure that it is entirely trustworthy in all particulars, a something which may leave us in the air, without a foundation? How do we know that the Bible is an infallible standard? We are told so by certain religious newspapers, and by certain teachers of religion, and in certain books which have credit among a limited constituency.

We are told so; but if we seek assured verity, if we are as anxious for verification as we ought to be in so serious a matter, we ought not to be satisfied by being told so. Religious newspapers have made mistakes, and perhaps in some instances might even acknowledge their fallibility. So of religious teachers, and books of a limited credit. Perhaps they all make mistakes. If so, possibly this assertion that the Bible is an infallible standard of truth is one of their mistakes. In so important an interest we ought not to rest on the fallible testimony of fallible men for adequate proof of the infallibility of a standard. Professor Shedd, a man of note in the religious world, tells us that the doctrine of his church is to this effect, namely, that the Bible is supreme in authority over the church and the reason, and free from error as it originally came from God, its author; that the Biblical miracles could not have been wrought by the operation of natural laws and forces; that no decree of God is ever changed, and no prediction of his fails of fulfillment; that man was created positively holy, and not merely negatively innocent, etc. This is the opinion of a religious man of note, and he says that it is the opinion of the religious denomination to which he belongs, as expressed in their symbols. Does this man of note know? Who told him so? Is he infallible? Or is his church entirely correct in all matters? If we ask him and his church, they will assuredly confess with a becoming humility that they are not infallible. They tell us that the Bible is, but then their testimony is insufficient, because they are fallible witnesses, and confess that they do make blunders. Therefore we have by no means reached the foundation of the matter, and perforce must go farther and deeper.

Very well, we can go farther than our contemporaries; we are not compelled to rely upon them: they point us back to the reformers. We may readily discover that the reformers were compelled to assert the infallibility of the Bible as the standard of truth. Who and what were the reformers? How did they know? They were men of whose excellence, and even heroic excellence, we are bound to approve. Brave men, learned men, some of them, and in many respects able men; some of them among the greatest men produced in the history of the world. Yet who told them that the Bible was the infallible standard of truth? No one told them so. They arrived at the conclusion after debate. There is no question that they were largely influenced to their decision about the infallible character of the Bible by a necessity laid upon them, to maintain their cause. In place of infallible church and infallible pope, we must have another infallibility, and they decided that the Bible was such an infallibility. Were they right in this decision? If they were infallible men, incapable of making mistakes, then of course they were right;

but they were not infallible men, for they distinctly denied that they were. They denied the infallibility of the church. Therefore their testimony must be taken with much allowance. We cannot be at all sure they were right in this matter, or in other matters, unless we can approve their deliverances on rational grounds.

So we are driven back beyond the reformers to seek our surety, because we cannot find it in our contemporaries, nor can we find it in the reformers. That great church from which the reformers revolted does not shed any light upon the subject, because it did not teach the doctrine.[1]

There certainly was a time when there was no New Testament, when there was a considerable body of literature, portions of which were read in the assemblies of the Christians. The Apostle Paul had written letters to the saints in various localities. It was natural that these letters should be read when the saints came together on the first day of the week, and at other times. These letters of Paul, like the sermons of more modern times, were not thought of as new parts of the Bible. Besides the letters, there were Christian documents which took a strong hold upon the feelings, and greatly stimulated the religious life of the Christians. Before anything was decided in regard to the New Testament, before the New Testament was thought of, a great deal of literature was afloat in Christian communities. The Christians would no

---

[1] The Church of Rome recognizes ecclesiastical tradition as of coördinate authority with the written records, holding that God's "supernatural revelation is contained in the written books, and unwritten traditions which have come down to us." Professor J. H. Thayer, *The Change of Attitude towards the Bible.*

more have dreamed of attaching these writings to the Bible, as a part of it, than we would think of making a still newer Testament (and binding it in with the Bible), composed of the discourses of Schleiermacher, Robertson, Spurgeon, and Beecher.

The time came when the idea of the New Testament arose. There was plenty of material for it. Just as the Hebrews of the older time had attributed to Moses a large body of writings, and to the various prophets another large body, and had gathered them into a collection known as "Moses and the Prophets," so it would have been most desirable for the Christians of the third century of our era to have had autographs of the apostles. How much more desirable to have an autograph of Jesus himself! That was manifestly lacking. Mark was not an apostle, but he had been a companion of the apostles. Luke was not an apostle, but he had been in company with some of the apostles. There was a writing which bore the name of Matthew, and he was an apostle; another writing which bore the name of John, and he was an apostle. There were the letters of Paul, who claimed apostleship to the Gentiles. There was also a curious book of the sort called apocalyptic, similar to that remarkable book written during the heroic period of the Maccabees, and a large number of other writings, like the Shepherd of Hermas, the Gospel of the Hebrews, the Acts of Pilate, the Protevangelion, the Gospel of the Infancy, the Epistle of Barnabas, etc. From this considerable body of material, judicious selection must be made. How can that selection be made but by putting at that business the men best fitted to do it? It would be necessary for representative men to meet, and consider the wishes and feelings of their respective localities in regard to the matter.

A canon is simply a rule. It is a kind of law. Now the laws we have, and the laws all people have made, first grow up in the necessities of the case, and in the minds and habits of the people. Thus it was with this canon. Certain portions of the Christian community were particularly fond of some of the extant writings. In the west, the Shepherd of Hermas had a strong hold,[1] and the Apocalypse, though it found much favor at first, was later regarded with disfavor. The Epistle of Jude, the Second of Peter, the Second and Third of John, the Epistles of Barnabas and to the Hebrews, and some others, were received by some and rejected by others. Following the example of the Jews in making their sacred canon, it became necessary for Christians to make theirs.

Now, a subject of such great interest would certainly be talked over by a vast number of people, and particularly by the religious teachers, or the clergy, as we now call them. A matter of the kind being thus in discussion, a public opinion would gradually grow up favorable to certain parts of the Christian literature and unfavorable to others. To almost every intelligent person, some writings would seem to be better, more authentic, and more divine than others. In regard to some, all would be practically agreed: as to others, there would be wide differences of opinion. Some would be universally accepted, some universally rejected from the proposed canon, and some would be held in suspended judgment.

Finally, we will assume that during the fourth century, representatives of the church in various portions of the Roman empire come together and make, after due deliberation and argument, an official list of the

[1] See note, p. 312.

books which are to constitute the New Testament. They pass a rule that the books which are not included in this list shall not be read in the public assemblies of the Christians. The last book of our New Testament, called the Revelation, they did not include, and therefore they made it wrong to read that in the religious services of the Christians. It was made wrong to read that book in public, because the very same authority which determined what the New Testament was, said that Revelation did not belong to the New Testament. We differ from these men, and say universally that Revelation is part of the New Testament. We read it in public religious service as part of the Bible. By so doing we proclaim in act, which speaks louder than words, that the men who first decided about the New Testament were mistaken in their decision. They were not infallible. On other ground we are persuaded to the same effect: it has never been claimed, so far as known, that these men were not as liable to mistakes as we are.

Therefore the doctrine of the infallibility of the Scriptures of the New Testament, which has been so strongly held, and is to-day so insisted upon by many religious teachers, lacks the proper evidence to sustain such a doctrine. A sentiment grew up in the early Christian centuries; this sentiment was held by a great many fallible men. Representatives of these men, chiefly their clergy, met in convention and settled that we should accept the list of books they approved, as being the New Testament. These were the books to be read in the churches. Before that, other books had been read, but now these only must be read. I do not reject the inspiration of these persons who decided upon the material for the New Testament; I would strongly affirm it. No good work can be done in this world apart from the Spirit of God. That the work of these inspired men was faultless is reasonably to be denied. The history of the occasion justifies us in the denial of an infallible outcome from it. Later in the history of the world, good men have often met for the discussion and decision of religious matters of weight. That their discussions and decisions were without flaw or fault, all Protestants deny. (Why one council should be singled out as an infallible council is more than any reasonable soul can tell.)

What we need in our religion is certainty. It is more necessary to us in our religion than in our other interests; but certainty that the Bible is infallible is the one thing inaccessible to us. On the contrary, the certainty is, that there is no proof of the infallibility of the Bible. If any man of eminence assures us that the Bible is infallible and in all its portions true, we may believe him, because we respect his character; but in order that our confidence in him may be justified, we ought to make a sure discovery of absolute truth in him, not only as respects his honest intention, but also as respects his information, and his ability to grasp such a subject. For infallibility is a very great matter, and the fallibility of man is an accepted belief of all men.

What shall we do with the Bible if we find that it is not an infallible standard? Shall we throw it away? That will doubtless be the first impulse of many. Those who have regarded the Bible as an infallible standard of truth, and have not much acquaintance with its contents, discovering that they were mistaken about it, will perhaps throw it away. (That will be because they have never been acquainted with its true value, but only with an assumed and a fictitious value. I venture to say that those who have become acquainted with its spirit and value — the revelation of it — will never throw it away. For the proof of the truth of the New Testament lies in itself. There is a certainty, a practical certainty, which, if we are sincere and simple-minded, is readily accessible to us. Only those things which are axiomatic are practically certain. After the axioms are found, only those deductions from them which are accordant with them can be called valid. Mathematics and logic have their axioms. We begin with axioms: they are fundamental. Religion has its axioms. All axioms are simple. The axioms that a whole is greater than any of its parts, and that a whole is equal to the sum of its parts, appeal to us. When once they are understood, there is no getting away from them. The books or scriptures in which they are written may all be burned; they remain, our inalienable possession. They are properly to be called infallible. There is no fault in them. They are verities, and the things which properly grow out of them are our practical certainties.

I take it that Jesus was the most axiomatic of any religious speaker in the history of the world. He does not seem to have argued very much, perhaps because he busied himself in laying the axiomatic foundation. Now, the axioms of Jesus are so arranged by the writer of the first Gospel of our New Testament that we are confronted by them at the outset. These axioms are the very things which, given in a simple way, will remain in the minds of men who hear them. We do not need any one to confirm us in our acceptance of them. The blessedness of purity of heart, for instance, is a truth we are created to feel. If the clergy gathered in consultation at Laodicea in 360 A. D. had set forth that purity of heart is blessed, it would not add one atom's weight to the authority of the axiom, to one who has understood it. If, on the contrary, such a convention should have decided that impurity of heart is really blessed, that would destroy the axiom for no one who has understood it. That is, therefore, one of the certainties of religion; and out of it grow many other practical certainties. The thing is infallibly true, whoever said it, or if no one had ever said it until now.

On the other hand, suppose we begin with the genealogy of Jesus as given in our first account. From Abraham to Joseph, the father of Jesus, the number of generations is forty. Is this the correct number? In the third account there are forty-one generations. If Luke is right, then Matthew has not given a correct genealogy of Jesus: it has the fault of leaving out one generation, and that is a serious flaw in a genealogical record. If Matthew is right, then Luke has committed the fault of adding a generation. However one chooses to explain it, there is a fault somewhere. Now an infallible writer does not commit a fault of that kind. A perfectly honest and trustworthy writer may. Explanations have been offered, but none of them prove satisfactory. What religious difference does it make whether there were forty or forty-one generations between Abraham and Joseph? None whatever. Therefore, for the purposes of religion, the chapter of genealogies might precisely as well be stricken out. If we desire genealogical knowledge, we cannot acquire it with certainty, because the authorities, inspired authorities, differ. If we desire religious knowledge, that is another matter. The first chapter of Matthew contains no religious information to impart: also, it contains no sure genealogical information.

In the fourth Gospel is an account of the first miracle performed by Jesus. The first of a series of wonderful events would not be likely to be overlooked by writers giving an account of a man's mission. Other miracles of course might be forgotten, but the first one would probably be remembered. This first miracle, however, was not heard of by Luke, as he makes his investigation, or it was not regarded important enough for record. The same is true of the other two evangelists. From seventy-five to a hundred years after the death of Jesus the story of this first miracle is written. Jesus went to a wedding in Cana, in Galilee, and the wine supply failed. He was one of the guests, his mother another. She mentioned to him that the wine was gone. Six water-pots, in the customary place, he caused to be filled with water. That which was put into the water-pots was water, but we are assured that what was drawn out of the same vessels was wine. It was not only wine in appearance, but it was such in reality, and was commended as good wine by the steward of the house.

This is plainly of the magical order; such things are not unfamiliar to the magicians. Now this story is absolutely unverifiable. There are really many things against it; but there is nothing for it, except that the convention assembled in Laodicea in 360, and other conventions, did not prune it out. They did prune somewhat; they rejected writings approved by the common consent of a multitude of Christians, but they did not leave out that story. Now, if we put the utmost reliance upon their judgment, we are not proceeding safely. They at least were not infallible. Then, because the story cannot be verified, and because it has but a secondary or illustrative connection with religion, why are we not at liberty to reject it as a fact? Why cannot we take it as a growth in the latter portion of a period most rife with such growths? From the efforts of total abstainers to explain that the wine was not intoxicating, we should imagine them to be glad if the whole story were out of the New Testament.

There is another story, introduced by the same author, which stands by itself, having no reinforcement from the earlier writings, and that is the most astonishing miracle performed by any one. It is the raising of Lazarus from death, after he had been entombed four days. Thither went Jesus and his disciples, and many were said to be the witnesses of the strange event. This event is said to have attracted the attention of the authorities at Jerusalem, and they undertook to kill Lazarus because they feared the influence which would accrue to Jesus from so great a proof of power. Luke in his investigations failed to reach that story. It was not told in his time, or he surely would not have omitted it; and that is equally true of the other evangelists. If, therefore, we seek verification of that incident, we fail to find it. There is nothing in the story to commend it to our minds as axiomatic. It is not self-verifying. There are truths connected with it which are self-verifying. But that which is not self-verifying cannot belong to the certainties of religion. To my mind, that particular Gospel, in which these stories are related, is the grandest and most helpful religious book in the world. It seems to me to contain more self-verifying truths than any other book. The things in it which are not capable of verification, except by that pseudo method which rests everything on the decision of the councils which determined the canon, are to be distinguished from the things which make direct appeal to our heart and conscience and reason.

The things of religion which do not belong to the practical certainties are not the things which in these times we can safely hold to. We have given a primary place to the secondary and unessential things of religion. We have regarded these unverifiable matters, such as the raising of Lazarus, and the turning of water into wine, as truths to stand by and maintain, as though they belonged to the religion of Jesus. Now they do not, and in the nature of the case cannot, belong to the religion of Jesus, but to the religion of those writers who failed to understand Jesus. The real subject-matter of the religion of Jesus has been fatally obscured by common faith in these unverifiable statements.

I have heard of a woman who kept a little coat, worn by her little boy, long after he had grown up and was away engaged in the business of the world. She loved to look at the little coat, and it was because the little boy had worn it, although he had long outgrown it. She would sometimes be glad to have her little boy back again, and able to wear the little coat, but that is impossible. Better is it that it is impossible. I confess to a love for the stories about the turning of water into wine, and the raising of Lazarus, because the religion of Jesus has worn, as a garment, those legends and others like them. I am persuaded that the religion of Jesus has outgrown such garments. It is better so. The lover of the Bible will have an affectional interest in the legends, but he will see that they are not the garments in which the religion of Jesus can practically work.

XIX.

PAUL AND THE SECOND ADVENT.

Long before any official list of the books which constitute the New Testament was made, there were catalogues of writings which held a high place in Christian esteem. The first list, the authorship of which is unknown, contains most of the books in the New Testament as we now have it. About the same time Irenæus made a list of a different sort. He thought that the First Epistle of Peter and the Second of John were of doubtful character, and to be ranked with the Shepherd of Hermas. He did not consider Hebrews, Jude, James, nor Second Peter and Third John, worthy of a place in his list. Also Clement of Alexandria made a list of superior and inferior books. Later, say about the middle of the third century, Origen divided the Christian writings into three classes: the authentic, the non-authentic, and the doubtful. Eusebius, the famous courtier, theologian, and historian, made his list about a century later than Origen, but agreeing with Origen's.[1]

But we have the evidence of three ancient copies of the New Testament, the most ancient yet discovered. The manuscript known as the Sinaitic, which was discovered by Tischendorf in 1841 in a convent of Mt. Sinai, is reckoned to be of the fourth century, or possibly of the fifth. That manuscript includes some

[1] See Dr. Gladden's *Who Wrote the Bible?* p. 318.

books which we reject, namely, the Epistle of Barnabas, and the Shepherd of Hermas. One of the other most ancient manuscripts includes material not contained in our Bibles. Moreover, when the Reformation came on, there was much dispute over portions of the contents of the Bible. Some of the prominent reformers rejected the book of Revelation, and others felt doubtful about other books. Thus in those far-off times of the Reformation, and in those still more distant times of the early church, there was a greater freedom of judgment in regard to the Bible than our conservative teachers would like to accord to us now. Whereas, both because we can study the matter under a greater light now than was possible formerly, and because freedom of judgment in regard to all matters whatsoever ought to be greater now than formerly, we are advancing to the use of great liberty in our opinions concerning the New Testament. The one thing of great importance to all Christians at present is that according to the best opinions, the different books of the Bible have a different value. Some books are better than others, and portions of each book are better than other portions. For each intelligent reader, therefore, the value of a statement is to be tested by the individual judgment.

(The mere fact that a statement is contained in the Bible is no proof of the truth of the statement. We are thrust back on a personal responsibility which we have not greatly cultivated in religious concerns. It is a deficiency in responsibility that makes so many of us afraid to think; but a religion which renders us afraid to think will surely work us a great mischief.)

Ordinarily, books are written in the order of their chapters. The first chapter is first written, etc: but in the Old Testament the book of Genesis, for example, was written long after later portions. In the New Testament it is equally true that the first books were not written first. Without going through the argument necessary to establish the truth of the proposition, it is generally agreed by scholars, including the conservative as well as the progressive, that the first letter Paul wrote, which remains to us, is his first letter to the Thessalonians. As Paul was the first writer of the New Testament literature, we have a reasonable probability that the part of our New Testament which was first thought out and written is this letter, which occupies a rather obscure place in the Testament. It is estimated by Dean Alford that Paul wrote the First Epistle to the Thessalonians in the autumn of the year 52 of our era. Others put it earlier, but it does not signify. Suffice it that the start of the New Testament was made by the writing of a letter by an apostle. Paul was an apostle, not because he had followed Jesus about in Galilee and Judea, and had listened to his teachings, but because he had been called to be an apostle by the command and voice of God uttered in his own soul. He obeyed that call, and did not ask leave of the other apostles, who had been disciples. He did not consult with them about it, for he probably knew that they would not consent to such an arrangement. He took up this work, just as previously he had taken up the work of persecution, because he believed that God wished him to do it. In the prosecution of it he had gone about Asia Minor, visiting various cities and planting churches. He had a dream one night, as Luke tells us. In his dream he saw a Macedonian, and heard his voice imploring the apostle to come over to Macedonia. Paul took that as a divine intimation that he must cross the sea and plant the new gospel among the Greeks. Accordingly he went across the sea, and visited Philippi, where he and his companion were imprisoned on account of a riot occasioned by their visit. Then they went to Thessalonica, where there was a Jewish synagogue, and there for the space of three weeks Paul preached to the Jews out of their Scriptures. The Jews were too tenacious of their traditions to give heed to what he said, but there were many Greeks who were more tractable, and they formed a Christian community. Now Christianity was so new to them that all sorts of difficult questions would arise in regard to it, after Paul went away. There was no such thing as a written gospel to refer to. So far as these Greeks knew, there were no books bearing upon the subject. Therefore they had discussions about various things, and did not know what to think. They were very much troubled, and word was either sent to Paul, or in some manner he heard of their state, and wrote them an epistle.

This letter tells us in general the view of the religion of Jesus which Paul gave the Greeks at that place. It tells us what Paul's notion of the gospel was at that time. This is interesting, not only in itself as a piece of information, but it is also much more interesting in showing in what a crude way the gospel took form at the first. There was one great permanent effect produced by Paul and his preaching. The Greeks, who had been idolaters, were turned away from idolatry to serve a living and true God, instead of the idolatrous images. They had also been taught to wait for God's Son, who was soon to come from heaven, and this Son was none other than Jesus, who had been raised from death, and who was the appointed deliverer from the wrath to come.

This was nothing strange at that time. The Jews supposed that certain who had died would come back again to the earth. They had that expectation in regard to the ancient prophet Elijah, although we may suppose that Jesus did not share the expectation. It is quite evident, also, that the Jewish Christians expected the revival of Nero after his death, and his reinstatement in imperial power for a time. No doubt the expectation of the return of Jesus to set up his kingdom and punish his enemies and persecutors and the enemies of the church was exceedingly comforting to the Christians. They were compelled to endure privations and the hatred of stubborn Jews; but all that would last only a brief time. The day of judgment, or of wrath, was fast approaching; and they must maintain patience and sobriety until that time.

Paul had adopted the feeling which had been growing among the Christian communities. He had not yet become very well informed about the actual teachings of Jesus, such as we find in the Gospels. They had not yet been written, and he had no means of knowing. Therefore he felt sure, about the middle of the first century, that a great change was impending; that the old order of things would pass away, and the new order would be instituted. But that new order, he supposed at that time, would be connected with the coming back again of Jesus in the clouds of the sky, to assume the command of all things, and to destroy the Antichrist, which many reckoned to be Nero.

The real substance of this letter of Paul's has reference to the conduct of these converted Greeks. He wishes them to be most careful of all to maintain a good behavior, so that at the coming of Jesus with all his saints, they may be ready. He speaks in particular of some of those gross vices to which, we are informed, the inhabitants of the cities of the Greek peninsula were addicted. He exhorts them to purity of heart and of life; for that, he says, is what God has called them to. Now the Greeks were not used to the Jewish idea, and no doubt Paul's preaching about the coming of the Son of God from Heaven had thrown them into a ferment of excitement. Such ferments are not unknown to us, arising from the same cause; and these Greeks, who had not enjoyed the high moral training which the Jews had, were undoubtedly less affected by the moral teachings of Paul than by his visions of the coming of Jesus in the clouds.

Therefore Paul, in this letter, is cautionary. He wishes them not to pay sole attention to the coming of Jesus in the clouds, but to grow morally, and to have the ambition of being quiet, and work at their various occupations, which probably many of them had neglected. They were to work at their occupations and make an honest living, as if there were to be no such coming of Jesus. Under the excitement caused by Paul's visit and his preaching many questions had arisen. His converts were filled with the idea of that appearance in the clouds; and some of them were sorry for those that had died before they were able to partake in that great triumph. It was so great a loss not to see the glorious advent! Thus the joyful expectations of these people were greatly lessened by the thought of those who had died and lost it all. Paul knew of these discussions, and he undertook to settle the matter. He wrote that there need be no sorrow for the dead,—that is, for the good among them. They would have as much to do with the triumph as anybody. "For this we say unto you by the word of the Lord, that we that are alive, that are left unto the coming of the Lord, shall in no wise precede them that are fallen asleep. For the Lord himself shall descend from heaven with a shout, with the voice of the archangel and with the trumpet of God; and the dead in Christ shall rise first; then we that are alive, that are left, shall together with them be caught up in the clouds to meet the Lord in the air; and so we shall be always with the Lord. Wherefore comfort one another with these words."

Such is the teaching which embodied itself in the first of the New Testament Scriptures. This is the message Paul bore to Jews and Greeks; the message concerning a scene soon to occur in the sky, and simultaneously a breaking of the graves, so that the bodies of those who had been buried would come forth and ascend to the sky, while a host of living men and women would also join the ascent. Then would come a final overthrow of the powers of evil on the earth.

Paul believed all this to be true, just as William Miller and many others have believed it to be true. Only, unlike some of the modern advocates of the theory, Paul would have the Christians neglect none of their affairs, and he would have them study to be quiet and give particular attention to sober and right behavior. However, in spite of all exhortations, the people could not help being excited at such a prospect. They wished to know the time when this magnificent panorama would open to view; but Paul reminded them that they knew that it would come unexpectedly, like a thief in the night. Therefore it was useless for him to tell them anything further, except that when wicked persons had settled themselves in an evil content, then the great day would come, and there would be no escape from it.

These enthusiastic teachings bore fruit. The Western people began to entertain the hope of the resurrection of their bodies. They had been careless about the disposal of the bodies of the dead. They were not affected by the Egyptian feelings on that subject, but delivered the bodies to the flames. In due time the primitive notion of Paul with reference to that matter obtained such a hold in the West that the Christians began the construction of those catacombs which belong to the wonders of the world. They were no longer indifferent to the disposal of the dead, but, with a religious and affectionate care, laid them away, in the sure hope of the resurrection. Such was the deep sobriety of Paul, and such his earnestness in the real moral teachings of the religion of Jesus, so far as he had heard them, that he laid great stress upon the daily conduct of his disciples. He wished them to admonish the disorderly, to encourage the faint-hearted, to support the weak, and to be long-suffering toward all. He would not have them repay evil with evil, but to be always following that which was good. He wished more for their moral improvement, what is called their sanctification, than anything else. He wanted to have them ready for Jesus, when he should appear, by being blameless and worthy.

This is the first thing that was written for the coming New Testament,— this about the advent of Jesus in the clouds, with the sound of a trumpet, and the raising of dead bodies; but to the fundamental authentic teachings of Jesus this bears faint resemblance.

Now something happened, and it is of the utmost importance with reference to these visions of Paul. While great events did come to pass, and while a changed order did supervene, it was not at all in the way Paul expected. Jesus did not descend from heaven, with the voice of command, and with the voice of an archangel, and with the trumpet of God, and raise the bodies of the dead, and catch up Paul and others who were alive at the time. A certain somewhat obscure Dutch author and some few American writers of no prominence have indeed claimed that these things actually happened at the time of the destruction of Jerusalem. If they did happen, however, we have no means of knowing it, — and therefore it is the same as if there had been nothing of the kind. Paul supposed that it was all true, and that he had received these visions from the Lord; but they were visions which he evidently outgrew. Comparatively few of the Christians of any age, after the apostolic, have given any heed to these teachings about Jesus coming in the clouds. Some of those who have more tenaciously held to the infallibility of the Bible have been greatly scandalized because the churches have been so careless of distinct teachings of an inspired apostle.

We are surely justified in the conclusion that Paul's first preaching differed materially from his later. If nothing more, he changed the emphasis from one doctrine to another. Another thing is certified to by one of his letters, and that is his abandonment of the expectation of being caught up to meet the Lord in the air. He may still have believed that Jesus would come at some period in that manner; but at all events he lost interest in the subject. As he ceased to care for the outward shows of royalty and conquest he acquired interest in other and more substantial matters. This is testified to by the letter to the Romans, which was written a few years later. It may be inferred that that letter was written to those who had been Jews, and might still indeed have considered themselves such. Hence the theological character of the writing. I suppose such questions were familiar to the schools of the rabbins; the schools of Schammai and Hillel. Paul shows a new tendency to go deep into the meanings of things and to reason subtly upon them. He is no longer to be satisfied with anything that is merely outward, in the flesh. He has become more spiritually minded; and, too, we may discern, if we attend carefully to his line of argument, the loss of the old expectation of the coming of Jesus in the clouds. He has acquired a far better idea, and one far more consonant with the religion of Jesus.

He does not look for a revelation of the wrath to come, but he sees the wrath of God already revealed from heaven against all ungodliness, and particularly against the craft of religious men. After a lengthy elaboration of the office and effect of faith, he perceives that the world is not waiting for the coming of Jesus upon the clouds, and that such a coming would really effect nothing of value. What the world is really waiting for — and it is filled with groans and tears and trouble while waiting — is the manifestation of men who have the spirit of Jesus. He does not look for the Son of God in the clouds of the sky, but for the sons of God walking the earth, and bettering the moral condition of it.

We have read the Bible under a wrong impression. We have supposed that all the things a man may have said or written are equally true or equally mature. It is the habit of students to grow, and therefore to change their minds. It was the way of Paul to grow. While exhorting others to make advance he was not himself idle. He was a greater man, and a better teacher of God's truth, in the year 58 than in the year 52. His fertile mind and his thorough earnestness did not permit him to linger in the old crudity and error. He evidently outgrew it. His experience was that of a progressive man, that is, of a growing manhood.

What he had written to the Corinthians, or the Ephesians, or earlier to the Thessalonians, did not debar him from writing a better message to others, when he had learned it. In him is illustrated, too, the wisdom of Jesus, who said that the kingdom of God is not immediately developed to full proportions in mankind, or in any member of the race, but that it grows in the mind and heart of mankind as it has opportunity. The stage of to-day is not the standard for to-morrow. So Paul changed his mind about that very peculiar phenomenon which we have learned to know as the Second Advent. It faded away from him, as doubtless it has faded away from many another. While the Thessalonian Greeks had turned from idols to serve a living God, he had taught them to wait for the Son of God from heaven; in other words, to expect the return of Jesus. They were clear of the wrath to come because they were in this state of mind. To the Roman Jews he said something which cannot be reconciled with the early enthusiasm. They were taught that so many as yield to the guidance of the Spirit of God are already, and while living on the surface of the earth, the sons of God. And they need not look with longing eyes to the sky, for the appearing of the Son of God, who had departed from the earth. With that Son of God they had not to do, except spiritually; but with the spirit and mind of Jesus they had everything to do. The prevalence of that spirit and mind upon the earth would bring its redemption from bondage.

The growth of Paul suggests that there was growth elsewhere also among the early Christians. In fact, all things of all sorts come into phenomenal existence in this world by growth. The kingdom of heaven is no exception to the general rule of development. It is not first the full corn in the ear, but first the blade. The kingdom of heaven was in the soul of Paul first as a blade of promise. It must needs have been so with all his associates. We are forced to discriminate between the earlier and the later development. The expectation of the coming of Jesus upon the clouds of the sky, attended by celestial beings, to which the first writing of Paul testifies so strongly, was the very thing which prevented the writing of a thoroughly authentic history of the acts of Jesus. From the time when he had been put to death, the days slipped by and there were newcomers in Jerusalem. Questions as to the difference between Paul's notions about the Gentiles and the contrary notions of the apostles who had been with Jesus arose. History was making itself rapidly. There were persecutions, and flights away from Jerusalem. There was the question of idols, and whether a follower of Jesus could eat that which had been offered in sacrifice to idols, after it was exposed for sale in the market.

By the zeal and insight of Paul great questions concerning the validity of keeping the Sabbath, and the rite of circumcision, and performing vows in the temple, and the like were forced upon the attention and decision of the men in authority; and meanwhile, too, strange stories about Jesus were growing, and gaining wide currency in Judea, and adjacent countries, — stories concerning his birth, and the events precedent thereto; strange stories of what he did as a little child. The age was emphatically an age of wonders and miracles. At every step the miracles were interwoven in the stories told and retold, and they gathered weight and size with each repetition. Meanwhile no man was attempting to soberly write the story of Jesus simply as he knew it, telling only what he actually knew Under the circumstances it seems, therefore, to have been one of the impossibilities to write a history of Jesus in the plain, matter-of-fact way of modern times.

What then? In place of the sober biography we have a growth in the mind of the first century which is unlike the historical Jesus; but the growth produces as its flower that ideal character, to know and love which is life and peace. You do not have to ask questions of history in regard to the value and glory and excellence of that character. It shines for itself like the dawn of day. It shines by a light which puts all other light in shade. It appeals to us as a radiant, divine, and earth-redeeming truth. This is the light that lighteth every man.

XX.

THE APOCALYPSE OF JOHN.

AFTER Paul had written his letters to the saints in various localities, other kinds of literature came into vogue among the Christians. Of these none is more puzzling, none apparently more inscrutable, than that found in the last book of the New Testament. Many readers have cast that document aside as useless. Others have regarded it as a collection of the vagaries of a person on the verge of insanity. It may safely be said that the majority of the people to whom the Bible is the infallible revelation of God do not get much revelation, infallible or other, out of the book which especially bears that name, the last book of the Bible. It is true that its writer declares him blessed who reads it, as well as those who hear it and keep the things which are written therein. Yet with the exception of the first three chapters and two or three passages near the close of it, there is nothing edifying in it to the average reader.

For that there is an excellent reason. The book was not written for us. We do not acquire any blessedness by reading it, because its application is not to us. If in some manner we can be made to feel that the book has a great revelation for us of things that must shortly come to pass, then of course we shall become greatly interested in it, and try to find out, if possible, what it means; but it was written so long ago, and had such distinct reference to things about to transpire, that we fail to find it interesting. There are truths in it which remain forever, but they are merely incidental in the book, and do not constitute its main theme.

It seems probable, contrary to the settled opinion of earlier students, that this book may have been one of the earlier of the Christian writings. It is not impossible that it was written before any of the Gospels. If the books of our New Testament were arranged chronologically, in the order of their composition, the First Epistle to the Thessalonians, as before suggested, would take the place of Matthew. Other epistles of Paul would follow that. Perhaps the next book to them would be this Apocalypse of John. So that if all the letters of Paul were combined in one book, and that book were placed at the beginning of the New Testament, then it is quite probable that the second book of the New Testament would be the one which now closes it. This does not profess to be an accurate opinion, nor one that can be substantiated by clear proof, but I believe it to be approximately true.

If the first contribution to the New Testament was written about the year 52, there is something to show that this contribution by a (possibly) second writer was made within fifteen or twenty years thereafter, because we may well suppose that only a dire and immediate necessity would call forth such a writing. Such a necessity is plainly visible in the condition of the Jews and the Jewish Christians in the latter half of the sixth decade of the first century.

A bit of history may be gleaned from many writers. One Florus was the Roman procurator of Judea, and exhausted the ingenuity of a man of some talent in devising exasperations for the patriots of his province. The people were insulted and made to feel the weight of the foreign power as heavily as possible, and the result was a revolt. Nero sent two of his generals to suppress the revolution; and they, beginning with Antioch, swept down toward the capital, leaving only misery, death, and destruction in their wake. Whether the Roman empire at that time was at its worst or not, it certainly was worse than modern imagination can easily picture. Nero has always been subjected to the execration of mankind, and his tools and favorites were men of the ferocious martial type. The Roman armies were the scourge of the world. The Jews, roused to the defense of their country, contested the advance of Vespasian with the courage and fury of despair. They were in no wise inferior to their conquerors in courage, but were deficient in military organization, and so they were driven back, inch by inch, toward the holy city. In it they were finally penned, Vespasian establishing his army in winter quarters in the vicinity. Then broke forth such terrors in Jerusalem, such atrocities, such sufferings, as elsewhere the astounded world has not looked upon. The French revolution, with its busy guillotine, its drowning of priests in the river at Lyons, its far-reaching Jacobin murder-society, was but child's play, compared with the destruction of Jerusalem. In its wildest days, Paris was a regulated city, compared with Jerusalem in its worst days, after the circumvallation of Titus. So dreadful a fate was accorded to the Jews that the tongue refuses to speak it, and the pen to write it.

The Christians fled out of the doomed city, went across the Jordan to Pella, scattered everywhere, so far as they were able; and everywhere they carried the tidings of the most terrible times that had ever, they thought, darkened the world. Either because banished to a small island in the Ægean Sea, or wishing to seclude himself, John, the writer of the Apocalypse, was at this time leading a solitary life in the Island of Samos, of the group of the Sporades. This is said to be a desolate island, about thirty Roman miles in circumference, and may have furnished subsistence for a very scanty population. Thither John had betaken himself, and there his visions came to him. It is possible that he had undertaken in that solitude to write letters of affectionate greeting, warning, appeal, and instruction to churches of Asia which he had become deeply interested in. He may have felt that the example of Paul, in that respect, was worthy of imitation. At any rate, he begins his letter to the seven churches of Asia, but in a style widely different from that of the more educated and argumentative Paul. One might be quite within the probabilities to suppose that he had made the plan of his letters, and was slowly working them out, adapting them to the needs of the various localities, when the news of the calamities of the fatherland came to him. The fervid imagination of the Hebrew, coupled with the faith of the Christian, forces him to send out a great message of the last times to the Christians not only of Asia, but wherever it may find them. The vision is not for all men. It is for those who can understand it. It is for those who have the knowledge of signs and figures of speech peculiar to the Jews.

We shall go astray in our interpretation of this book of visions if we fail to note that the seer devotes himself only to the things which must shortly come to pass. What more natural than for John, hearing the awful tidings from Judea, to see an end of the old disorder, the crash of it in a final chaos, its reduction to ashes, and the rise of an orderly cosmos, a beautiful kingdom, to be ruled by the Lamb? The anguish, pain, and terror of the time were to him like the final pains of death, and like the pains of birth, as well; but the keynote of the whole vision is in the anticipation that the events noted are about to transpire; not after centuries, and not after weary and bloody decades even, but at once. How one scene treads upon the heels of another, each pushing itself forward upon the stage to be itself crowded off without delay!

The main subject of the book is not a doctrine, properly so called; it is not a gospel, nor a treatise upon any topic, but a schedule of things about to happen. If John began with the idea of writing a pastoral letter to the churches of Asia, and had gone as far in that enterprise as the first three chapters (exclusive of the introduction, which may well have been added later), he abandoned it. The times were too pressing. If we combine all the scenes into one, it is contained in the words, "Behold he cometh." All is an expansion of those words.

Our religious teachers have had dogmatic uses for all the books of the Bible, and they have made it appear to the readers of this last book that the author was talking about the last things, or about the Second Advent, whenever it might be. He tells us that his vision is not of a second advent, or a last day, or anything of that nature, to occur in some remote period. What he saw was the immediate occurrence of events like the siege of Jerusalem.

After the apocalyptic method, he sees all these

things, as it were, in heaven. Everything is planned there, and symbolically represented, before it occurs on earth. There is a door opened in heaven, so as to permit the seer to perceive what is going on there. Through the door he beholds a throne, and he immediately hears a voice bidding him come up and see the things which must come to pass. On the throne is One who shines with an indescribable glory. A rainbow spans with its arch the awful presence. Figures arrayed in white, and crowned with golden crowns, surround the throne; and out of the throne proceed voices, lightnings, and thunders. The picture is certainly a sublime one. Golden lamps are burning; a multitude of eyes are gazing. The One sitting on the throne holds a book sealed with seven seals, but to remove the seals is beyond the power of any one, until a Lamb appears (also called the Lion of the tribe of Judah), who is able to open the seals. This book evidently contains the things which are shortly to come to pass. There is no one who can open the book of coming events, except the Lamb. He opens the seals one by one. At the opening of the first, there rides forth a rider upon a white horse, one who comes to conquer the world. At the opening of the second seal comes forth a red horse, probably representing, quite fittingly, war. At the opening of the third seal, a black horse. At the opening of the fourth seal, a livid horse, possibly representing famine. At the opening of the fifth seal, the voice of souls is heard, calling for vengeance upon tyrants, oppressors, and murderers. Then an earthquake, together with the turning of the sun into blackness, the moon red as blood, while the stars of heaven fall from their places. The heaven is removed as a scroll, when it is rolled up; and then appears the day of the wrath of the Lamb.

After the seven seals come the seven trumpets and then the seven vials or bowls containing God's wrath. These are one by one emptied of their contents upon the earth. Upon the pouring out of the first bowl a disease falls upon the inhabitants of the earth. The second bowl is poured upon the sea and it turns to blood. The third turns the waters of rivers and springs into blood. The fourth renders the sun hot with intolerable heat, etc.

The Jewish character of the vision is shown in the sealing of the twelve thousand from each tribe, and in the name "Lion of the Tribe of Judah," as applied to the Lamb, and in other ways. But there emerges to view the Beast, who sets a mark upon all men, bond and free, rich and poor, without which no one is permitted to buy or sell. This Beast is to be recognized by the initiated as the Cæsar, Nero. In a mystic manner, the seer spells out the name for those who can understand. Pestilence, bloodshed, famine, every possible evil, betrays its dire presence in these visions. The very sum and head of all evil, the dragon, or devil, having but a short time, bestirs himself to the utmost in doing all the mischief possible while space serves.

Such is the writing of a man who, in his cave on the lonely island of the Ægean, can see the panorama of the final conquest of good over evil. He sees not only the glories of the opened heavens, and the activities of spirits good and bad, but he sees the great dragon, the devil, at length laid hold of by a powerful angel, in whose hand is the key of the bottomless pit; and the fiend is thrust down into the nether depths, there to abide a thousand years. Then he is let loose for a brief season, but it does not interest the seer, because that period is so far away. What does interest him is the event of the time, — the coming of Jesus in the clouds, to be seen by every eye, to be hailed by all mouths, to be worshiped by all men; and that is shortly coming to pass.

So vivid are the waking dreams of this man, so huge the disasters he sees, so bloody the color of all things, so lurid, so awful, that we wonder if this man could have walked about in the quiet paths of Judea or Galilee with the Son of Man, and learned of him; but we must recall the things which were transpiring in Judea at that very moment. We must put ourselves in the place of the seer, as well as we may, and think of the ruthless Roman carrying fire and slaughter and desolation through the fair land of the promise, — the sacred city sacked, its holy places invaded, its inhabitants brutally slain. We must think of the deadly hatred such things must needs evoke in the breast of the Jew. We must think of the anguish of soul, the despair, except for the vision of the coming triumph, when all shall be reversed. Then the Beast, and the false prophet, and the dragon, and all the enemies of the sacred race will be shut up in the fire of the wrath of the Lamb, and the smoke of their torment will ascend forever and forever. Could any pain be too great for Nero and his hordes?

Looked upon without sympathy and without knowledge of the circumstances, the book of Revelation is an insanity. There is an order, a method in the scenery, but the total is a frightful phantasm; yet it is redeemed by one of the sweetest and most entrancing pictures of hope ever written by human hand. The seer does not see through the open door of heaven the wreck of a world. He does not see purposeless agony of human souls, a meaningless martyrdom; rather there is an issue from it all of a world at last fit for the habitation of gentle and just men. After all the death supervenes life; after all the darkness and gloom comes an unfading light. For the diseases which have afflicted men there blooms the glorious tree, whose leaves have healing power. The hunger and the thirst, and the groaning, and the terrors, the bloodshed, oppressions, falsities, are all going, and they are going soon. That is the thing which must shortly come to pass. The golden city which is the true capital of the world, the New Jerusalem, descends from God out of heaven, and becomes at last an earthly city. The nations rejoice, and walk in the light of it; the time of crying and groaning and mourning is over. "Behold I make all things new," is the voice which thrills every heart.

This book, strange as it is, had its uses; but they were for the most part exhausted in the lifetime of the writer who wrote it. Like that other apocalyptic book which was sent forth in the period of the Maccabees, to nerve the heart of the despairing with courage and inspire hope in the hopeless, this message of the seer of Patmos must have been the great divine book of its day to those who could read its mysteries. For those of a later time who have read it unintelligently, it has been far other than a blessing. For the most part it has been out of date since the century in which it was written, and not only out of date, but the inspiration of disordered dreams, and the cause of religious frenzy in many.

Now it is this kind of religious literature which has a transient value. It is not for future ages, but only for the age in which the writer lives. When it is taken to be a schedule of the events of the ages of the world, to wind up finally with the triumph of the Jews, it will be sure to be misunderstood, and to produce insane visions and baseless expectations.

There is another thing to be taken account of. With the exception of the first three chapters, which are advisory and appealing, and passages near the close of the book, which are hopeful, there is not very much which corresponds with the known facts. It is impossible to identify the fulfillment of these predictions. If we assume, as we must, that Rome, and the Cæsar, and the legions, and all the imperial power are set forth in various vivid imagery, they on the one hand, and the Lamb, or Jesus Christ, on the other hand, with the hosts of heaven fighting under his banner, what are we to think of the result of their conflict? The victorious rider on the white horse, coming forth conquering and to conquer, is to utterly annihilate the power and pomp of the enemy. Babylon, the mystery of iniquity, the infamous woman, arrayed in scarlet, and drunk with the wine of her fornications, falls prostrate, and is thrust down to destruction, and the smoke of her torment ascends, the sign that she was, but is not. This is the expectation of the seer, but Babylon stands clearly enough for imperial Rome, the mistress of the world. She upon her seven hills, ruling with wide-stretched arm the destinies of the habitable world, hated beyond all by the Jew, fell not. The Jew and the Christian did not conquer her. By that slower process of downfall which has happened to all nations, she after a long period came to the end of her imperial power. The ardent prediction of John was not fulfilled, and can never be fulfilled, because the times have gone by.

He who starts with the notion that the Bible is an infallible book, and true in all of its statements, including its predictions, is forced to one of two courses with respect to this book of John the seer. He must hold that the predictions were accurately fulfilled, although we have no historic account of it, or else that when the seer spoke of things shortly coming to pass, he did not mean shortly in our sense of the word. He meant shortly from the standpoint of God. I believe that is the course usually followed by interpreters who believe in the infallibility of the Bible. In support of that theory is the fact that at the close of the splendid scene, the triumph of God and the sovereignty of the Lamb is described as the descent of the holy city, New Jerusalem, from heaven: then the redemption of the world is accomplished. That shows that the seer did not limit himself to events near at hand. Yet is there any trouble in supposing that the seer did expect the ending of the old world in his own lifetime? Is it difficult to imagine that he, in his fervid faith, and with his soul aglow with the promises of Christ, not understood by him, should see the end of things at hand? Indeed, he takes the pains to say as much over and over again. The plain fact is that he was mistaken, as many another good and inspired man has been, both before and since his time.

The body of his message is full of incongruous imagery. The seer lets loose his imagination to riot in the scenes of conflict and triumph. There is an absence of that moral teaching which makes the substance of the instruction of Jesus. "The end of things is at hand." There is required no longer the setting forth of the quiet and blessed ways of life. The man is in a delirium. He has reached the climax of that frenzy which has acquired the name of the Second Advent. Yet that frenzy finds no real foundation in him, because he is dreaming of the things of his own time and not of our time.

In the three Synoptic Gospels which have been given a place in our New Testament, we find something of the same idea attributed to Jesus. We hear him not only predicting the overthrow of Jerusalem, but he is represented as saying a few of the things spoken of in the Apocalypse. So strong a hold had these ideas concerning the coming of Jesus in the clouds upon the popular imagination, that we may well conclude that some of these elements were put into the mouth of Jesus, as predicted by him; but it is difficult to reconcile them with his authentic teachings. It is easier to think that from this very book, if it was earlier than the Gospels, were taken the solemn words of the Gospels about waiting and watching for the Son of Man.

The historic criticism of the New Testament thus opens to our view the necessity for a change of opinion with respect to the contents and meaning of the Scriptures. There may be many who are declaring that since the fathers fell asleep all things remain as they were since the beginning of the world. That is a serious error. Nothing remains as it was, but all things change in the order of creation. It is the order of creation that all things should change. Therefore many seem to be taken unawares with the influx of the new opinion which the close of our century witnesses. They do not know what they can do. There is a kind of watchfulness to which they have not been addicted. The old view of the Bible is utterly untenable. Watchful souls have discovered it, and have sought a better view. Perhaps it were most wise in all religious men to be watchful of the present ways of God in the continuing creation. They who are watchful will surely see that if creation goes on from one stage to another, revelation must also increasingly go on from age to age.

XXI.

THE CERTAINTIES.

Referring incidentally to the genealogies given respectively by Matthew and Luke, we discover ample reason to be dissatisfied with them. They do not agree. In Matthew the line of Joseph is traced to Abraham, but the ancestor of Joseph who belongs to the line is Solomon, the son of David. In Luke, however, the progenitor of Joseph is Nathan, the son of David. (If the matter were important, we should find at once that we cannot trust the narrative.) (It is not of consequence, except to those who believe in the infallibility of the Bible, and to them it certainly ought to be weighty, because it disposes finally of their dream of infallibility.) The simple, honest, and honorable way to treat the case is to conclude that one or the other or both of the evangelists were as liable to be mistaken as other honest men, and that one or the other of them was surely mistaken in tracing the line of Jesus through Joseph to Adam or Abraham. (Solomon was not the progenitor of Joseph, if Nathan was.)

(From a strictly religious standpoint, this is of small moment.) The religious bearing of the ancestry of Jesus is nothing to one who has once apprehended that religion. If, however, Matthew and Luke are not to be trusted in an unimportant matter, are they to be trusted in matters of real religious consequence? If they differ, by what means shall we decide which is right? If they agree concerning any matter which does not seem accordant with the teachings of Jesus, how are we to know what the truth in the case is? These are serious questions, for which we need not search unavailingly for answers.

We have seen already that during the period which elapsed before the writing of the Gospel according to Luke, at least, — if not before the writing of any Gospel, — there came to be a feverish expectation of the second advent. This expectation rose to the height of delirium, as shown in the Apocalypse of John. The heart of the Christian community was all engaged with the second advent; and out of the abundance of the heart the mouth speaketh. It became natural for the people to put into the mouth of Jesus discourse concerning the second advent, because they were so full of it themselves. Yet it is in those passages which touch upon that subject, in the three Gospels, we find the sayings of Jesus which strike us as least in his method, and least in accord with the tenor of his other teaching. As largely contributing to the fever of second adventism at the time, we may be sure the book of Daniel was influential. In the book of Daniel are found words of accurate prediction. "From the time of the removal (or change) of the perpetual sacrifice, when the abomination of desolation shall be set up, there shall be a thousand two hundred and ninety days." It is supposed that the abomination of desolation was either some image, emblematic of the Roman sovereignty, or something connected with the idolatry of that people. It is related by Matthew and Mark that toward the end of his life Jesus went into the temple, and was passing out of it, when his disciples wished to call his attention to its beauty, and especially the adornment of it. He assured them that the overthrow of that temple was imminent: not one stone should be left upon another. It is further related that, returning to the Mount of Olives, his disciples privately asked him about the destruction of the temple and the end of the age when he should have come again. In answering these questions he is made to refer to the book of Daniël: "When, therefore, ye see the abomination of desolation spoken of by Daniel, the prophet, standing in the holy place (let him that readeth understand), then let them that are in Judea flee unto the mountains; let him that is on the housetop not go down to take out the things that are in his house," etc.

Luke, in giving his account of this conversation, does not make Jesus refer to the book of Daniel. He does not think of the desecration of the temple by the introduction of the Roman ensign or some idolatrous image into its holy place; and therefore he is not obliged to have Jesus say: "Whoso readeth let him understand," because what he says is plain to any one. "When ye see Jerusalem compassed with armies, then know that the desolation thereof is nigh. Then let them which are in Judea flee to the mountains," etc. It is therefore evident that while these three accounts are all colored by ideas of the second advent, they do not agree. Matthew and Mark say that Jesus referred specifically to Daniel, and his enigmatical words about the abomination of desolation; while Luke tells us that he spoke of the armies encompassing Jerusalem as the sign that the desolation of it had come. It is idle to urge that they mean the same thing; they do not, because in one case the sign is the introduction of some heathen symbol into the holy place of the temple, and in the other case it is the appearance of armies around the walls of Jerusalem. (Thus is indicated to us the probability that there was some common stock of apocalyptic literature from which the three quoted, only Luke changes the quotation to suit the facts, which, when he wrote, had already transpired.)

(There is abundant evidence that the people of the time when the Apocalypse of John and the three Gospels were written did not understand Jesus. They make him say things inconsistent with his real mission, which was spiritual. That is largely because they are filled and fevered with the splendors and horrors of the second advent. They contradict themselves, therefore, for they tell us that he talked of signs in the sun and moon and stars; (while at the same time they record that he had already said that no sign should be given to that generation.) They make him foretell a great tribulation (upon which John dwells much in the Apocalypse), and that immediately after it the sun shall be darkened, and the moon shall cease to yield light, and the stars shall fall from heaven. If we contend that this tribulation is some final catastrophe in the still future history of the world, we are told that he said that the generation then alive should see the fulfillment of all these predictions. The tribulation was soon coming, the darkening of the sun and moon and the fall of the stars. If it be still further urged that by "generation" he did not mean what is commonly meant, but rather the race (of the Jews), note that Matthew makes him say that there were some standing by him while he was speaking who should not taste death until they had seen the Son of Man coming in his kingdom. That is to say, there were some living at that time who should (as Matthew says) continue to live until the Son of Man came in the glory of his Father, with the angels, to judge the world.

These are the things in which it is quite evident that the writers of the Gospels misunderstood Jesus: for those writers, following the popular idea about the second advent, lost sight of the moral regeneration of the world, as the only thing befitting the character and mission of Jesus, and thought of the conquest of the world in some outward way, as by the advent of Jesus with armies of angels in the clouds of the sky. Whatever may have been their opinion, this one thing remains by which to test their insight, or their lack of it, namely, the fact that the Son of Man did not come with the angels so that every eye saw him and all the tribes of the earth mourned. What did happen in that generation was nothing unusual in the clouds of the sky, but something unspeakably dreadful upon the surface of the earth; and that was the siege of Jerusalem by Titus, and the awful scenes of famine and madness inside the walls of the devoted city. The judgment did not sit, with the Son of Man upon the throne of his glory, in the sense which the words of the evangelists imply. The nations were not gathered to be separated from each other as a shepherd divides the sheep from the kids. Those nations which had not been kind to the brethren of the King were not sent into the eternal fire with the devil and his angels. Yet these are the events which the enthusiastic Jewish Christian expected would happen in the near future, — these are the things which the words of Jesus, as the evangelists report them, would lead any one to expect.

Now it is no pleasant task to show the deficiencies of any one, least of all the faults of those who have performed the inestimable service of giving the New Testament to the world; but the deficiencies are there, open to the inspection of any who have eyes to see. We are forced to deal with them, as best we may; but we shall not deal well with them if we slur them over, or construct some theory by which we continue to accept things mutually irreconcilable. The task is being laid upon us of distinguishing between the actual teachings of Jesus and those teachings which have been credited to him, but which do not accord with his method. All things in the world which appeal to us for our trust and confidence must be tested. If in so important an interest as religion we do not prove all things, we shall not be likely to hold fast to that which is good.

Two incidents are related in the evangelists from which lessons are to be learned. The mother of the sons of Zebedee came to Jesus with a request. "Command that these my two sons may sit, one on thy right hand and one on thy left hand, in thy kingdom." Jesus told them that they did not know what they were asking, as surely they did not; and the ten were indignant that the two sons of Zebedee should thus undertake to get the start of them in the coming dignities. The scene gave occasion to Jesus to teach them that those who are really first in the kingdom of God are not those who have the best seats, but those who do the best and most service. This lesson is obvious, from the standpoint of Jesus, and it is given in different forms by the several evangelists. On another occasion Jesus took a little child and presented him to the disciples as an example of the hu-

mility they ought to have. It becomes evident that
Jesus discouraged the ambition of his followers, so far
as it related to having seats or thrones of authority in
the coming kingdom. As to authority, that at any
rate was God's matter, and he would attend to it as
seemed wise to him. Jesus would not give such a
promise as was demanded of him. He preferred to
promise that they should partake with him in the labor
and sufferings incident to his mission. All this seems
clear enough. (We would suppose that no one could
be so blind as to err in respect to these solemn lessons.) Yet that the evangelists did err in respect to
them is perfectly plain.

A young man who had great possessions came to
Jesus to learn of him the way of life. Jesus told him
what the way of life would be for him, but he could
not bring himself to undertake to walk in it, and
went away sorrowful. Then Jesus told his disciples
how difficult it must be for the rich to enter his
kingdom. Peter supposed, after his usual fashion,
that for such great sacrifices as this young man was
called upon to make there must be great reward. He
had the notion, so common among men of the less
spiritual sort, that one does everything for a reward;
so he said, substantially, to Jesus, "We have done
what you told that young man to do. We have left
everything behind in order to follow thee, and now
what shall we have?" If Jesus answered as Matthew tells us he did, then his answer to the mother
of Zebedee's sons must really pass for nothing. They
were wishing for thrones on either hand of his throne.
He would not grant that. When Peter asks for something by way of reward for leaving their fishing business and following Jesus, Matthew declares that Jesus

said: "Verily I say unto you, that ye which have followed me, in the regeneration, when the Son of Man shall sit on the throne of his glory, ye also shall sit upon twelve thrones, judging the twelve tribes of Israel." Probably some have supposed that in the other world, beyond the grave, the twelve tribes of Israel would be again reëstablished; but that notion has only to be examined to be abandoned. The establishment of a tribal relation, an old primitive and provisional arrangement in heaven, is not satisfactory to the mind. What the evangelist undoubtedly meant was the restoration of Israel, as a community of twelve tribes, on the earth and in the land of Palestine. Such restoration is plainly contemplated in the Apocalypse of John. These tribes were to have one imperial king, the Lion of the tribe of Judah; and the twelve followers corresponding with the number of tribes were to be assigned thrones over the tribes, and so the ambition of the disciples, the sons of Zebedee and the ten who had been indignant with them, would be gratified. Their sacrifices would be most gloriously rewarded.

That Jesus should once in a while say things of this sort, absolutely contrary to his own deep convictions expressed at other times, or build up the things he was mainly engaged in tearing down, is not probable. (How much more probable is it that his disciples, and afterward the persons who undertook to write his biography, fell into grave error and misunderstanding of him, than that he should have so grossly misunderstood himself.) To put the case compactly: in one breath he declines to promise the two sons of Zebedee the thrones they asked for, through their mother, and in the next breath he emphatically promises them these thrones of authority and dignity. I therefore hold the statement of Matthew to be incredible. It is difficult to find an inner and deeper sense in which the words may be true. The reward promised is of the very kind Jesus did not believe in.

It may be asked if any one has a right to set up his individual judgment against a plain declaration of the New Testament ; (and I answer, not only a right but a positive duty.) Those who hold to the infallibility of the Bible may be said to give an equal value to these two mutually destructive teachings of the New Testament. In so doing the teachings necessarily reduce to nothing. (It is our right and duty to see that the true teaching may be recognized as such, and the false teaching be so classified, otherwise the word of God is made of none effect by our tradition of infallibility.)

(If Jesus characteristically teaches unworldliness and a distrust of worldly ambitions, he cannot once in a while countenance, much less stimulate, such ambitions.) Whoso tells us that Jesus promised thrones to his disciples, as their reward for making the sacrifice of following him, convicts himself, not Jesus, of error.) Very well, some one will say, if the evangelist errs in such ways, how may we be sure that he does not err in all ways? In answering that question we ought to heed the principle that the truth which is assured to us is self-evident. It is characteristic of Jesus that while he lacks the authority of the scribes, he has the far higher authority of the self-evidence of what he says. One asks: "How do I know that purity of heart is blessedness? May not that prove to be an error, if Jesus is not infallibly reported?"

If we cannot see that purity of heart is blessed beyond all peradventure, we could not be sure of it if a dead man were to rise from the grave and tell us so. We could not certainly know it if an angel were to fly down out of the sky and alight visibly before our eyes and tell us so. It is a self-evidencing truth, or it is nothing. So it is of that teaching concerning humility and service; having once grasped the idea of it, it is evident. We know it is true just because we see it to be true. That other statement about sitting upon twelve thrones and judging the twelve tribes of Israel, and all like sayings attributed to Jesus, not only do not carry any evidence of truth in themselves, but they are contrary to the self-evidencing truths we see in the other sayings of Jesus. Therefore the one is to us an authentic saying of Jesus, and the other is not. In the one we detect the truth of Jesus, in the other the error of the evangelist.

Such discrimination is made obligatory upon us at the present time. We simply have to exercise the same kind of discrimination that those men did who determined what should go into the Bible and what should be kept out. Are we less responsible than they? Have we not as grave cause as they to distinguish between wheat and chaff?

All of the sayings of Jesus which have come down to us in the New Testament were first committed to oral tradition. They were repeated from mouth to mouth. They were of the kind which do not pass into oblivion. They were also of the kind that preserves the sense, even if the wording be somewhat changed. It is quite possible that not one in ten of these sayings of Jesus has been recorded in our Bible, for it is evident that Jesus was a copious talker. Paul, for instance, was familiar with a saying of Jesus which none of the evangelists record. "It is more blessed to give than to receive;" but many or most of these sayings attributed to Jesus, and committed to oral tradition, were not so self-evident as that one. Some sayings supposed to have come from Jesus are sensuous, like that saying concerning the twelve thrones. Irenæus, one of the earliest of the Fathers, quotes one of these sayings believed to have been uttered by the mouth of Jesus. There was a Christian pastor or bishop named Papias, earlier than Irenæus, who diligently collected the "sayings" of Jesus which were current in the early churches. The writings he seems to have held in small esteem, compared with these oral traditions. They came from the "living voice," and therefore he valued them. Now here is one of the sayings attributed to Jesus, which he and Irenæus were sure Jesus uttered. It was precisely as good in their view as that about the twelve thrones, and was in fact of the same order. After the second coming of Jesus the saints would be put in possession of the earth, but it would be a new earth, and much more beautiful and fertile than the old earth. The saints would have vineyards, and the vineyards would be immeasurably better than the old ones. Here is what Jesus is reported to have said of them: "Then will grow vines having ten thousand shoots, and each shoot ten thousand branches, and each branch ten thousand twigs, and each twig ten thousand clusters, and each cluster ten thousand berries, and the juice of each berry will make twenty-five measures of wine:" 2,500,000,000,000 measures from each vine!)[1] That was one of the sayings supposed to have come from

---

[1] See Cone's *Gospel Criticism*, p. 275.

Jesus. The people believed it; Papias believed it; so did Irenæus. Because they believed it we may concede that there is considerable evidence for its authenticity; but its meaning does not correspond, as we may easily see, and as some of the later Fathers did see, with the moral teachings of Jesus, and they rejected it. We may with equal certainty declare that it is foreign to Jesus to say the words about the twelve thrones upon which the twelve disciples are to sit in the regeneration. (As well believe in the marvelous vines, each one capable of pouring out rivers of wine, as to believe in such a regeneration of the world as that the twelve tribes shall reappear and have twelve kings.)

(A gold mine is not composed exclusively of pure metal. It is partly gold and partly other things. A certain worthless metal, pyrites, resembles gold. The people who work in the mines dig out the material, and then they separate the gold from the refuse. They sift, or wash, or try by fire, but in any number of ways they seek to differentiate between the excellent gold and the things which are not gold. Some are more skillful in this than others, and the unskilled cannot determine the difference between gold and pyrites. At all events, the exceedingly necessary process, before the gold is put into the money circulation of the world, is to separate the gold from the grosser or cheaper materials.

(I believe the Bible to be a mine of truth, and in particular the New Testament and the four Gospels are rich veins in this mine.) Some way or other, by the cultivation of our faculties, we are to learn to discriminate the real from the seeming; the truth of Jesus from the dross of the misinterpretation of his biographers. If men can learn to recognize the precious metals wherever they see them, and are able to test them, there is no reason except indolence or superstition, why they should not learn to recognize the truth of God, the truth of Jesus, wherever it may be found. The way of taking everything in the Bible as the truth, even when shown that some things cannot in the nature of things be true, is a way of laziness; and not over conspicuous for its honesty. We do not acquire the wealth of revelation in that way. Only as we freely test the Bible, and learn how to test it, shall we get its truth free from its dross, and be able to enjoy and live that truth.

XXII.

THE FOURTH THE GOSPEL OF THE PRESENT TENSE.

A MULTITUDE of questions arise respecting the doctrines of the New Testament, after one has become a little acquainted with the results of historical criticism. If Jesus did not promise his disciples that they should sit upon twelve thrones, judging the twelve tribes of Israel, did he promise the success of his enterprise of saving the world? The three Synoptic Gospels give us grand pictures of a judgment day. In the first we witness the gathering of all nations before the Son of Man, who sits upon the throne of his glory. In the second Gospel we hear Jesus saying: "Whosoever shall be ashamed of me and of my words in this adulterous and sinful generation, of him also shall the Son of Man be ashamed when he cometh in the glory of his Father with the holy angels." In the third Gospel we hear the same words, but do not find given such a picture of judgment as is given in the first. Nevertheless, in the first three Gospels we are led to expect a judgment day, when the Son of Man shall appear with the holy angels and consummate the judgment of the world.

The judgment and other events associated with it are to occur in the lifetime of those who live in that generation. Now we reckon the life of a generation to be about thirty or thirty-five years. That is the average duration of life for the generation. By reason of other sayings ascribed to Jesus, however, we are not limited to so short a period as that for the fulfillment of the predictions. We are permitted to take the life of the man who survives his generation, and he may live, as tradition asserts the Apostle John did, to be a hundred years old. Therefore, we may conclude that the judgment of the nations, when the Son of Man " shall sit upon the throne of his glory," will transpire within the century. So that according to the predictions contained in the first three Gospels, as well as in such portions of the New Testament as Paul's earlier letters, the Apocalypse of John, and the Epistle of Jude, the judgment day must certainly be before the year 150 of the Christian era.

Two things are evident: (1.) That if the prediction of the coming of Jesus in the clouds of heaven with the angels were really announced to take place in that generation, that is, within a century, that fact would not be forgotten by the people. Friends would tell friends of it, and parents dying would bequeath that promise to their children. The sufferings, privations, and persecutions incident to the time would be the more patiently borne because the day of judgment and of vengeance was not far away. (2.) If, however, the generation passed entirely away, and these things did not come to pass, and if the harrowing scenes of the Roman conquest of Jerusalem became less dreadfully real to the people by the soothing effect of time, and if instead of the end of all things there seemed rather to be a new beginning of things, not in the sky, but on earth, then surely a different notion of the meaning of judgment would grow up. Other ideas, such as the gift of thrones to the twelve, in the coming regeneration, would lose their hold upon the imagination of the more intelligent portion of the church. Moreover, ideas of those very wonderful events of which Paul writes to the Thessalonians, such as the raising of the bodies of the sleeping, or dead, and their ascent into the sky, and the catching up of the living, to make their abode in the sky, would be materially modified. In three of the Gospels these ideas found very full expression, and especially in the Gospel of Matthew. Indeed, Matthew in particular is everywhere colored with these thoughts of the impending judgment and irruption of angels. The color is quite deep in some of the last chapters.

There is, however a book of the New Testament which gives a very different conception of judgment, the resurrection, and the coming of Jesus; that is, the fourth Gospel. This is the book which seems always to have puzzled the students. It puzzled the early Fathers. German criticism has long played itself out in force upon it; and no wonder. It is unlike any other book in the Bible.

An immigrant in a new country compares the land with the tales that have been told of it. He sees virgin soil, great forests, plentiful water, and other natural advantages. If he has been led to expect that all manner of fruits and good food will present themselves ready to his hand upon his advent into that country, he will suffer great disappointment. The fruits and the food are there, potentially, and even beyond all that he has been told, but he must make his own effort toward their development. He must proceed to put his own labor into the clearing of the forest, and the tillage of the soil, and the actual raising of crops, and then he will realize how true the stories were which had been told him. They were true, only they had left out a very important element of truth, and that was the personal labor part.

The early Christians were hearing all the time about the new kingdom of Jesus; they were for the most part looking to see it drop into their hands, as it were, from the skies, — a ready-made kingdom coming with sudden pomp of judgment. Angels were to fly down with all the blessings and rewards and retributions of which Jesus had been understood to talk. They watched for these events to come to pass because they had been solemnly assured of their early arrival, and they did not come. The delays were unaccountable, and hard to endure; the century in which it was necessary for them to occur was waning, perhaps had already waned, when a different Gospel was written. Not different indeed from the authentic teachings of Jesus, but a better exposition of those teachings.

Recur to Paul's first contribution to the New Testament, and what he said about the rising of the dead: "For the Lord himself shall descend from heaven, with a shout, and with the voice of the archangel, and with the trump of God; and the dead in Christ shall rise first; then we that are alive, that are left, shall together with them be caught up in the clouds to meet the Lord in the air," etc. In the fourth Gospel the truth Paul misconstrues is given, clear of that air-castle element which Christian imagination added. There is the Lord, not descending from heaven, but present upon the earth, and there is the voice, and the effect of the voice is the rising of the dead; but the scene is transferred from the future to the present, and from the sky to the ground. Much more than that, the transfer is also from the outward to the inward.

"Verily, verily, I say unto you, the hour cometh and now is when the dead shall hear the voice of the Son of God, and they that hear shall live." A great current of religious thought and feeling had been running toward the hour which was assumed to be coming; and the present hour, with its possibilities, its resurrections, its judgments, had been neglected. It is quite possible that the fourth Gospel was written partly to counteract the religion of expectation, the religion of sky-gazing. For in it the Son of Man is taken out of the clouds, and his religion made to be no cloud-land religion but the religion of the present hour and place. We do indeed see the angels in this last Gospel and last contribution to the New Testament, but even the angels are not cloud dwellers; they ascend and descend upon the head of the Son of Man.

Great attention has been given this fourth Gospel by the critics. For long it has been discerned to have a different method, and perhaps even a diffcrent truth from other Gospels. They are narrations of events, and of brief sayings of Jesus, each saying more or less disconnected from the others. When we undertake to discourse, we take our subject and develop it, as we are able. We argue and illustrate that particular theme. Not so the discourses of Jesus as given in the Synoptic Gospels. He is nowhere represented as speaking consecutively at length. In the sermon on the mountain, as well as in the sermon on the plain, he speaks in short and more or less disconnected sayings.

A mass of bones, each perfect in itself, would undoubtedly have an interest for us, but would not impress us in the same way as if girt in a living frame, bound together, and vitally coöperating. It is in the fourth Gospel that we reach the discoursing Christ, — the Christ who has so much to say and do that books cannot contain the record. Therefore in this fourth Gospel we may conceive ourselves as possessing a few of the discourses of Jesus, or the sayings of Jesus constructed together. It is the book of the talking teacher, rather than the book of aphorisms.

A multitude of opinions have of course arisen as to the authorship of this book, and the time when it was written. It is probable that many of these opinions are erroneous. Of one thing we may be certain, and that is that the uncritical opinions concerning the book which obtained in the past are no longer to be rationally held. As to what new opinion may be adopted, that will probably appear as one studies more deeply into the nature of the book and the time of its composition. But the fourth Gospel is such that, when we are reading it, and feel the inspiration of its sentiment, we care not to ask about its authorship or the time of its composition. Indeed, it is free from time and sense, because it sees the whole mission of Jesus, not more in futurity than in the present, and not more really in either than in the past. "In the beginning was the Word," and the Word is always speaking, has always spoken, will always speak. It is when we study the structure of the Bible and its various parts that we become interested in the authorship of the fourth Gospel; and then it is that we may possibly discover in it a key which will unlock many doors.

Let us go back to our immigrant, who has come to a new land and is disappointed at its failure to correspond with the stories he had heard of it. He sits down and waits. He will see if these rich promises are coming to pass. He provides himself with a rude shelter, and contrives to get a scanty subsistence out of the brook, and from the wild game; but he engages himself, for the most part, in waiting for the spontaneous bounty of the new world to drop into his lap, and it fails to drop. Then some one, having knowledge of his forlorn state, writes him a letter, bidding him note that he has misapprehended the nature of the information he received. The information is substantially true; the bountiful harvests are really there, — fields of corn, widespread and abundant; but they are there to be wrought out into actuality by him. Before he will ever see the promises fulfilled, he must address himself to the necessity of doing his part toward fulfilling them. Above all he must stop waiting and watching for these things which will never come by being waited for. The sooner he stops that, and goes on to develop the bounties of the earth into harvests, the better.

I take it that the fourth Gospel is such a message as that addressed to a mistaken church. It revises their truth, or their apprehension of it. The truths of Jesus which had not theretofore been clearly expressed, or which had been so connected with clouds and futurity as to be neutralized in effect, were now brought into the foreground. Let us note specifically how: —

Said the religion of the time: "The judgment of the world is coming; the Son of Man will soon appear in the clouds, and sit upon the throne of his glory." Said Jesus in the fourth Gospel: "Now is the judgment of this world." Said the religion of the time: "When Jesus comes in the glory of his Father, and all the holy angels with him, then shall we know the truth and see all things." Said Jesus in the fourth Gospel: "Not when the Son of Man shall come in the clouds, outwardly in the sky, but when the Spirit of truth shall come unto you to be in you, then shall you know the truth, and shall be free, and shall know the things to come." Said the religion of the time: "There shall be great power and glory hereafter, and thrones for those who have suffered with the Son of Man." Jesus in the fourth Gospel said: "In my Father's house are many abodes." In the religion of the time were the ceremonies of the new religion, and in the three Gospels were to be read the consecrating words of one august ceremony: "As oft as ye eat this bread and drink this cup, ye do show the Lord's death till he come." In the fourth Gospel Jesus does not appoint a ceremony; he rather says: "Except ye eat the flesh and drink the blood of the Son of Man, ye have no life in you." "He that hath the Son hath the life." These are words of inward meaning, — words not related to the time when the Son of Man shall come, but to the transfer of the mission of Jesus from himself to his disciples, which would come whenever they sufficiently partook of his spirit.

The structure of the fourth Gospel differs from that of the others sufficiently to attract the attention of any one. The fourth Gospel introduces ideas from a Greek philosophy. As in the older time when the Jews came in contact with the Greeks, and were influenced by them, so it happened again. Only the Greek influence, shown by the fourth Gospel, appears to be unlike that exercised upon the writer of Ecclesiastes; but the structure, which is a proper subject of study, may for the present be passed over. The difference between the fourth and the other Gospels is in part this: (that it is not tinctured by second advent pictures and expectations.) More than that, in place of the second advent expectations it puts the mission of the Spirit.) If you search the three evangelists, you will fail to find more than an incidental promise of the Spirit. We see the Spirit, indeed, descending from heaven and abiding upon Jesus. It comes like a dove, or as though it were some outward agency, something to abide upon the Son of Man, rather than to be in him. The Spirit drives Jesus into the wilderness to be tempted of the devil. It influences Jesus to go into the temple, or into Galilee; but there is slight notice of the Spirit in these synoptics. The hope of being filled with the Spirit, and enlightened, and empowered, the three evangelists do not aspire to. In the place of the Spirit, they have the vision of the Son of Man coming in the clouds of heaven, humiliating and punishing his enemies, and rewarding his friends.

(On the other hand, in the fourth Gospel we have distinctively the gospel of the Spirit. In the first and third we find the disciples begging their Master to teach them how to pray, as John had taught his disciples. Perhaps John had taught his disciples one or more forms of prayer. If we are to credit the evangelists, John did not belong to the new kingdom, but to the old Jewish dispensation; and he acted in accord with the old order of things. Jesus taught the disciples how to pray. It was not of his own motion that he taught them, but by their persuasion. He taught them to pray to the Father and to pray for the coming of the kingdom. In John is introduced a different teaching. This teaching was not addressed to the disciples, being perhaps too large and spiritual for them; but it was addressed to a woman, half or more heathen, — one devoted to the worship of Jehovah in Mount Gerizim, and after the manner of the Samaritans. To this learner, Jesus said that God does not desire the Jerusalem worship, nor the Gerizim worship, but the worship in the spirit. "Neither in this mountain, nor yet at Jerusalem, shall they worship the Father." "The hour is coming and now is." All Jewish attention was fixed upon the coming hour, but Jesus adjourns nothing. If the hour is coming when spiritual worship is in order, it is in order now.

So in many ways the fourth becomes the Gospel of the present tense. It calls attention from the bodily form and presence of Jesus, and concentrates it upon his spirit. It dissolves the clouds upon which religious imagination had held the Son of Man was soon coming; there had been those who expected, with Paul, in his earlier days, to be taken out of the world, to meet the Lord in the air, and so to be ever with the Lord; but in this fourth Gospel Jesus is made to say, "I pray not that thou shouldest take them out of the world, but that thou shouldest keep them from the evil."

It was understood by the early Christians that on one or two occasions Jesus had taken a few little loaves of bread, and had magnified them into a simple banquet for a multitude. This was made much of as a sign of great power, and power, too, of the kind most attractive to men. In the fourth Gospel this miracle is accepted, because upon it can be based the doctrine of the Spirit, and the discourse of the bread of life is given. The Christians had been fond of reading Daniel, and his visions of the Son of Man coming on clouds of heaven, and coming to the Ancient of days. In the fourth Gospel their attention is directed to another kind of prophet. Ezekiel has his dreams as well as Daniel; and in his dreams the writer of the fourth Gospel sees more than in the ambitious spectacles of Daniel. The prophet is brought to the door of the temple, and he beholds a spring of water issuing from the threshold. This little spring in the temple flows outward, deepening and enlarging as it flows. It becomes a river, and it proves to be a river of life to every region into which it finds its way. One can conjecture that the prophet felt so about Israel; that from its religion and its teaching, or its spirit, would flow forth in due time influences which would give life to the world. Now it is precisely this kind of prophecy which is in accord with the man who wrote the fourth Gospel. He does not think about the domination of the Son of Man by reason of his glorious advent upon the clouds, when every eye shall see him, and all the tribes of the earth shall mourn. (He does think about the diffusion of the influence and Spirit of Jesus throughout the world.)

In the fourth Gospel, we see Jesus standing in the temple on the last and greatest day of a national feast, and lifting his voice to say: "If any man thirst, let him come unto me and drink. He that believeth on me, as the scripture hath said, out of his belly shall flow rivers of living water." (But this spake he of the Spirit, which they that believe on him should receive.) The common feeling of the people had been that Jesus would rule, just as other rulers did, by force, only that his force should prove irresistible, but the idea of the writer of the fourth Gospel was that Jesus should rule, not by force, but by influence. Therefore the great discourses recorded in the fourth Gospel are discourses of the Spirit. (The kingdom shall come by the Spirit. The earth shall become the abode of righteousness by the Spirit, or by the influence of Jesus.) So will be realized the vision of the prophet who saw the spring bubble up at the threshold of the temple, and flow out in a widening river to bless and heal, and give life to the world.)

In the Epistle to the Hebrews the courage and patience of the Christians were stimulated by such words as these: "Cast not away therefore your boldness, which hath great recompense of reward. For ye have need of patience, that, having done the will of God, ye may receive the promise. For yet a very little while, he that cometh shall come, and shall not tarry." That expresses the feeling which it was the object of the fourth Gospel to counteract. Is it not specifically counteracted in such words as these, found in the fourth Gospel, as coming from the lips of Jesus, "A little while, and ye behold me no more; and again a little while, and ye shall see me"? All the time Jesus is talking about the Spirit. It is the Spirit which is to complete his work. It is the Spirit which is to be born into the world, by being transferred from him to them. They will be full of rejoicing because of that Spirit, and not because they expect to see the Son of Man coming on the clouds.

The critics tell us that they are dubious about this fourth Gospel, dubious about its history, — it differs so greatly from the simple tales of the other Gospels. There is such an air of elaboration about it, that they do not credit it. Very well, but the fourth evangelist, whoever he may have been, is trying, as best he can, to reveal the spirit of the character and mission of Jesus. He will take historical incidents, as they have recorded themselves in the Christian traditions, and make them serve his purpose, of exposing the heart of Jesus. He does not care for geography, as is evident, and he does not care to locate any incident in its proper historical setting; he will open the heart of the matter. So he tells us that Jesus says, "He that believeth on me believeth not on me, but on the one sending me;" that is, the Spirit.

The age was not ready for the work of Jesus, and weary ages have passed since the days of the Son of Man on earth. The adjournment of all things until the Son of Man should come on the clouds has had its fatal effect for a long time. Perhaps the world will soon be more ready for the gospel of the Spirit, the gospel of the present tense. But before any of us will be ready, we will have to discredit those visions which filled the imagination of the first Christians. When once we have boldness enough to credit the gospel of the Spirit, we shall have boldness enough to discredit the sayings of the writers of the epistles and of the three Gospels about the coming of Jesus, with all the holy angels, to judge the world. We shall perchance be ready to have our judgment of the world and its ways as we go along. Perhaps then there will be some real belief in the Spirit of Jesus, as saving the world.

XXIII.

AUTHORSHIP OF THE FOURTH GOSPEL.

STUDENTS have long recognized this difference between the fourth and the other Gospels of the New Testament: that while in the former are given the discourses delivered in public, the parables and such teachings as those contained in the sermon on the mountain, in the latter the sayings of Jesus to his disciples, or on private occasions, are treasured up. It is related in the Gospels that Jesus uttered his parables on the shore of the lake to the crowds there congregated, and that his disciples afterward asked an explanation of these somewhat mysterious teachings. That was accorded them: "To you it is given to know the mysteries of the kingdom of heaven, but to them it is not given."

There would seem to be a peculiar fitness in John's giving us the picture of his Master's inner life. He was the beloved disciple. He came nearest his Master's heart. Christian art has presented to us this young man with the angelic countenance; a gentle, winning man, just emerging from youth to manhood. While it is true that Christian art has doubtless erred in so depicting John (one of the sons of thunder, Jesus called him), nevertheless no figure in the apostolical college proves so attractive to all people as that of John. While Peter is aggressive, and takes the place of command in emergency, and while Paul, afterward connected with the apostles, is incomparably more able to do the necessary work than any other, perhaps than all others combined, we find something in John we do not find in these others. Peter may represent the truth and period of law, Paul of faith, but John is representative of a still future period of love.

The ideal John is perhaps widely different from the real. We fail to find the ideal man in the three Gospels. The real John is intense in his devotion to his Master; but equally intense in his anger against anything and anybody found in the opposition. He is not even tolerant of that kind of friendship which does not drive a man into personal following of Jesus. "Master," he says, "we saw one casting out demons in thy name, and we forbade him because he followeth not with us." He will make no concessions, and despises neutrality. If a man does not belong to Christ, he must belong to the enemy. There is no middle ground of suspended opinion. An enthusiastic son of thunder is he, — not the mild and benignant man it seems that he became late in life. There is a tradition that he wished to call down fire from heaven upon certain Samaritans who were not hospitable to Jesus. He was an ardent hater, — a man who would see his enemies burn in fire.

In the Apocalypse the imagination of the writer runs riot in scenes of fire, famine, blood, and earthquake. That book is not the production of a mild and gentle spirit; it has not in it the sovereign feeling of Jesus: "Forgive your enemies." Experience shows, however, that good men, vehement in their goodness, become milder as they grow older. Clement of Alexandria tells us how John, grown old, at Ephesus took a special and loving interest in the younger members of his flock. He was deeply solicitous for their faithfulness and spiritual welfare. Even if they went astray, he did not abandon them, nor excommunicate them. One of his young men fell away from the good ways of Christ, and became a bandit. He rose to be chief of a robber band. (John did not abandon him to his evil fate, but succeeded in winning him back to truth and righteousness.) After the apostle has become very old, and incapable of work, when he can no longer teach, his spirit is strong within him, and it is a spirit of long-suffering love. He is able to do no more than sum up the religion of Christ in a few words, which he repeats over and over: "Little children, love one another." Hate has been quenched in his breast, and all the simple philosophy of his soul is that of love. One can hope that the ghastly and grim images which thronged upon his middle life, when he was on the island, and when tidings came to him from Judea, had altogether faded from him.

We form our judgments of men by their characteristic sayings, partly. (To all men is attached an individuality which distinguishes each from all others.) While there are strong resemblances, there are distinct points of difference. We know the faces of our friends, and their gait, and numerous other characteristics. While men change from ruddy youth to pale and gray age, we still recognize them by those things in them which are most characteristic. We learn to recognize men also by their mental characteristics. If the last poem of Lord Tennyson were attributed, by way of jest, and in all the press, to such a man, for example, as Mr. Herbert Spencer, those acquainted with these writers would at a glance discover the jest. The thought and the style of each are as peculiar to himself as his countenance.

If any person with an appreciation of the meaning and use of words were to carefully read the Apocalypse, and master its contents, so far as they can be mastered, and then if he were to read with equal care the fourth Gospel, neither scripture having any author's name connected with it, he would say with positive assurance that the two were not written by the same hand. Of course he might be mistaken, but following the ordinary common-sense method of discernment, he would have no resource but to declare the writings produced by different men. (The critics of fifty or more years ago were so impressed with this common-sense conclusion that they, or some of them, came to another conclusion, which is not so obvious. They concluded that the fourth Gospel was a forgery, perpetrated by some man, possibly of the third century, who gave it out as the work of the Apostle John; and in its ignorance the church accepted it as genuine, and gave it the sanction of a place in the sacred canon.)

(That is the way it is with many.) If their notions in regard to anything are shattered, they seem to renounce having any notions whatever upon that subject. They declare the thing itself to be a falsehood, or a deceit. If John did not write the fourth Gospel, it is assumed by the impatient thinker, it is a fraud and a delusion. If Matthew did not write the first Gospel, that is also a falsity. Some high authorities tell us that if Moses did not write the Pentateuch, then it is all an untruth. This is the feebleness of an impatient and hasty learning. This is resting everything on some unintelligent assumption. It is parallel with supposing that if but one error is detected in the Bible, anywhere, — an error which is unexplainable, — then the whole Bible goes to pieces, and is of no value.

If one is able to see the force of the oft-asserted statement of John in the Apocalypse, that the things there predicted are to take place at once, and sees thereby that the writer was mistaken, he is solemnly assured that he is destroying the Bible. (Fifty years ago there were people still in existence, and possibly a few may survive to this day, who felt that if the world was not constructed out of nothing, in a week's time, then the whole fabric of revelation was undermined. Yet the world, at least, is here, and we stand upon it, undismayed at all discoveries in regard to its creation. It witnesses to itself with sufficient power to command our assent. (Is it not so with truth?) However it came to be spoken, by whatsoever mouth, or written down by whatsoever pen, is it not its own most convincing witness? It must be to such as are capable of understanding and believing a truth.

Were the fourth Gospel not written by John, it is a foolish alternative to pronounce it a forgery. In respect to the Epistle to the Hebrews, which in our Bibles is called the Epistle of Paul, a critical opinion is held by many devout scholars that it is not Paul's epistle; but that opinion does in no wise invalidate the writing. (It stands for what it is worth.)

The book of Ecclesiastes, in the Old Testament, is largely supposed to have Solomon for its author; but, as we have seen, there are very strong reasons for believing that Solomon never saw it nor heard of it. There are marks in it which identify it with a later age. There are marks in the fourth Gospel which make it all but impossible for John to have been the writer of it. Yet that it is "according to John," or represents the essential doctrine which was left over in John after the failure of his wild visions of plagues and judgments and all the like, is very credible.

Every one is entitled to his hypothesis. The hypothesis of forgery, or a deceit practiced upon the early church may be offset by another more reasonable. We may concede that such a man as the Apostle John would not only teach the churches of Asia by personal ministrations, but that he would draw around him a few disciples, to whom he would be able to open his mind in the fullest manner. We are informed by tradition that he had disciples, peculiarly attached to his person, in his later days, — Polycarp, Papias, Ignatius, and probably others. Among the number we are at liberty to suppose the presence of some man of Greek descent, possibly educated in the schools of Alexandria, more or less an adept in the doctrine of the Logos. In the earlier half of the first century of our era, a philosopher and author had flourished at Alexandria, Philo by name, a man who achieved a remarkable celebrity. This Alexandrian Jew is said to have had a philosophy compounded of Platonism, Stoicism, and Pythonism, taken from the Greeks, and of Emanationism, borrowed from the East, all of which he annexed to the doctrine of the Old Testament. He was the mediator between monotheism and polytheism. The central point of his philosophy is the doctrine of the Logos, or the Word.

(When we open the fourth Gospel, at its threshold we confront the Logos doctrine) It is not necessary to suppose that the idea of Philo is transmitted, complete, to the author of the fourth Gospel. Indeed, it is difficult to see how so compound a system could well be entertained by any one except the compounder. At all events, its central truth appears in the last Gospel. It is not impossible that in his maturer years the mind of John may have imbibed the sublime views of the Alexandrian, in place of the fantastic visions of earlier manhood. It would seem impossible, however, that the Jew should have completely lost the Jewish method, and have been born into a method of expression foreign to him and his race. There is nothing strange in supposing that a disciple of John, entering most heartily and intelligently into the real heart of the man and his gospel, attaining that profound and at that time difficult doctrine of the Spirit which we see in the fourth Gospel, undertook to set forth the real meaning of Jesus, and his mission, "according to John."

Tradition has it that John spent his declining years at Ephesus; and that his friends and followers pressed him to give his recollections of the sayings of Jesus. Those which were widely current were different from those which John rehearsed in his maturity. The other evangelists had neglected these most weighty things, so that there was danger, as it seemed to the elders at Ephesus, that these most important sayings of Jesus would be lost to the world. To that effect tradition speaks.

We may not be able to rely on the tradition, but it accords with our hypothesis, which I hope is a reasonable one. We strain no point in thinking that the elders of the Ephesian church must have felt the superiority of these sayings of Jesus over those which were everywhere repeated. The religion of Jesus, as it was apprehended by the people generally, was a kind of body religion. An extreme reverence for the person of Jesus, coupled with the expectation of seeing him come to set up his empire in the world, would naturally distract attention from his real teachings, and go far to neutralize them. It is evident from the tenor of the fourth Gospel that this feeling on the part of the followers of John at Ephesus went to the extent of proposing a kind of antidote for the prevailing religion. It is quite possible that John, like other men who feel their last days on earth approaching, did, as opportunity served, write, in detached portions, notes of particular discourses of Jesus. That he should remember the exact words of these sayings is in the last degree improbable. That he should rather give in his own Hebrew method, in detached parts, these recollections is more probable. That he should propose to some fittest of his followers the work of arrangement is according to the mode common among his people. The work of the editor had been of the utmost importance in the history and religion of the Jews. In the fourth Gospel we seem to have the foremost specimen of editorship in the Bible, or perhaps in all literature. This is not a thing to be affirmed with the confidence one would have in affirming the correctness of an addition or a multiplication in arithmetic, carefully revised. It is the kind of hypothesis which we are accustomed to make to see if we can account for a phenomenon. Now, when we come to the end of the fourth Gospel we find a kind of a postscript. This postscript is like the indorsement of a committee: "This is the disciple which beareth witness of these things, and wrote these things, and we (the committee) know that this witness is true." An author would not speak in that way about himself, of course.

The work of reducing those sayings of Jesus which John remembered, and in which his faith grew great in his later days, was committed to others. These others would in turn commit the chief labor of arrangement, and of composition, to that one of their number best fitted by education, and by sympathy with the subject, to do the work. In the main, the critics tell us, the work is by one hand. This editor, however, does not content himself with stringing together, as may happen, the fragmentary writings of John, — he proposes to be an editor who edits. The conversations of the aged apostle he may find of more importance than the fragments of his writing; moreover, he is a man possessed of his own personal feelings and philosophy. He has his idea of Jesus, and he has his philosophy, learned of Philo Judæus. In place of that genealogy of Jesus, which may very well have seemed to him, with his exalted conception of the mission of the Son of God, to be flat and childish, he puts forth the sublime postulate of the Logos. Jesus, to be sure, was born and took his beginning in the world as others of the children of men did. But what about the Spirit of which John, in his last days, had so much to say? Had that a beginning? Ah! that was in the beginning with God. That was God. It was that which had become flesh, in Jesus, and manifested God to men. So his prologue, almost identical with the doctrine of Philo, does not necessarily represent John, for it came not from Jesus but from Philo; and it is the key of the fourth Gospel. In this Gospel we are not interested in the person of Jesus so much as in the Spirit which guided him. It is the spirit, not the flesh, which profiteth.

Perhaps a question will arise as to the profound

change which transpired in John. Certainly it was a most profound change which happened to him. The belligerent apostle; the seer of Patmos, driven almost wild with grief at the calamities of his nation, attempting to play over again the part of the Maccabean prophet, and saturated with the popular notion about the return of Jesus, in the clouds — very quickly; how could he become the benignant father of the Ephesian church, and the advocate of the Spirit? It is such a change in him, under the circumstances, as we might reasonably expect. Not a change in method of writing so that he could possibly write the fourth Gospel, but a change from the apostle of the flaming advent to the apostle of the Spirit. Jesus did not come; the holy angels did not fly in the sky; and while plagues devastated the earth in some portions, the visions of the Apocalypse were in no degree realized. Would not this failure to a man who loved and believed in Jesus, in spite of everything, prompt him to seek for a better interpretation of Jesus? Would not this seeking lead to a finding? Would not those sayings of Jesus, which had made so little impression, even upon himself, now be brought more vividly to his mind? The man who has been most thoroughly in the glamour of the second advent is the one of all others to learn a profound distrust of it; that is, provided he is a seeker for truth, and not the mere advocate of a scheme. It is the enthusiastic and devoted man who goes to an extreme, as John did; and when he finds his error, he is likely to go as far away from it as possible. (He who has found no redemption of the world by means of outward displays, but only in a renunciation of our own interior evil, will cheapen all outwardness, and declare nothing of worth, except the spirit.)

It is impossible even to hint at the many opinions of this fourth Gospel which have been held by wise men. They have been as diverse as possible. One cannot take the time to examine the reasons why a particular scholar should deem the prologue of the Gospel as characteristically the work of the Apostle John, while others see in it exactly the opposite. It will suffice for our purpose to see simply the fact that this fourth Gospel is peculiarly the Gospel of the Spirit. It is a distinct modification of the Gospels of the body, as we may call them, which precede it. It introduces, as of the highest import, and makes large, that which is small in the preceding evangelists. New incidents come in, but their arrangement is of secondary importance. The author does not care for them except for the purpose of building his structure of "sayings." Not only is it true that the incidents are dealt with loosely, but they are dealt with inaccurately. As Matthew Arnold has pointed out, the writer speaks as if he did not know the relative position of the cities of Judea. He places Bethany beyond the Jordan. He talks of the "manner of the Jews." He says that such an one was high priest that year, as if that office were annual, which it was not at that time. He is manifestly foreign to the drapery of his subject; but then he does not care for the drapery. He cares for the spirit of the subject. Thus he neglects the things the other writers have taken the most pains with; and in particular he dismisses that subject which was uppermost in their minds, — the second advent. The one great subject they had neglected, namely, the subject of the Spirit of truth, he magnifies.

Here is the creation; and here also, as part of it, is

the human mind to contemplate it. What shall we think about this creation? Is or is there not a Creator? Does the Creator take any means of manifesting himself? Has he anything to say to us? Is there any way by which we can discover his location, or in any wise approach him or get speech with him? These are questions which not only the philosopher, but the plain thinker would wish to ask. The Jew, such an one as John the apostle, would have his answer to these questions, but they would not be the answers of the prologue of the fourth Gospel. He would say that there is a Creator of this world, and of the stars of heaven; that this Creator does manifest himself to men through prophets and wise men; that he has caused his will to be written, and thus has he spoken. Here are the sacred oracles containing words of God. The writer of the fourth Gospel, however, goes far beyond any such concept of things. To him all creation, and every part of it, and from the very beginning, is speech of the Creator. The Creator speaks by creation.

To him God is not a being sunk in slumber, as an Oriental philosophy declares; nor is God a creator who creates from a distance. The sublime old thought, "Day unto day uttereth speech, and night unto night showeth knowledge," commands his assent. A day, the sky, the mountains, the sea, and all things are divine expressions. More than that: the Word which has always been with God and is God becomes the rocks of the world, the waters of the oceans, the stars of the sky, and in due process becomes flesh, and dwells among us, full of grace and truth. Nothing is made without that Word. (Jesus certainly did not build the worlds, but that manifesting Spirit, which became flesh in him, has always been uttering God. This is the fundamental idea of the fourth Gospel.

Herder, one of the founders of modern German literature, says that the fourth Gospel "is the echo of the earlier Gospels, in a higher key."[1] They are keyed to flesh and sense, in some measure. They bind us to incredibilities, and unless we are cautious, make us superstitious. In them an unnatural order is made to play a ruling part. In the fourth Gospel the natural order is restored, and takes its place as divine. It is true we have still the miracles, some of them not recorded in the synoptics, but they are always subordinate. We must not expect a writer of those times to be free from the notion of miracles; but the writer of the fourth Gospel does not care for the miracle (the story of which has floated down to him), so much as for the lesson and spirit of every incident he uses. It is this fourth Gospel which above all other books really preserves for us the religion of Jesus. It delivers us a message which, in our doubting times of religious transition, gives rest and peace to our souls.

[1] Pfleiderer, *Development of Theology.*

XXIV.

CONFLICT AND HARMONY.

An age of comparative freedom, or of awakened thought, is also an age of great diversity of opinion. If any powerful impulse is at any time given to thinking, an inevitable variety shows itself. If people are left in ignorance, only as they are kept in ignorance is there unity of opinion. When the thinking of a community is let out to some one person, there is no difference of opinion. Indeed, it may almost be said there is no opinion.

The work of Jesus was moral and religious in the truest sense; and yet by it a great impetus was given to thinking, especially to those of the most active minds. The age which begins to think in a new way is an age of stir, and is likely to be an age of revolution. Such an age was that of the beginning of the Christian era.

Among the disciples of Jesus were a few men of strong intellectual force. It would of course be too much to say of any of the apostles that they were men of an independent way of thinking. On the contrary, they were men whose capacity for thinking had not been developed. The fisherman, the tax-collector, and the peasants were all involved in the settled modes of thought, or of so-called thought, of their time and place; there was cast into their minds new seed sown by a divine thinker. Although this new element was not immediately productive of result, in process of time it became a powerful force in the world.

Just what the relation of Paul of Tarsus was to the earlier disciples and apostles of Jesus it is very difficult to determine. Certainly we do not err in recognizing him as different from the other apostles, not only in temperament and character, but in a marked degree in education and in native force of mind. They were more like sheep, adapted to follow a shepherd; he more like a shepherd, fitted to lead the sheep; and it is significant that he worked out his problem of the religion of Jesus by himself. He did not refer his difficulties to them for solution. He says that he did not confer with flesh and blood. He had already received a training in the use of his mental powers, which enabled him to be independent of human sources.

Were we to attempt a chronological arrangement of the experience of the apostle to the Gentiles, it would perhaps be something like this: being on the road to Damascus, in the enterprise of persecuting the new religion, he is stricken with a sudden blow, is shocked out of his old pursuits, becomes a convert to Jesus, and goes on to Damascus. From Damascus he does not go back to Jerusalem to consult with the leaders of the Christian community there, but retires into Arabia. What he did in Arabia is a matter of no public concern; the common inference is that he retired into solitude, to ponder the subject in its depths. Then, after three years, he returns to Jerusalem, and there abides with Peter for fifteen days. He sees none of the other disciples except James, but he has nothing to do with the churches of the region. (He grasps the idea of a world-wide religion. He proposes to cut loose from the trammels of Judaism, and carry his message to the nations.

This manifests the breadth of his mind, and his comprehension of the religion of Jesus. If Jesus did say, as he is reported to have said, that he was not sent save unto the lost sheep of the house of Israel, Paul did not hear of it, or, having heard, did not believe it. His mind and heart are set on more comprehensive things: he will leave Israel and go to the Gentiles. Accordingly he proceeds to Upper Syria and Cilicia, where he prosecutes his work on the new plan.

Meanwhile Peter has broadened. He is in a limited way thrown into contact with Gentiles, and reluctantly recognizes them as subject to the mercy and promise of God, but he feels that the case demands utmost caution. Peter is brave, but he will not endanger anything by haste. He has neither the courage nor the greatness of mind to enable him to abandon Judaism. It is perhaps better that he has not. In fact, as to the essential truth of it, Paul himself never did break with Judaism, but only with its formal observances, its rites of consecration and sacrifice. Judaism is the root out of which naturally grows the plant of the religion of Jesus; but this root had produced chaff as well as wheat. Jesus winnowed the grain out of the chaff; so in a degree did Paul, and so in a lesser degree did Peter.

Differences of opinion arose between Paul and the other apostles. It was natural that they should look upon him with suspicion. His " call " to be an apostle was not one they would be likely to recognize. Jesus had not called him as he had called them; it was the Spirit of Jesus which had called him. He felt the call in his soul; he had no outward call. Finally, however, the chief apostles, James, Peter, and John, "reputed to be pillars" of the new church, gave Paul and his colaborer, Barnabas, the "right hand of fellowship," and they departed on their way rejoicing. Yet there was a difference which drove the apostles asunder. Peter, being politic, did something at Antioch which roused the indignation of Paul. Peter found friends at Antioch, and was on pleasant and familiar terms with them, eating at their tables. When friends of James, the strict constructionist, came from Jerusalem, Peter drew away from his Gentile friends, and declined to eat at their tables. He conducted himself as a Jew, not because of conscience, but because of policy. Such action failed to command the respect of Paul, but roused his indignation, and he withstood Peter, chief of the apostles, to his face. Peter was a "pillar of the church," but Paul did not care for that. It was more important for even a pillar of the church to be sincere in his conduct than for him to be successful, and avoid scandal. Therefore Paul asked Peter a question: "Why do you seek to make the Gentiles conform to Jewish usage?" He who believes in Jesus Christ is free from that usage. In this is indicated the beginning of a separation into two great parties of the Christian church: Paul, with his doctrine of freedom, leading in one direction; James and others with their doctrine of the "works of the law," — the ceremonies, circumcision, and the rest, — leading in another direction.

Paul and Barnabas, however, being of one mind for the time, went on their Gentile mission. Yet even they were not free from differences of opinion, and

Luke tells us, in his simple-minded way, that on one occasion they parted, after having a sharp contention. Such were the divisions and subdivisions among these early promoters of the gospel of Jesus. It is well for any one who would know the Bible not to overlook its difficulties; not to evade the facts, but to try to understand them. If, in our endeavor to understand them, we suffer the distress of seeing the unity of the Spirit in the bond of peace broken, nevertheless even that gives us its valuable lesson.

From such men as John and James, not to say Peter, take away the stimulating presence and daily contact of Jesus, and there may easily come a relapse from the truth of his teaching. Paul could go alone, without the consent or countenance of anybody, but they were not of such strong stuff. And there resulted something of mutual distrust. This distrust speaks for the intellectual activity of the time. It tells us that while good men could not think alike, they could at least think to some purpose. The progressive man was obstructed by the conservative men. Hints of this we get in the epistles of Paul, and elsewhere. It is well known that the Hebrew Christians, especially those of Jerusalem and Judea, were under a strong conservative influence. They demanded of heathens that they should become Jews in order to be Christians; they should submit to the rite of circumcision. It came to be noised abroad that Paul made no such terms with heathens; the leaders of the church at Jerusalem sent out some of their number to investigate that matter. Paul boldly and somewhat harshly calls these brethren spies. They were trying to spy out this liberty of which Paul was an apostle. He would not yield to them, no, not for an hour.

He would go his way,—they should go theirs. Moreover, Paul manifestly rejects all authority of the leading men at Jerusalem, no matter what their reputation or high place may be. John and James and Cephas are to him by no means infallible men. They are not only liable to be mistaken, but he points out their error. (Note, then, that to these founders of the religion of Jesus, after the departure of Jesus, there is no notion of the infallibility of an apostle.) Paul does not dream that they are infallible, and they certainly do not dream that he is; yet they all had to do, directly or indirectly, with the making of some portion of the contents of the Bible.) The Reformation theory of the infallibility of the Scriptures finds a most scanty proof in the pages of the Bible itself, but there is much to disprove it. The fact that the apostles made attacks upon each other furnishes a startling evidence of the fallibility of all concerned.

Paul claimed to be an apostle of Jesus: the claim was disputed. At one time he seems to maintain that his accusers are over-apostolic, taking too much upon themselves, etc. He reaches the summit of severity when he talks of these conservatives, probably numbering among them some of the Jerusalem apostles; but they are equally severe in their judgment of him and his work. It was natural for them, because they cared so much for some formulas and usages, that they should be harsh to a man who had outgrown their formulas. (In fact, there is nothing in the whole history of the founding of the church which does not testify to its naturalness by showing how ambitions and notions ruled then, very much as they have ruled since.

Paul propounds the doctrine of justification by faith.

He lays it down in the form of an elaborate argument, and illustrates it historically: Abraham was justified not by works, but by faith. Paul is ready to dispense with all rites, and to say that circumcision, which is outward in the flesh, is of no value. Not works but faith is Paul's great dogma. This was not accepted by the Jerusalem party; it awakened their strong dissent. Of this dissent the Epistle of James apprises us. "Was not Abraham justified by faith?" asks Paul. The Epistle of James answers, "What doth it profit, my brethren, if a man say he hath faith, but have not works?" Can faith save him? "Was not Abraham our father justified by works in that he offered up Isaac his son upon the altar?" Now it may be supposed that James means by "works" those deeds of righteousness which have nothing to do with ceremonial performances; but he points here to a work of sacrifice which belongs to the ceremonial order. Abraham offers his son upon the altar. He is justified by that act, his faith led him to it; and faith without works (such works) is dead. Here, then, is James, the righteous man (probably not the apostle of that name), who distinctly opposes Paul in a letter to the whole of Israel. Paul maintains that Abraham was justified by faith, apart from works, and James contends that Abraham was justified by works. Here is an issue, and it was because of this issue between Paul and James that the great reformer Luther wished to cast aside the Epistle of James. He saw the real superiority of the doctrine of Paul; he had no patience with the conservatism of James. Truly, if the Bible were to be regarded infallible, the Epistle of James and other such material should have been kept out of it. But the

Epistle of James, while it has its defects, has its great value. Moreover, the apostle to the Gentiles is not without his defects; he does not claim to be without them, but confesses them.

In that portion of the New Testament known as the Second Epistle of Peter, certain of Paul's writings are characterized as hard to understand and liable to divert the unstable from the truth. This may, or may not, represent the feeling of the Apostle Peter. John may well have reference to Paul, in his messages to the seven churches of Asia. He speaks to the Ephesians of persons who had called themselves apostles. He severely animadverts upon the eating of meat offered to idols, which Paul had taught was entirely harmless in itself. He denounces God's fiery judgments upon those who are misled by such un-Jewish teachings.

These, and more instances which might be adduced, sufficiently show the diversity of opinion, rising to the point of violent denunciation, which obtained among the first apostles. These are not things to be prudently hidden, or explained away, but to be considered in all their bearings. With such facts staring us in the face, we must seek a better idea than the Reformation has furnished of the real nature of the Bible. Men's opinions are not infallible. Inspired men are subject to the same infirmities which other men have. They may misjudge each other; may fail, as the apostles did fail, to heartily coöperate in their work.

If the matter were left there, — and many critics do leave it there, seeing only the evidences of frailty and blunder in these men of the Bible, — much would be lost. There seems to me to be a grand proof of the divinity of the Bible, its divine purpose and mission, in connection with these very things. When men meet on friendly terms and agree to coöperate in any great work, and for the most part find themselves in sympathy and accord, they will subordinate many individual preferences, and perhaps some individual convictions, to the "cause" in which they are engaged. A distinction of one of the great Christian churches of the world lies in its unity. It is catholic, and in a way comprehensive, and individual notions are subordinate to the interest of the organizations. Perhaps men of more than ordinary intelligence can be permitted to entertain their personal opinions on many or most subjects, but it would be harmful to permit a public assertion of them. Such methods, however, always suppress truth. Unity is desirable in the last degree. That we should all be one family, and have one religion, and one faith, and one spirit, is certainly a consummation to be devoutly hoped for; but such unity will not come by suppression: it will come by free expression of differences.

If, now, we regard the fourth Gospel as "according to John," representing his wisest and best days, we may perhaps be startled by the fact that the highest of John and the highest of Paul are one thing. These two who may have been opposed to each other, teaching doctrines the one against the other, yet arrive at the point where they see chiefly one truth, and in this they are united. It may be that John had warned the churches of Asia against Paul, as one of those who called themselves apostles, and were not. The identification of Paul with the object of John's attack seems sufficiently clear if we remember that Paul had called the eating of meat offered in sacrifice to idols a harmless thing. John writes to the church at Pergamum, as well as the church at Thyatira, in stern condemnation of such teachings. He mentions no names; it is not his habit to do that. John is narrow, and Paul is broader.

The narrow man and the broad man tell us at last the same story, and it is the story of the Spirit. Paul says that whensoever Moses is read, a veil lieth upon the heart of the hearer. He cannot see the real meaning of Moses. Why? Because he is bound by the letter or the writing of Moses; but, adds the apostle to the Gentiles, whensoever the man shall turn to the Lord, the veil is taken away. Very well, who is the Lord? Let us see if we can gain the hint which Paul gives. We can easily see how much of the Mosaic Scripture was concerning things which have no particular relation to a man's moral conduct or his spiritual life. Here, for example, is the book of Leviticus, which belongs to the books of Moses. Minute instructions in regard to things of no importance are there given, — ritual, the cult, the performance of ceremonies; altars, priests, robes, things outward, and tending to outwardness. When Moses was read, these things were read.

Now the real spirit of Moses is not found in these regulations, but in truths which belong to our inner life, our relations with God and each other. However, every Sabbath day Moses was read in the synagogues, and a veil rested upon the heart of the hearer. Now Paul declared that when the hearer turned to the Lord, the veil would vanish. Well, were not the Jews always turning to the Lord? Was not that their distinction? Alas! no; for, as Paul goes on to say, the Lord he is talking about is the Spirit. That which is properly of authority in Moses is the spirit of his teaching, not the letter of it; and as for Moses, and all teachers, the commanding fact is not that they wrote this or that, but that there was truth in what they said. The Lord of all is not a visible God, having a man's name, but the Spirit; and where the Spirit is, there is liberty. More than that: " We all, with unveiled face, beholding as in a mirror the glory of the Lord, are transformed into the same image from glory to glory, as from the Spirit, which is the Lord."

All this in Paul corresponds with John in his maturer years. It agrees with that saying of Jesus which the other evangelists failed to note : "It is expedient for you that I go away, for if I go not away the Spirit will not come;" it corresponds with the axiomatic teachings of Jesus which all the evangelists give us. The outward is principal, it may be, in the three evangelists, but the inward is there as well. For when Jesus, in the synoptics, tells the Jews to make clean the inside of the cup and platter, and that those who seek for the Holy Spirit shall receive the Holy Spirit; when he tells of the Good Samaritan, and speaks of fasting and the Sabbath, the strain is the same as that of Paul and the fourth Gospel. The things which come from the unclean heart, they are the things which defile, but eating with unwashed hands is nothing; the kingdom of heaven is within you; judge not according to the appearance, but judge righteous judgment, — all these words of Jesus, given in the synoptics, are exactly in line of the maturer judgment of Paul and John; and these are the very things which are in line with the better judgment of everybody; they prove themselves.

We are accustomed to the notion that the Jews somehow made a great mistake in their religion.

They were all astray; the proof is that they rejected Jesus. How were they astray? If we say that they were unfaithful to their trust and did not live in accordance with their religion, we shall do them an injustice. For Paul, who seems to be an unprejudiced witness, bears testimony that they were religious, according to their method, and very zealous; but he finds fault with their method. "They went about to establish their righteousness, which was of the law." The law, as it had come down to them, was largely a commandment about performances. They tried unsuccessfully to establish a righteousness on that basis, and, in the nature of the case, that is impossible. The real mistake of the Jews is the mistake of the Christians as well. It shows itself in such a passage as that in Matthew, about the Son of Man sitting upon the throne of his glory, and gathering the nations to judgment. It shows itself in the promise to the twelve that they should sit on thrones of judgment. As if the world could be made better by having the Son of Man seated on a throne; or as if the twelve tribes could be made better by having the apostles on thrones. Against all this outward business, be it what it might, it was the work of Jesus to protest. It is in his protest against these things, as well as in his positive teachings of the blessedness of the good life and the good heart, that Jesus is identified. The spirit is all. Out of the evil heart proceed the miseries and ills of the world. Out of the heart which changes from evil to good proceed the blessings of the world. It is in this good heart, this repentant heart, this life of inward truth and rectitude, that God, who is a Spirit, works the works of creation.

Some one wrote the Epistle to the Hebrews. In

that there is a mass of reference to priesthoods and sacrifices, and all the like. It was adapted to the Hebrew, for whom it was intended ; but for us it is dross. Mixed with the dross glitters the gold of truth. There was an outward law engraved on stone tablets; that passes away. With its departure comes a new covenant, the covenant of the inward law, which is engraved on our inward life. The fastings and mortifications, the sacrifices and altars, belong to a period which ought to pass away. To do the outward things of worship belongs to the old childish order. To be inwardly bent upon righteousness is to belong to the new order; and that is the real order.[1]

Thus it is the spirit, or inward life of man, with which the Spirit of God has to do. To that agree all the prophets and apostles. So long as the body, letter, formula, or other outward thing fills the field of faith, the Spirit is excluded. Wherefore, beneath all the superficial show of disorder and disagreement in the evangelists and apostles, their disputes about meat offered to idols and circumcision, and their ambitions concerning places in the coming kingdom, there is a unity; and in that unity we may discover the gold of their real subject-matter.

---

[1] That the men of faith who lived under the old order really belonged to the new is attested by the words of Jesus : "Your father Abraham rejoiced to see my day," etc.

XXV.

THE SOCIOLOGICAL RELIGION OF JAMES.

What is religion? A host of answers may be offered, but all may resolve into two: both advocate and adversary may answer that religion is a doing of something by which God, or the Superior Power, is affected in feeling toward us. This answer comes out of human experience. We may well conceive that the experience of primitive men who were conscious of having done ill caused them to feel that something must be offered to the gods to avert disaster, or retribution. The doing of this, which ultimately takes the form of sacrifice, is religion. Thus religion springs out of a sentiment in us that we are ill-deserving, and out of an imagination that if we have done ill there is some way of averting the due retribution. All the part of religion which belongs to sacrifice, or a propitiation of the anger of God, rests upon the imagination. It is because of the prevalence of the sacrificial idea in religion that many men of strong judgment have rejected it. The sacrifice of a beast on an altar, or of a Son of God upon the cross, for the purpose of averting just retribution from any one, is seen to rest upon a purely imaginary basis. Not only so, but it belongs to the less developed imagination: the imagination of the man who is trained in reasoning does not respond to it.

Suppose we say that religion is not a matter of the

imagination, but of the heart; that however much the imagination may be concerned in it, the man who turns from that which is evil to that which is good is really the religious man; we may be the better able to understand some of the things which the Bible has to say to us. "With the heart man believeth unto righteousness;" that is to say, in striving to obey the demands of right, in striving to go clear from the rule of evil, one is living a religious life in the true sense of the term. Of course such a man may be more or less confused in his ideas of right and wrong, may be far astray in his reasonings; but be he who he may, wise or simple, he is truly religious.

It seems to have been natural that religion should have been regarded as for the most part theological, or mainly concerned with our relations with God. Temples, altars, votive gifts, vows, and all the paraphernalia of religion have hitherto been strictly Godward. The priest or medicine-man has been our agent to adjust things between us and God. Having in some manner achieved that adjustment, all is done that need be done. Yet a change comes, involving religion: while some fear that religion will disappear, others perceive that it is undergoing that change which perpetually increases its reasonableness and usefulness and decreases its futility; because the old theological religion does, more than all else, demonstrate its futility. Now it appears to have been conceived by some of the early Christians that religion is not theological, or Godward, chiefly, but sociological, or manward. Changes do not need to be effected in God. It would be better to accept outright the dogma of the Hebrew prophet that God is the unchangeable. Changes in man, and in his conditions, and in the mutual relations of men, are the very things which are required, in the nature of things. It is therefore hopeful to observe that in our own times religion is undergoing the most serious modification, — it is shifting its ground from the theological to the sociological aspect of things. This shifting of the ground is anticipated by some of the wiser of the early Christians. Indeed, it is the natural result of the teachings of Jesus, when those teachings are understood. It comes from ceasing to think of God as a transcendent Being stationed aloft above nature, and learning to think of him as immanent in nature. (It comes ultimately from faith in a Being who immediately works in every department of force and matter.) Of this change from the theological to the sociological religion we see evidences in James, the writer of a Christian epistle, whose contribution to the Bible is characterized more by practical common-sense than by flights of imagination. It is this writer who says, "Pure religion and undefiled before our God and Father is this, to visit the fatherless and widows in their affliction, and to keep himself unspotted from the world." Or, the religion which meets the approval of God seeks chiefly to better human conditions.

As to James, the author of this epistle, he is one of three or four of that name, some of whom we catch but passing glimpses of in the Gospels. The first James whose acquaintance we make is the son of Zebedee, one of the twelve, and the brother of the Apostle John. The second is James the son of Alphæus, also one of the twelve, and possibly brother of Matthew the publican, the name of whose father is Alphæus. There is also a James rather mysteriously spoken of as the "brother of the Lord;" and there is "James the Just," a citizen of Jerusalem. It was surmised by Luther that still another James existed, and that this other was the author of the epistle. Like Luther, we are left somewhat to surmise; but the most reasonable surmise is that James the Just is the author. The man who could properly bear such a noble title would be the one to write such a letter. It is supposed that James the son of Zebedee was beheaded by Herod a few years after the martyrdom of Stephen, and before the letter could have been written.

Now the writer of that letter, as compared with Paul, had a limited horizon. He addressed his letter only to the Israelites. To the mind of emancipated Paul, circumcision was nothing but a formal ceremony, and had ceased to signify anything. To the mind of James, circumcision was a commandment of Jehovah. It was to be practiced, not because we find it necessary, or because it is in any wise useful, but because God commanded it. It is thus many good men seem to think about immersion and other forms of baptism, — we would not practice such ceremonies unless they were divinely commanded. Inasmuch as we have the commandment, we are assured that it becomes a part of righteousness to perform the rite. Paul was less solicitous than others about such commandments. He wanted to know the reasons for them, and whether they were binding in their nature to all time. Having satisfied himself that they were not, he had little use for them. Paul, however, became a man of the world: James was the man of Jerusalem. His sympathy could stretch as far as the seed of Abraham, or that portion of it included in the covenant of Abraham. Further than that he was not prepared to go; but of the real essence of Israel's religion he had nevertheless the true idea. To him, Jesus was a Jew, and had never ceased to be such; but to Paul, Jesus was a man, and with his mission commensurate with the human family, not with the family of Abraham alone. James gloried in his lineage. Paul declared that though a Hebrew of the Hebrews, and of the tribe of Benjamin, and circumcised the eighth day, after the regular order, he counted such things as mere refuse, compared with other things.

So then James has the limitations which Paul does not share: nor is he limited in respect to one class of subjects alone. In many ways he shows a narrowness. He has not been able to comprehend the meaning and blessedness of faith. For a man to believe in God is no great achievement. Demons believe that God is; but they are not thereby improved. To believe things is a matter of theory, or speculation; and one who lays emphasis on belief lives a life as it were in the air. It is very much, as he explains, like telling a hungry and naked man, who applies for help, to be clad and fed. It is a kind of mind-cure for poverty: he thinks it absurd. To feed the hungry and clothe the naked, and to do the things of charity in general; to speak soberly and with genuine sweetness, that is what is necessary. "What doth it profit, my brethren, if a man say he has faith, and has not works?" Faith is visionary to this man; and yet he has it. Only he does not comprehend what is said about it by such a man as Paul. This doctrine of being justified by faith does not meet his approval. A man is justified by what he does. If he is commanded to sacrifice his only son on the altar, and proceeds to do it, he is justified. Rahab of Jericho was justified by taking care of the Hebrew men who demanded protection. She was not a person of stainless character: on the contrary, a fallen woman; but by her works was made a just woman. Paul elevates faith above works, James the Just elevates works above faith. Each has his point of view; each honestly speaks from that point.

What chiefly distinguishes this just man, this strict man of Jerusalem, is his feeling that religion is mainly the regulation of our social relations. The sacrifices have their importance, but fall nevertheless to a secondary place. He is troubled by the disparity of condition among the children of Israel. There are the poor, who are suffering their poverty, their life embittered by it; and over against them the rich, who enjoy the good things of life, and oppress the poor. This is of vastly more importance to this good man than anything that Paul can say about the sin of Adam, and the consequent sinning of all his descendants, and the passing of death upon all for that reason. That is in the region of speculation or the realm of "faith," and James the Just is impatient with that whole department of thought. If James were our contemporary, possibly he would object to it all as belonging to the field of dogma. The president of a great college and a representative of conservative thought has said: "Now I say, I dare to say, would to God that men would heed me, that if I must choose between life and dogma, I will say that Christianity is not a life, but a dogma. You cannot live the Christian life without holding the Christian dogma. The one emanates solely from the other. This dogma's great supposition is that man is a sinner, and that without the shedding of blood there is no remission of sin. Its great fact is that Jesus was the propitiation for our sins, and not for ours only, but for the sins of the whole world." [1]

It is conceivable that James the Just would have even less patience with that than with justification by faith; and I am sure that Paul, after all his argumentation about sin introduced by Adam, and death as consequence, would maintain Christianity to be a life. He seems to forever dispute our learned conservative by his ringing words, — "For me to live is Christ." Our learned conservative, who tells us that Christianity (if one has to choose), is not a life but a dogma, would go far to rouse the wrath of James the Just, who is endeavoring to clear the mind of Israel from mischievous notions of that sort. The theological aspects of religion he diligently seeks to replace by the sociological aspects. "See," he says, "how it is with the poor and with the rich." The social condition, actual not theoretical, fills his soul with grief and indignation. Such a respect of persons, such sycophancy on the part of the poor, such haughty pride and vanity on the part of the rich, as may be seen in the synagogue itself, he cannot bear. He asks if God cares for the rich more than for the poor. Visions of harvests, owned by the rich, and reaped by the poor, and the wages withheld, torture him. It is all unjust, and he in the soul of him is just; therefore it is unendurable. (A sturdy democrat is he; a man of practical common-sense, and of a warm and indignant heart.) He is far more concerned with the evil conditions of Israel's religion, and its social life, than with the new notions of faith which are beginning to make themselves known.

[1] *Baccalaureate Address of President Patton*, Princeton, May 7, 1891.

Those notions are of great consequence and will bring result in due time, but the time is too serious in its delinquencies, in its corruption of religion, to permit him to think of a doctrine of faith.

There is another thing of interest to us, and that is the feeling which this just man had in regard to the second advent. He could not have been unfamiliar with the current interest in that matter; but here again his common-sense and his abounding interest in the social state of Israel led him to modify the popular idea. James does probably look for a coming of Jesus in the clouds, but more clearly sees a violent revolution coming on earth; he is very sure that is coming, and shows his sagacity in taking the common-sense view; he proclaims the judge at the door, rather than as coming in the sky; he waxes vehement in his denunciations of the careless levity and corruption of the rich. They are preparing revolution. This is the sort of prophet who might have cried to the landed gentry of France in the middle of the last century, "Weep and howl for the miseries which are surely coming upon you." It is the social maladjustment, rather than the coming angels, which will cause the fiery and terrible days; and they are not far away. This man speaks more in the tone of the ancient prophets than does Paul. He sees a threatened ruin. Neither fear nor favor restrains him from utterance of the truth as he sees it, — a most brave and faithful man, scorning all such notions as are conveyed by the modern saying that if one has to choose, Christianity is not a life but a dogma. To him the whole matter is one of vital meaning; that is, a matter of life and death.

The descendants of Abraham are destroying themselves and their heritage by their bad living. It is evil conduct which makes for death. Not Adam and his sin, but falsity, injustice, respect of persons, and all the rest of it, bring ruin. It is possible that no philosopher or political economist has ever put the case more strongly, tersely, and intelligibly than did James the Just. "Such and such a course, in our social life, leads to the pit of social destruction. A nation, be it Abraham's nation or another, cannot stand if it goes not clear of these social wrongs." That is his message. Yet he does not counsel to take up arms. "Do not the rich oppress you?" he cries to the people. We should look for him, then, to advise them to strike down the oppressor, to break the strong arm of tyranny, but he does not. He does not say to them that they will do well to rouse themselves, and combine to resist the rich, and destroy their property, and sweep them from the earth. On the contrary, he tells them that if they will obey the royal law, "Thou shalt love thy neighbor as thyself," they will do well. He would free them from the baleful influences of oppression, the most baleful of which is to tempt the poor to be the tools and sycophants of the rich. He would teach them not to respect persons; but to revenge themselves upon their oppressors is foreign to his mind. He is not a maker of revolution; he discerns the things which do make it, points them out, and warns as best he may against them.

One is reminded here of the attitude of Paul toward slavery, which at that time was nearly at its worst in the Roman empire. He proclaimed the brotherhood of man, with fidelity; and all that is involved in that condition he believed in. Yet he did not counsel insurrection of the slaves. He said, "Slaves, obey your masters; not with eye service, as men pleasers, but with singleness of heart." These men, James and Paul, are not men of violence and passion; they see that wrong brings retribution. They stand by the peaceable methods of Jesus. Both are reformers, but they do not expect to reform murder by murder, nor theft by theft. They will reform evil by means of good. "Be not overcome of evil, but overcome evil with good," says Paul.

Now for the most part reformers are subject to that kind of limitation which shuts them up to one object. Having found one great evil in the world, they are disposed to think that it is the one curse of humanity; and that if it is abolished, all will be well. The temperance reformer refers almost all the evils to intemperance. To reform that out of existence will clear the state of the one affliction which degrades it in every department. "Wipe slavery from the country and we shall be a most happy people," was the feeling of the anti-slavery reformer. We have wiped out slavery, and still are not a supremely happy people. There is something yet to be done; slavery was but one form of evil. The oppression of the rich over the poor in ancient and modern times has been but one of many causes of public unhappiness and discontent. To change these conditions without changing from other evils which distress us is to fail of accomplishing enough. Wherefore James the Just, clearly seeing the line of cleavage running through the entire Hebrew community, with accompanying respect of persons, and other mischiefs, could also see that there were evils of a radical sort, for which all men were responsible; and if they were not put down, the social life would prove a dismal failure. If there should ever come a time when there would be no rich and no poor, but when abundance would smile upon every corner of the world, and if the pest of the unbridled tongue remained, we should still suffer from an intricate and all-pervading evil, which would set the world afire, as with the flame of hell. One can imagine how the soul of this just man was vexed immeasurably by the endless clatter and jargon of splenetic, peevish, slanderous tongues, — a rain of bitterness, always deluging society.

Here is no theory, and no attempt to account for a condition, but a vivid exposure of the condition: Hebrew society everywhere was made all but unendurable by the poison of envenomed tongues. Had we a land flowing with milk and honey, with abundant springs pouring out of our mountains, and watering all the pastures; had we fruit growing in tropical luxuriance, and every man sitting under his own vine and fig-tree, a pleasing prospect on every hand of us, and labor reduced to a mere pleasant exercise; had we Paradise expanded to all portions of the habitable globe, — with the human tongue let loose to perform its favorite work, our Paradise would be a miserable failure. A wilderness with some government of the tongue in it would be preferable. We imagine our fellow-men of the older countries to be groaning under the weight of czars, sultans, kaisers, and all the like; to be spied upon at every moment by intrusive police; to be liable at a moment's notice, or without notice, to deportation from their homes to the wastes of Siberia; to be shut up in prison, or set at hopeless work in the mines. Such evils are unspeakable; but to burn all thrones from under all despotic rulers, and to set up some other form of government, or no-government, gives us no effective clearance of our evils. Every man and every woman, able to talk, and therefore to sweeten or embitter the lives of their fellow men and women, possesses the power to contribute to the continued reign of wretchedness.

Thus the reformation contemplated by James the Just is one which purifies society of an evil everywhere prevalent, and which is not imposed by one class upon another. His religion is fundamentally practical, shunning metaphysics, and in a remarkable degree social. He does not denounce vague judgments against vague iniquities, and he does not have to ask only the wise to listen to him. The iniquity he chiefly speaks of is one from which all suffer, and in the propagation of which almost all are implicated; and no one can possibly fail to understand what he is talking about. Let every person, therefore, give heed to do his personal part, putting the bridle upon his own tongue, and so reduce the evil of the world.

Nevertheless, it is evident that the conduct and teaching of Jesus had produced a strong feeling in the early church respecting wealth. Jesus had been understood to bless the poor, and to declare that it was next to impossible for a rich man to have part in his kingdom. James the Just shares this impression, and believes the poor to be specially favored of God. Apart from the bitterness, he seems to have had the same feeling about the rich of his time that the modern social reformer has about the millionaires. It is for that reason he lays so much stress upon the coming revolution. It is unquestionable that wealth gained by injustice, by the withholding of proper wages, by chicanery, or by cunning, is at all times a menace to any society which permits it. Great wealth, such as we see piling itself up in enormous bulks in modern times, is at best a deplorable fact; one cannot intelligently look upon it without anxiety.

The feeling of the early Christians is expressed in the Shepherd of Hermas,[1] a book which Irenæus and others deemed worthy a place in the sacred canon, and which was publicly read in many or most of the churches at one period. This is a very ecclesiastical book, and may have contributed much to the development of the papacy afterward, but otherwise is of considerable merit. The writer has visions, and in one of them beholds six angels building a tower upon the water. These angels are assisted by a host of others, who bring them stones for the tower, and the stones which are thus employed are found to be exactly square, and to fit each other to a nicety. Some stones are cast far away, and it is noted that others — white, round stones — are left near the base of the tower. The writer is told that these round stones represent the rich, and that they cannot be built into the tower, which is the church, until their riches are taken away. Their impoverishment alone will make them also square stones, fit for the sacred edifice.

Aside, however, from the prevalent feeling of the church concerning wealth, this is evident: that the Epistle of James the Just is in no wise a theological

[1] "As respects [the Shepherd of Hermas], the conservative Zahn remarks: 'It enjoyed alike in the West and the East all the rights of a Biblical book. . . . As respects circulation, acknowledgment, and influence, the Shepherd surpassed, at the close of the second century and beginning of the third, more than one document which to-day belongs to the New Testament.'" — Professor J. H. Thayer, *The Change of Attitude towards the Bible.*

work. His religion — the religion he seeks to teach — is social in its reference. However mistaken in theory — as concerning the sin of Adam, or the passing of death upon all, and the position of Jesus in the rank of being — any one may be, if his religion has the social reference, that is pure religion and pleasing to God. Perhaps there is nothing better for our time, rife with just criticism upon the Christian religion and making honest effort to do without religion in the reformation of the world, than the letter of James the Just; for in it he tells us the thing we most need to know, and that is that the religion which is not sociological is vain; and that all effort toward the uplift of our race, done in the spirit of charity, is religious, — and it is divinely religious.

www.ingramcontent.com/pod-product-compliance
Lightning Source LLC
Chambersburg PA
CBHW030801230426
43667CB00008B/1013